Praise for *Thi*

"*Think and Grow Rich!* has had a tremendous impact on my life. My company, Contours Express, would not exist if not for this book. And now, seven years, 15 additional readings, and more than 350 fitness centers later, I still find new personal and business applications each time I read it. Without question this is the greatest business book ever written."

> -- Daren Carter founder of Contours Express fitness centers, located in six countries

"Dr. Hill's original work transformed the 20th century. This newly revised version will do the same for the 21st century. No writer, thought leader or guru of personal growth and development comes close to Napoleon Hill. This landmark work takes his stature to an even more monumental level."

> -- Bill Brooks, author of *The New Science of Selling and Persuasion*

"I thought Think and Grow Rich! was a classic and could never be improved. I was wrong. I am sure Dr. Hill would be greatly pleased to see how his work has been honored and enhanced by this outstanding new edition."

> -- Wally Amos, founder of Famous Amos Chocolate Chip Cookies, author of *The Cookie Never Crumbles: Inspirational Recipes for Everyday Living*

"Reading Think and Grow Rich! many years ago helped me to become the World's Greatest Retail Salesperson. A must to read if you want to become somebody. You'll love it; I know I did. Thank you, Napoleon Hill."

> -- Joe Girard, World's #1 Retail Salesperson, as attested by *The Guiness Book of World Records*

"Unfortunately, we don't learn success principles in school. Fortunately, we can learn the keys to success by reading *Think and Grow Rich!*. Napoleon Hill masterfully explains concepts such as definite purpose, positive mental attitude and handling adversity. When you apply these concepts, your life is going to improve dramatically! I am forever grateful to Napoleon Hill for writing this remarkable book."

-- Jeff Keller, author of *Attitude is Everything*

"I was introduced to *Think and Grow Rich!* as a high school student. This book was recommended to me by my teacher who taught a class called 'Everyday Living.' At that point in my life I suffered from low self-esteem, and this book was a motivating factor for me. It gave me a new lease on life when I realized I could do anything if I had the desire and believed I could achieve my goals."

-- S. Truett Cathy, founder, Chairman and CEO of Chick-fil-A, Inc.

"*Think and Grow Rich!* is timeless and will continue to change lives. It's powerful in turning people's dreams and passions into life-long realities. It did mine and still remains my number one reference book."

-- Don L. Price, professional speaker, author, sales/ marketing & positive change solution provider

"My first copy of *Think and Grow Rich!* by Napoleon Hill cost me 25 cents (yes, two dimes and a nickel) in a used book store. Dr. Hill's words in that book have inspired me for more than 35 years—and they still do. It's a classic at any price."

-- Dr. Jim Tunney, former NFL referee, educator, speaker, author of *It's the Will, Not the Skill*

"The book that changed my life."

-- Tom Hess, virtuoso guitarist and composer for the band HESS

"I first read *Think and Grow Rich!* 30 years ago at age 18. I found it to be the most fascinating book I had or have ever read, excluding the word of God. It is much more than instructions on how to obtain wealth. It strengthens your spirit, your soul, and promotes the proper attitude to achieve peace, endurance, and a loving family—the real measures of success in life. My life has been richly blessed as a result of reading and rereading *Think and Grow Rich!*. Dr. Hill performed a wonderful work for mankind and was a useful vessel for God when he wrote this book for all people and all ages. I know all readers will be enriched upon reading this new edition of *Think and Grow Rich!*.

-- Emerson B. Hall, president of TruBody Shaving Gels

"I just bought a new edition of *Think and Grow Rich!* by Napoleon Hill. It's a collection of interviews with the richest people in the world, to find out the secret of their success. I must've read it 20 times."

-- Michael Flatley, dancer and choreographer (*Riverdance*)

"If you follow the principles in *Think and Grow Rich!* and allow it to become a part of your life, you will be successful in all of your endeavors. I read *Think and Grow Rich!* more than 50 times over the years while creating the world's first premium pest elimination company, servicing thousands of restaurants, hotels, hospitals and cruise ships halfway around the world."

-- Al Burger, co-founder, with wife, Sandee, of Bugs Burger Bug Killers

"I am a fifth generation exterminator and second generation 'think and grow richer.' The stories in *Think and Grow Rich!* are both memorable and inspiring. I strongly recommend this book to all who are seeking instant motivation."

-- Andrew Burger, President, "Bugs" Burger Bug Killers

"Personal development isn't something that just happens; you have to work for it. This book cuts to the quick in the way of leading you down your own path toward individual freedom."

--Karen E. Spaeder, freelance business writer and former Managing Editor of *Entrepreneur* magazine

"As a teenager growing up in the rural south, I never dreamed that I could ever accomplish anything financially other than earn a good living. Even though I graduated from Emory University, I majored in psychology, which didn't qualify me for a job that paid a substantial income. In 1969, however, I was introduced to *Think and Grow Rich!* by Napoleon Hill. This book entirely changed my economic mindset. Dr. Hill taught me that by studying successful people and heeding their advice, anyone, including Bill Lee, could accumulate wealth. I pray that as a result of this updated edition of Dr. Hill's work, many other young people can receive the blessings of his research."

> -- Bill Lee, CSP, founder of Lee Resources, Inc., author of *30 Ways Managers Shoot Themselves in the Foot* and *26 Factors Affecting Your Bottom Line*

"Think and Grow Rich! was one of the first motivational books I ever read. Often I pick it up and read a chapter....the ideas NEVER go out of date."

> -- Patricia Fripp, CSP, CPAE, keynote speaker, speech coach, sales trainer, Past President National Speakers Association

"Ross Cornwell has made it easier than ever to learn from a giant of a leader and thinker. Napoleon Hill's wisdom applies to us all, any generation, any background and station in life! Napoleon Hill has served as Mentor to Millions. Why not you?"

> -- Ty Boyd, CEO of Ty Boyd Executive Learning Systems and author of *The Million Dollar Toolbox*

"Napoleon Hill's writings have influenced my life to understand that our God-given destiny is to soar on eagles' wings. You have to stretch yourself before you can soar, and once you have a burning desire, a significant goal you can stretch much farther than you previously had thought possible. Beware: Every time an eagle raises its wings to fly, someone will put an arrow to the bow, but remember, eagles can soar higher than any arrow can fly. May this revised and updated edition of Napoleon Hill's *Think and Grow Rich!* enable you to Reach—Stretch—Soar!

> -- Father Brian Cavanaugh (Third Order Franciscan), Franciscan University of Steubenville, editor of *Appleseeds* and author of *The Sower's Seeds* series

"Zen teacher Richard Rose said a spiritual seeker could find Enlightenment by following Napoleon Hill's *Think and Grow Rich!,* and substituting 'God' or 'Truth' wherever the book says 'money.'"
> -- August Turak, founder of Raleigh Group International, Elsinore Technologies, Inc., and the Self Knowledge Symposium Foundation

"A classic! If you haven't read it, read it! If you have read it, read it again!"

> -- Thomas Crum, author *The Magic of Conflict* and *Journey to Center*

"I believe and trust in God. He will use many things in life to get your attention. I believe he used this book to get mine. I have without a doubt been endowed with the power to **THINK** of ways to optimize every situation in my life, whether positive or negative, and to **GROW RICH** spiritually, physically, financially, and emotionally."

> -- Corey Honore, professional body builder and fitness expert

"It's so simple and yet we need to be reminded again and again, 'What we think about is who we become.' Each time we open this book we begin a most rewarding journey. Of course the key is to open it — what are you waiting for?"

> -- W Mitchell, member of the CPAE Hall of Fame, author of *It's Not What Happens To You, It's What You Do About It*

"For over 10 years we have applied the principles of *Think and Grow Rich!*, especially the MASTERMIND GROUP concept. We formed a Mastermind Women's Group, and we set and monitor goals in all areas of our life — spiritual, family, financial, health, education, business, recreation, personal, and civic. As a result, hundreds of lives have been changed, especially financially through forming investment clubs. This book is the success system that cannot fail."

> -- Ann McNeill, President, MCO Construction & Services, Inc.

"Here comes the all time classic self-help bestseller gently adapted to be most relevant for the challenges we all face today. If you believe pursuing self-improvement is important for enjoying a full and meaningful life, you will want to make sure you have this book in your personal development library."

> -- Charles C. Manz, author of *Temporary Sanity: Instant Self-Leadership Strategies for Turbulent Times* and co-author of *Fit to Lead*

"*Think & Grow Rich!* is at the top of its genre. No book is as complete and thorough as this classic. It gave me, as an immigrant, the hope and the knowledge I needed to fulfill my dreams. Anybody who reads this book will learn Napoleon Hill's wisdom and turn around their life. It's a must for self-help book readers."

> -- Tony Alcázar, author of *La Nueva Raza Latina en América* (*The New Latino Race in America*)

"*Think And Grow Rich!* has helped thousands of Americans to become financially free even beyond their wildest imagination....By just putting into practice all the things Napoleon Hill recommended in his book, I made up my mind to become an entrepreneur within a month of getting hold of and reading *Think And Grow Rich!*. About a year later, November 1984, that dream became a reality."

> -- Sunny Obazu-Ojeagbase, founder of Success Attitude Development Centre, publisher of *Complete Sports*, Nigeria's largest circulating daily sports newspaper

"I consider *Think and Grow Rich!* the 'bible' of personal development, whose teachings, principles and wisdom are timeless. I have read it several times and continue to recommend the book to clients and audiences everywhere. Read it if you want to be successful!"

> -- Allan J Kleynhans, performance coach, professional speaker, South Africa

"*Think and Grow Rich!* is THE granddaddy of all self-help books. It was the most important book I read at the time of a career change 30 years ago. The concepts I learned have served me well all these years. Attitude adjustments, affirmations, visualizations and Mastermind Groups — Mr. Hill helped us all learn to think on a higher level about the principles of prosperity. Many thanks to a great mentor!"

> -- Bobby Covic, author of *Everything's Negotiable! How to Bargain Better to Get What You Want*

"I was introduced to *Think and Grow Rich!* by an alcoholic member of our cemetery sales team. I had a wife and three children at the time, and we were just barely making it. My only source of income was the commissions I made knocking on doors selling cemetery property, and they were hard to come by, especially since almost nobody was a permanent resident in the Miami area.

"Reading *Think and Grow Rich!* gave me a crutch to lean on as I forced myself out to pound those doors where the potential prospects were. If my family was going to eat, I had to convince people to buy cemetery property 30 or 40 or more years before they would need it. The Six-Step Success Formula helped me to realize that there was a way even for an uneducated lunkhead like me to make it like the big guys. I followed the success formula faithfully, and, lo and behold, my whole life turned around.

"Two of my most useful tools in the book were the poem 'My Wage' ('I bargained with Life for a penny…') and 'If You Think You Are Beaten' ('Life's battles don't always go to the stronger or faster man…'). I truly believe that Dr. Hill had the same message the Bible has for us. It was just little easier for me to apply. I went on to build the largest cemetery organization in the country starting out from my basement on Concord Ave. in Anderson, S. C. In 1970, we sold 30 cemeteries to Service Corporation International, making it possible for them to become the largest funeral-cemetery company in the world. I served as President of their Cemetery Division for three years.

"I'm now 85 years old, living comfortably on the shores of Lake Hartwell with my wife of 65 years. Almost all my good fortune came about because I had the good fortune to be introduced to *Think and Grow Rich!* in 1953. I have given away many cases of this great book. It was required reading in my company and in my family, and it has made a difference in a lot of the people's lives who were given the opportunity to make it part of their lives.

"Thank you, Ross, for giving me this opportunity to look back and appreciate how really important all of this is and what a difference it has made in my life and the lives of so many others."

> -- Dick Herbert, founder of National Heritage Corporation, former President of the Cemetery Division, Service Corporation International

For more testimonials, see page 386 and following.

Think and Grow Rich!

Think and Grow Rich!

By

Napoleon Hill

The Original Version, Restored and Revised

With Revisions, Editor's Foreword
and Annotations

By

Ross Cornwell

Aventine Press

Third Printing, July 2008

This book is affiliated solely with
The Mindpower Press
and is not officially endorsed by or affiliated with
any other institute, foundation or organization.

Special Discounts: Copies of this book may be purchased at special discounts for educational, business, or sales promotional use, or for the establishment of Master Mind Alliance study groups. The book is also available at special discounts for bulk purchases as premiums or special editions, including personalized covers. For information, please write Special Markets Department, The Mindpower Press, P. O. Box 1732, Clemson, S. C. 29633, or e-mail: jrcornwell@mastermindpower.org .

LIBRARY OF CONGRESS
Library of Congress Cataloging-in-Publication Data
2004112184
Ross Cornwell

Teaching, for the first time, the famous Andrew Carnegie formula for money-making, based upon the THIRTEEN PROVEN STEPS TO RICHES.
Think and Grow Rich!: The Original Version, Restored and Revised, by Ross Cornwell, Napoleon Hill

Includes index.
ISBN 1-59330-200-2

Cover design by Ryan Ratliff; book design by Keith Pearson
Sketch (page 289) by Pam Latour

The Mindpower Press website address: www.mastermindpower.org
e-mail: jrcornwell@mastermindpower.org
Printed in the United States of America on acid-free paper.

Whatever the mind can conceive and believe, it can achieve.

—Napoleon Hill

Contents

SPECIAL FOREWORD BY BOB PROCTOR

You and I have something in common. We have both selected one of the greatest books ever written, *Think and Grow Rich!* by Napoleon Hill. However, it is almost 50 years since my mind was first exposed to the information that you are holding in your hands. The content of this book has the potential to improve the quality of your life to a degree that is very likely, at this time, beyond the scope of your imagination. You see, I probably know this book and what it can do as well, if not better, than most people alive today. Fifty years of studying the same book does something to you. Let me explain.

In 1963 my brother Al handed me a gift that I consider a true treasure. He gave me a copy of *Think and Grow Rich!* that he had bound in black Moroccan leather. Although I had already been studying another copy of the book for a few years, I have carried Al's copy with me every day, everywhere I go, since receiving it. So much in my life has changed for the better since that day.

Just a year ago Al sent me an e-mail explaining how grateful he was that I began studying *Think and Grow Rich!*. He went on to tell me that our entire family enjoys greater prosperity and joy today because of Napoleon Hill's wonderful book. The philosophy contained in the following pages is one of the best perspectives on success that you will find anywhere. It has worked itself into our family's way of thinking and into our way of living.

As I am dictating these words, I am sitting in my library surrounded by a few thousand books — great books, but none of them have had the impact on my life that Napoleon Hill's *Think and Grow Rich!* has.

Henry Ford, John D. Rockefeller, Thomas Edison, and Alexander Graham Bell were a few of the people who were close friends of Napoleon Hill. Even without any research, you have a pretty good idea of the impact that the work of these great individuals has had on the world. We're aware of their accomplishments because, in most cases, their name is associated with it. And yet, to my way of thinking, it is nearly impossible to accurately describe the positive impact that Napoleon Hill and his work have had on the world. Through his books, Napoleon Hill has transformed the lives of millions of people. Today, Hill's incredible research and the organized information that came from his years of dedicated effort, percolate in the mind of countless millions of people worldwide — many of whom have never heard of Napoleon Hill. Yet these same individuals enjoy the wisdom that has been shared by others who have been impacted by Napoleon Hill's great work.

When *Think and Grow Rich!* was first placed in my hands, I was sitting in a fire hall in a suburb of Toronto, Canada. I was a very confused, unhappy, and broke 26-year-old. I had virtually no formal education and no business experience. My mental focus was always on what I didn't have, what I was lacking, and why I couldn't do the things I dreamed about. However, Hill's work inspired me; it caused me to focus on what I *could* do. As I studied the powerful information shared in this book, I began to search for ways of how I could do things, rather than why I couldn't.

Think and Grow Rich! taught me to work at developing my strengths and managing my weaknesses. With the repetition of reading each chapter over and over again, I began to develop a healthy respect for my potential and my capabilities. Today I own a number of very prosperous companies that operate worldwide. I have attracted business partners with whom anyone would be proud to work. The LifeSuccess Group of Companies is focused on providing service in the same area in which Hill dedicated his life — helping people understand their potential and how to develop it.

I have formed the habit of reading a few lines from *Think and Grow Rich!* every day and have arrived at the conclusion that whatever challenge I may face, my solution will be found in the pages of this wonderful book. Another habit I have formed that I would urge you to follow is to read the chapter on "Persistence" every day for 30 days at least twice a year.

Recently, I traveled to Kuala Lumpur, Malaysia, to speak at the international conference of the Napoleon Hill Foundation, where the Prime Minister of Malaysia was presented with the Napoleon Hill Award. Although Napoleon Hill has moved on to the next phase of his eternal journey, the Napoleon Hill Foundation continues his great work. I clearly remember the moment I walked into the Foundation's library, which houses much of Hill's original work. A deep feeling of gratitude came over me; I felt indebted to him and to the Foundation for the abundant life that I enjoy.

Make up your mind right now — make a firm decision that you are going to harness the philosophy in this book to do for you what it has done for millions of people all over the world! I strongly urge you to do as I did some 46 years ago, to read *Think and Grow Rich!: The Original Version, Restored and Revised* over and over again until it becomes a part of your way of thinking, your way of being. You will be richly rewarded for doing so.

Bob Proctor, best-selling author, *You Were Born Rich*
June 22, 2007

DON'T WAIT.
THE TIME WILL NEVER BE JUST RIGHT.

THE EDITOR'S FOREWORD

IF THIS IS your first exposure to *Think and Grow Rich!*, I urge you to stop reading at the end of the third paragraph below and turn immediately to "The Author's Preface" on page 1. The beginning of a life-altering experience of the most profound kind awaits you there — an experience that has given thousands of men and women the key to success every year since Napoleon Hill first published this landmark work.

Think and Grow Rich! is the ONLY "how-to" book or other resource on personal success that you MUST have. It will help you *grow rich* — it will enrich your life — in all ways that matter, not just financially and materially. The ideas behind *Think and Grow Rich!* are the wellspring from which all legitimate "Personal Success" and "Positive Mental Attitude" movements have flowed. Every book, tape, CD, DVD, or other product on personal success that has been produced since *Think and Grow Rich!* was first published does little more than rediscover Dr. Hill's ideas and principles.

If you are reading *Think and Grow Rich!* for the first time, pay no attention for now to footnotes, the extensive endnotes, and appendices. They provide information that will one day expand your appreciation for the book, but during your first reading, they will simply slow you down and interrupt your learning process. When you have completed your first reading (there will be many!) and thus begun your journey on the road to high personal achievement, financial independence, and outstanding success in life, return to this foreword for the additional insights it provides into *Think and Grow Rich!* and the philosophy it entails. Study the endnotes, where you will gain further insight into such things as Positive Mental Attitude, the era in which Napoleon Hill worked and wrote, the people he wrote about, and of course Napoleon Hill himself. So again, I urge you, the first-time reader: Do not hesitate. Waste no time. Turn to the "Author's Preface" to begin your study—and DO IT NOW!

If you are *not* a newcomer to Napoleon Hill's work and have already read another version of *Think and Grow Rich!*, a different sort of reward awaits you. The edition of *Think and Grow Rich!* you now hold, as its subtitle indicates, is the *Original Version, Restored and Revised.* Remember that Dr. Hill first published *Think and Grow Rich!* and the money-making secret it contains in 1937, at the depths of the Great Depression. In 1960, he published a revised edition of the book, which deleted many sections that appeared in the original. Much of this deleted material focused on specific matters related to the environment of an economic depression. These and other changes in the original manuscript evidently were made so as not to "date" the book. Copies of the 1960 edition and its subsequent printings have, until now, been just about the only ones available in bookstores and most libraries since the 1960s. Ironically, because of the enormous economic upheavals, dislocations, and uncertainties that have swept America and the world during the 1980s, 1990s, and into the new century, much of what was omitted from the 1960 edition turns out to be amazingly relevant to circumstances and conditions that prevail today. *Think and Grow Rich!* in its original form speaks as clearly and meaningfully to people in the 21st century as it did to those in the early and later 20th century—and perhaps more so.

The version of *Think and Grow Rich!* you are now reading restores the book to its original form by reinstating material that was edited out four decades ago. (A few original passages have not been restored in the main body of the text because of their obsolescence, but these passages are quoted and explained in the endnotes.) In addition, the original "look" of *Think and Grow Rich!*

has been re-created. The typeface that has been selected, combined with Dr. Hill's creative use of italics and "all caps" words, gives a vigorous, enthusiastic "visual quality" to the text.

While this new version, in the main, restores *Think and Grow Rich!* to its original form and look, the book has also been *revised* throughout. In every chapter there are minor changes in punctuation, terminology, and, occasionally, phrasing. Financial and economic data are updated where it makes sense to do so (for example, using today's dollar values in illustrations and figures), so that readers will not constantly be forced to do in-the-head calculations to make comparisons. Each such revision of word or figure is made solely to remove any artificial obstacles to a full understanding of Dr. Hill's ideas. The goal at every step has been to make *Think and Grow Rich!* as user-friendly as possible for today's reader.

This edition is revised also in that it is the first fully annotated version of *Think and Grow Rich!* ever published, the first with footnotes, endnotes, and appendices, and it contains the first comprehensive index to assist readers in using the book more effectively. Most of the annotations will be of interest primarily to the Napoleon Hill devotee who seeks greater understanding of the historical context in which Dr. Hill created *Think and Grow Rich!*. While his message itself is timeless, many of the persons, events, and circumstances he discusses in his commentary and illustrations are no longer familiar to most readers. *Think and Grow Rich!: The Original Version, Restored and Revised* aims — in the sense of a "revised standard version" — to make all of these things as clear as possible without in any way interfering with or disturbing the integrity and message of the original work.

What to make of *Think and Grow Rich!*? Dr. Hill's book is a publishing phenomenon. Year after year, people continue to "discover" it — tucked away inconspicuously on a bookstore or library shelf or passed along from a family member, friend, or associate — and they have read it, loved it, and used it to turn their lives around and their powers of creativity and imagination loose.

The first copy of *Think and Grow Rich!* was sold in 1937. Eleven years later, in February 1948, *Coronet* magazine polled 300 successful young men and women, asking, "What book or books most influenced your life and contributed to your success?" *Think and Grow Rich!* was ranked fourth on the list. In September 1986 – 38 years and eight U. S. Presidents later – *USA Today* published a list of the "10 top-selling paperback books about investments" in America for that month. Despite the fact that it is only in the most general sense an investment book, being primarily about investing in yourself and others, *Think and Grow Rich!* ranked No. 1 on the list. (Some books it beat? *How to Buy Stocks, The Only Investment Guide You'll Ever Need,* and *Getting Yours.*)

Some years ago the Library of Congress conducted a survey asking what books most influenced readers' lives. The top answer, by a wide margin, was The Bible. In second and third place were, respectively, *Atlas Shrugged* by Ayn Rand and *Think and Grow Rich!* by Napoleon Hill. In 2002, *BusinessWeek* magazine published "The BusinessWeek Best-Seller List" in its October 14 edition   Almost incredibly, *Think and Grow Rich!* ranked tenth on the list of the current 15 top-selling paperback business books – 65 years after the first copy of the book was purchased!

Walk into any well-stocked bookstore in America and you will find a few paperback copies of *Think and Grow Rich!* (usually the 1960 version in one of its manifestations) in the business or self-motivation sections. *Think and Grow Rich!* endures because it works.

For three years it was my privilege to serve (on an independent contractor basis) as the first editor-in-chief of *Think & Grow Rich Newsletter,* published by Imagine, Inc., for the Napoleon Hill Foundation, a charitable organization he established to carry on his life's research and work. My experience in that position not only provided me with the insight and confidence needed to undertake this restoration/revision of *Think and Grow Rich!*, but also introduced me to the living power of this book in changing people's lives. I was exposed to the kind of correspondence and phone calls that pour in daily from people throughout the world, in all walks of life and in all circumstances, who have read *Think and Grow Rich!*, applied its principles diligently, and attained self-confidence, self-understanding, and levels of success that most people only dare dream of. You may one day find yourself giving such a personal testimonial.

Yet there is more to *Think and Grow Rich!* than the power of the principles it explains. Part of the book's appeal is the uncanny, almost prophetic insights of Napoleon Hill about matters and issues that are very much "today." He talked about such concepts as networking, participatory management, excellence in customer service, visualization techniques, brainstorming, and the use of written goals and objectives long before any of these became corporate or psychological buzzwords—even before, in most instances, the terms themselves were created. He spends almost an entire chapter discussing the concept of mentorship, although he never refers to it as such and puts an unusual Hill twist on it. His speculations on human brain functions anticipate the whole area of right brain/left brain research. Any one of the numerous self-analysis tests scattered throughout his pages is thoroughly applicable today and well worth the price of this book alone. Fifty years before the word "downsizing" would come into vogue, Napoleon Hill spelled out in specific detail the perfect strategy and tactics to use when one finds oneself suddenly forced to look for a job or try to start a business. His analysis of what capitalism is and means (in Chapter 6) is the most compelling and persuasive ever made and should be required reading for everyone.

No matter what town, state, or country you may live in, no personal success library can ever be complete without this restored, revised, fully annotated, and fully indexed version of *Think and Grow Rich!*. It contains all of the book's original contents, edited for today's reader. It includes restored material that makes it more relevant and valuable today than it was when it was first created. Teaching the practical steps to the attainment of financial independence and even great wealth is one of the main purposes of *Think and Grow Rich!*. But the greatest value of this wonderful book is not that it can make you financially successful, but that it can help YOU—or ANYONE—achieve success *however* you may define it, and help you get whatever else it is that you desire from life.

To paraphrase what is perhaps Napoleon Hill's most famous statement:

"Whatever, friend, you can conceive and believe, you can achieve!"

Think and Grow Rich!: The Original Version, Restored and Revised shows you step-by-step just how to do it.

Ross Cornwell

If you like this new edition of Napoleon Hill's greatest work, please recommend it to others when the occasion arises. We also invite you to go online to Amazon.com, BarnesandNoble.com, Amazon.ca, Amazon.co.uk, or other booksellers to write a brief "reader review" of the book. It will take only a few minutes and is a good way to help spread the word about the new edition. As you read the book, if you come across any mistakes—factual, grammatical, whatever—please report them to the editor by e-mailing him at *jrcornwell@mastermindpower.org* . He is also interested in any other comments or suggestions you may have.

THE AUTHOR'S PREFACE

IN EVERY CHAPTER of this book, mention has been made of the money-making secret which has made fortunes for more than 500 exceedingly wealthy people whom I have carefully analyzed over a long period of years.

The secret was brought to my attention by Andrew Carnegie more than a quarter of a century ago. The canny, lovable old Scotsman carelessly tossed it into my mind when I was but a boy.[1] Then he sat back in his chair, with a merry twinkle in his eyes, and watched carefully to see if I had brains enough to understand the full significance of what he had said to me.

When he saw that I had grasped the idea, he asked if I would be willing to spend 20 years or more preparing myself to take it to the world to men and women who, without the secret, might go through life as failures. I said I would, and with Mr. Carnegie's cooperation, I have kept my promise.

This book contains the secret, after having been put to a practical test by thousands of people in almost every walk of life. It was Mr. Carnegie's idea that the magic formula which gave him a stupendous fortune ought to be placed within reach of everyone who does not have time to investigate how successful people make money. It was his hope that I might test and demonstrate the soundness of the formula through the experience of men and women in every calling. He believed the formula should be taught in all public schools and colleges, and he expressed the opinion that if it were properly taught, it would so revolutionize the entire educational system that the time spent in school could be reduced to less than half.

His experience with Charles M. Schwab and other young associates of Mr. Schwab's type convinced Mr. Carnegie that much of what is taught in schools and colleges is of no value whatsoever in connection with the business of earning a living or accumulating riches. He had arrived at this decision because he had taken into his business one young person after another, many of them with but little schooling, and by coaching them in the use of this formula, developed in them rare leadership. Moreover, his coaching made fortunes for every one of them who followed his instructions.

In Chapter 2 on "Faith," you will read the astounding story of the organization of the giant United States Steel Corporation as it was conceived and carried out by one of the young associates through whom Mr. Carnegie proved that his formula will work for all who are ready for it. This single application of the secret by that young man—Charles M. Schwab—made him a huge fortune in both money and OPPORTUNITY. Roughly speaking, this particular application of the formula was worth six hundred million dollars* to the people involved.

These facts—and they are facts well known to almost everyone who knew Mr. Carnegie—give you a fair idea of what the reading of this book may bring to you, provided you KNOW WHAT IT IS THAT YOU WANT.

Even before it had undergone 20 years of practical testing, the secret was passed on to many thousands of men and women who have used it for their personal benefit, as Mr. Carnegie planned that they should. Many have made fortunes with it. Others have used it successfully in creating harmony in their homes.

Arthur Nash, a Cincinnati tailor, used his near-bankrupt business as a "guinea pig" on which to test the formula. The business came to life and made a fortune for its owners. The experiment was so extraordinary that newspapers and magazines gave it more than a million dollars worth of laudatory publicity.[2]

---

* In today's dollars, approximately $12.5 billion.

The secret was passed on to Stuart Austin Wier of Dallas, Texas.[3] He was ready for it — so ready that he gave up his profession and studied law. Did he succeed? That story is told too.

I gave the secret to Jennings Randolph the day he was graduated from college, and he would go on to use it so successfully that it carried him to a seat in the United States Senate and a long and distinguished career in public service at the national level.

While serving as advertising manager of LaSalle Extension University when it was little more than a name, I had the privilege of seeing J. G. Chapline, president of the university, use the formula so effectively that he went on to make LaSalle one of the great extension schools of the country.[4]

The secret to which I refer is mentioned no fewer than a hundred times throughout this book. It has not been directly named, for it seems to work more successfully when it is merely uncovered and left in sight, where THOSE WHO ARE READY and SEARCHING FOR IT may pick it up. That is why Mr. Carnegie tossed it to me so quietly, without giving me its specific name. If you are READY to put it to use, you will recognize this secret at least once in every chapter. I wish I might feel privileged to tell you how you will know if you are ready, but that would deprive you of much of the benefit you will receive when you make the discovery in your own way.

While this book was being written, my own son, who was then finishing the last year of his college work, picked up the manuscript of Chapter 1, read it, and discovered the secret for himself. He used the information so effectively that he went directly into a responsible position at a beginning salary greater than the average person ever earns. His story is briefly described in Chapter 1. When you read it, perhaps you will dismiss any feeling you may have had at the beginning of the book that it promised too much. And, too, if you have ever been discouraged, if you have had difficulties to surmount which took the very soul out of you, if you have tried and failed, if you were ever handicapped by illness or physical affliction, this story of my son's discovery and use of the Andrew Carnegie formula may prove to be the oasis in the "Desert of Lost Hope" for which you have been searching.

This secret was used extensively by President Woodrow Wilson during the First World War. It was passed on to every soldier who fought in the war, carefully incorporated or "embedded" in the training he received before going to the front. President Wilson told me it was also a strong factor in raising the funds needed for the war.[5]

In the early days of this century, Manuel L. Quezon (then Resident Commissioner of the Philippine Islands) was inspired by the secret to gain freedom for his people, and he went on to become the first president of that free island nation.[6]

A peculiar thing about this secret is that those who once acquire it and use it find themselves literally swept on to success, with what seems to be little effort, and they never again submit to failure! If you doubt this, study the names of those who have used it wherever they have been mentioned, check their records for yourself, and be convinced.

There is no such thing as SOMETHING FOR NOTHING!

The secret to which I refer cannot be had without a price, although the price is far less than its value. It cannot be had at any price by those who are not intentionally searching for it. It cannot be given away, and it cannot be purchased for money, for the reason that it comes in two parts. One part is already in possession of those who are ready for it.

The secret serves equally well all who are ready for it. Education has nothing to do with it. Long before I was born, the secret had found its way into the possession of Thomas A. Edison, and he used it so intelligently that he became the world's greatest inventor, although he had but three months of schooling.

The secret was passed on to a business associate of Mr. Edison. He used it so effectively that, although he was then making only $12,000 a year, he accumulated a great fortune and retired from active business while still a young man. You will find his story at the beginning of the next chapter. It should convince you that riches are not beyond your reach, that you can still be what you wish to be, that money, fame, recognition and happiness can be had by all who are ready and determined to have these blessings.

How do I know these things? You should have the answer before you finish this book. You may find it in the very first chapter or on the last page.

While I was performing the more than 20-year task of research which I had undertaken at Mr. Carnegie's request, I analyzed hundreds of well-known individuals, many of whom admitted that they had accumulated their vast fortunes through the aid of the Carnegie secret. Among these individuals* were:

HENRY FORD	JOHN D. ROCKEFELLER
WILLIAM WRIGLEY, JR.	THOMAS A. EDISON
JOHN WANAMAKER	FRANK A. VANDERLIP
JAMES J. HILL	F. W. WOOLWORTH
FANNIE HURST	COL. ROBERT A. DOLLAR
GEORGE S. PARKER	EDWARD A FILENE
E. M. STATLER	EDWIN C. BARNES
HENRY L. DOHERTY	ARTHUR BRISBANE
CYRUS H. K. CURTIS	WOODROW WILSON
GEORGE EASTMAN	WILLIAM HOWARD TAFT
THEODORE ROOSEVELT	LUTHER BURBANK
JOHN W. DAVIS	EDWARD W. BOK
MARIE DRESSLER	FRANK A. MUNSEY
ELBERT HUBBARD	KATE SMITH
WILBUR WRIGHT	ELBERT H. GARY
WILLIAM JENNINGS BRYAN	ALEXANDER GRAHAM BELL
DR. DAVID STARR JORDAN	JOHN H. PATTERSON
J. OGDEN ARMOUR	JULIUS ROSENWALD
CHARLES M. SCHWAB	STUART AUSTIN WIER
ERNESTINE SCHUMANN-HEINK	DR. FRANK CRANE
DR. FRANK GUNSAULUS	J.G. CHAPLINE
DANIEL WILLARD	ARTHUR NASH

*Additional information about these individuals will be found throughout the endnotes, beginning on page 313. Many are discussed on pages 316-322

KING GILLETTE   ELLA WHEELER WILCOX
RALPH A. WEEKS   CLARENCE DARROW
JUDGE DANIEL T. WRIGHT   JENNINGS RANDOLPH [7]

These names represent but a small fraction of the hundreds of well-known Americans whose achievements, financial and otherwise, prove that those who understand and apply the Carnegie secret reach high stations in life. I have never known anyone who was inspired to use the secret who did not achieve noteworthy success in his or her chosen calling. I have never known any person to achieve true professional distinction, or to accumulate riches of any consequence, without possession of the secret in one form or another. From these two facts I draw the conclusion that the secret is more important, as a part of the knowledge essential for self-determination, than any which one receives through what is popularly known as "education."

What is EDUCATION anyway? This will be answered in full detail.

As far as schooling is concerned, many of these individuals had very little. John Wanamaker once told me that what little schooling he had he acquired in very much the same manner as a steam locomotive takes on water, by scooping it up as it runs.[8]

Henry Ford never reached high school, let alone college. I am not attempting to minimize the value of formal education, but I am trying to express my earnest belief that those who master and apply the secret will reach high stations, accumulate riches, and bargain with life on their own terms, even if their schooling has been meager.

Somewhere, as you read, the secret to which I refer will jump from the page and stand boldly before you IF YOU ARE READY FOR IT! When it appears, you will recognize it. Whether you receive the sign in the first or the last chapter, stop for a moment when it presents itself and celebrate — for that occasion will mark the most important turning point of your life.

We pass now to our "Introduction" chapter and to the story of my very dear friend who has generously acknowledged having seen the mystic sign and whose business achievements are evidence enough that he discovered the secret. As you read his story and those that follow, remember that they deal with the important problems of life such as all people experience—the problems arising from one's endeavor to earn a living, to find hope, courage, contentment, peace of mind, to accumulate riches, and to enjoy freedom of body and spirit.

Remember, too, as you go through this book that it deals with facts and not with fiction, its purpose being to convey a great universal truth through which all who are READY may learn not only WHAT TO DO, BUT ALSO HOW TO DO IT—and receive, as well, THE NEEDED STIMULUS TO MAKE A START.

As a final word of preparation, before you begin the next chapter, may I offer one brief suggestion which may provide a clue by which the Carnegie secret may be recognized? It is this: ALL ACHIEVEMENT, ALL EARNED RICHES, HAVE THEIR BEGINNING IN AN IDEA! If you are ready for the secret, you already possess one half of it, therefore, you will readily recognize the other half the moment it reaches your mind.

Napoleon Hill

Success comes to those who become
SUCCESS CONSCIOUS.

§　§　§

Failure comes to those who indifferently allow
themselves to become FAILURE CONSCIOUS.

Introduction

MINDPOWER

The Man Who "Thought" His Way

TRULY, THOUGHTS ARE THINGS — and powerful things at that when they are mixed with definiteness of purpose, persistence, and a BURNING DESIRE for their translation into riches or other material objects.

Edwin C. Barnes discovered how true it is that individuals really do THINK AND GROW RICH.[1] His discovery did not come about at one sitting. It came little by little, beginning with a BURNING DESIRE to become a business associate of the great Thomas Alva Edison.

One of the chief characteristics of Barnes' desire was that it was *definite*. He wanted to work *with* Edison, not *for* him. Observe carefully the description of how he went about translating his DESIRE into reality, and you will have a better understanding of the 13 steps which lead to riches.

When this DESIRE, or impulse of thought, first flashed into Barnes' mind, he was in no position to act upon it. Two difficulties stood in his way. He did not know Mr. Edison, and he did not have enough money to pay his railroad fare to Orange, New Jersey, where Mr. Edison's laboratories were located. These difficulties were sufficient to have discouraged the majority of people from making any attempt to carry out the desire. But his was no ordinary desire! He was so determined to find a way to carry out his desire that he finally decided to travel by "blind baggage," rather than be defeated. (In other words, he went to East Orange on a freight train.)

He presented himself at Mr. Edison's laboratory and announced he had come to go into business with the inventor. Years later, in speaking of the first meeting between Barnes and Edison, Mr. Edison said, "He stood there before me looking like an ordinary tramp, *but there was something in the expression of his face which conveyed the impression that he was determined to get what he had come after.* I had learned from years of experience with men that when a man really *desires* a thing so deeply that he is willing to stake his entire future on a single turn of the wheel in order to get it, he is sure to win. I gave him the opportunity he asked for *because I saw he had made up his mind to stand by until he succeeded.* Subsequent events proved that no mistake was made."

Just what young Barnes said to Mr. Edison on that occasion was far less important than *that which he thought.* Edison himself said so! It could not have been the young man's appearance which got him his start in the Edison office, for that was definitely against him. It was what he THOUGHT that counted.

If the significance of this statement could be conveyed to the person who reads it, there would be no need for the remainder of this book.

Barnes did not get his partnership with Edison on his first interview. He did get a chance to work in the Edison offices at a very nominal wage, doing work that was unimportant to Edison but most important to Barnes because it gave him an opportunity to display his "merchandise" where his intended partner could see it.

Months went by. Apparently nothing happened to bring the coveted goal which Barnes had set up in his mind as his DEFINITE MAJOR PURPOSE. But something important was happening in Barnes' mind. He was constantly intensifying his DESIRE to become the business associate of Edison.

Psychologists have correctly suggested that "when one is truly ready for a thing, it puts in its appearance." Barnes was ready for a business association with Edison. Moreover, he was DETERMINED TO REMAIN READY UNTIL HE GOT THAT WHICH HE WAS SEEKING.

He did not say to himself, "Ah well, what's the use? I guess I'll change my mind and try for a sales job." But he did say, "I came here to go into business with Edison, and I'll accomplish this end if it takes the remainder of my life." *He meant it!* What a different story people would have to tell if only they would adopt a DEFINITE PURPOSE and stand by that purpose until it had time to become an all-consuming obsession!

Maybe young Barnes did not know it at the time, but his bulldog determination, his persistence in standing back of a single DESIRE, was destined to mow down all opposition and bring him the opportunity he was seeking.

When the opportunity came, it appeared in a different form and from a different direction than Barnes had expected. That is one of the tricks of opportunity. It has a sly habit of slipping in by the back door, and it often comes disguised in the form of misfortune or temporary defeat. Perhaps this is why so many fail to recognize opportunity.

Mr. Edison had just perfected a new office device, known at that time as the Edison Dictating Machine (later the Ediphone). His sales staff were not enthusiastic about it. They did not believe it could be sold without great effort. Barnes saw his opportunity. It had crawled in quietly, hidden in an odd-looking machine which interested no one but Barnes and the inventor.

Barnes knew he could sell the Edison Dictating Machine. He suggested this to Edison and promptly got his chance. He *did* sell the machine. In fact, he sold it so successfully that Edison gave him a contract to distribute and market it all over the nation. Out of that business association grew the famous slogan "Made by Edison and Installed by Barnes."

The business alliance was a great success for more than three decades. Out of it Barnes made himself rich in money, but he did something infinitely greater. He proved that one really can "Think and Grow Rich."

How much actual cash that original DESIRE of Barnes was worth to him, I have no way of knowing. Perhaps it brought him two or three million dollars.[2] But the amount, whatever it may have been, was insignificant when compared to the far greater asset he acquired in the form of the definite knowledge that *an intangible impulse of thought can be "transmuted" into its physical counterpart* by the application of known principles.[3]

Barnes literally *thought* himself into a partnership with the great Edison! He *thought* himself into a fortune. He had nothing to start with except the capacity to KNOW WHAT HE WANTED AND THE DETERMINATION TO STAND BY THAT DESIRE UNTIL HE REALIZED IT.

He had no money to begin with. He had but little education. He had no influence. But he did have initiative, faith, and the will to win. With these intangible forces he made himself "number one man" with the greatest inventor who ever lived.[4]

Three Feet from Gold

Now let us look at a different situation and study someone who had plenty of tangible evidence of riches, but lost them — *because he stopped* three feet short of the goal he was seeking.

One of the most common causes of failure is the habit of quitting when one is overtaken by *temporary defeat*. Every person is guilty of this mistake at one time or another.

An uncle of R. U. Darby[5] was caught by "gold fever" in the gold rush days and went west to DIG AND GROW RICH. He had never heard that *more gold has been mined from the human brain than has ever been taken from the earth*. He staked a claim and went to work with pick and shovel. The going was hard, but his lust for gold was definite. After weeks of labor, he was rewarded by the discovery of the shining ore. He needed machinery to bring the ore to the surface. Quietly, he covered up the mine, retraced his footsteps to his home in Williamsburg, Maryland, and told his relatives and a few neighbors of the "strike." They got together money for the needed machinery and had it shipped. The uncle and Darby went back to work the mine.

The first car of ore was mined and shipped to a smelter. The returns proved they had one of the richest mines in Colorado! A few more cars of that ore would clear the debts. Then would come the big killing in profits.

Down went the drills! Up went the hopes of Darby and Uncle! Then something happened. The vein of gold ore disappeared! They had come to the end of the rainbow, and the pot of gold was no longer there! They drilled on, desperately trying to pick up the vein again — all to no avail.

Finally, they decided to QUIT.

They sold the machinery to a junkman for a few hundred dollars and took the train back home. Some junkmen are dumb, but not this one. He called in a mining engineer to look at the mine and do a little calculating. The engineer advised that the project had failed because the owners were not familiar with "fault lines." His calculations showed that the vein would be found JUST THREE FEET FROM WHERE THE DARBYS HAD STOPPED DRILLING! That is exactly where it was found!

The junkman took millions of dollars in ore from the mine because he knew enough to seek expert counsel before giving up. Most of the money which went into the machinery was procured through the efforts of R. U. Darby, who was then a very young man. The money came from his relatives and neighbors because of their faith in him. He paid back every dollar of it, although he was years in doing so.

Long afterward, Mr. Darby recouped his loss many times over *when he made the discovery* that DESIRE can be transmuted into gold. The discovery came after he went into the business of selling life insurance.

Remembering that he had lost a huge fortune because he STOPPED three feet from gold, Darby profited from the experience in his chosen work by the simple method of saying to himself, "I stopped three feet from gold, but I will never stop *because people say 'no'* when I ask them to buy insurance."

Darby in his day was one of a small group of fewer than 50 individuals who sold more than a million dollars of life insurance annually. He owed his "stickability" to the lesson he learned from his "quitability" in the gold mining business.

Before success comes in anyone's life, that individual is sure to meet with much temporary defeat and, perhaps, some failure. When defeat overtakes a person, the easiest and most logical thing to do is to QUIT. That is exactly what the majority of people do.

More than 500 of the most successful individuals this country has ever known have told me that their greatest success came just one step *beyond* the point at which defeat had overtaken them. Failure is a trickster with a keen sense of irony and cunning. It takes great delight in tripping one when success is almost within reach.

A 50-Cent Lesson in Persistence

Shortly after Mr. Darby received his degree from the "University of Hard Knocks" and had decided to profit by his experience in the gold mining business, he had the good fortune to be present on an occasion that proved to him that "no" does not necessarily mean *no*.

One afternoon he was helping an uncle grind wheat in an old-fashioned mill. The uncle operated a large farm on which a number of black sharecropper farmers lived. Quietly, the door was opened and a small child, the daughter of one of the tenant families, walked in and took her place near the door.

The uncle looked up, saw the child, and barked at her roughly, "What do you want?"

Meekly, the child replied, "My momma say to send her fifty cents."

"I'll not do it," the uncle retorted. "Now you run on home."

"Yes sir," the child replied. *But she did not move.*

The uncle went ahead with his work, so busily engaged that he did not pay enough attention to the child to observe that she did not leave. When he looked up and saw her still standing there, he yelled at her, "I told you to go on home! Now go or I'll take a switch to you."

The little girl said, "Yes sir," *but she did not budge an inch.*

The uncle dropped a sack of grain he was about to pour into the mill hopper, picked up a barrel stave, and started toward the child with an expression on his face that indicated trouble.

Darby held his breath. He was certain he was about to witness a horrible beating. He knew his uncle had a fierce temper. In those days, poor children, especially sharecropper children, simply were not allowed to exhibit such overt defiance. When the uncle reached the spot where the child was standing, she quickly moved forward one step, looked up into his eyes, and screamed at the top of her shrill voice, "MY MOMMA'S GOTTA HAVE THAT FIFTY CENTS!"

The uncle stopped, looked at her for a minute, then slowly laid the barrel stave on the floor, put his hand in his pocket, took out a half-dollar, and gave it to her.

The child took the money and slowly backed toward the door, never taking her eyes off the man *she had just conquered*. After she had gone, the uncle sat down on a box and looked out the window into space for more than ten minutes. He was pondering, with awe, the whipping he had just taken.

Mr. Darby, too, was doing some thinking. That was the first time in all his experience he had seen a black child deliberately master a white adult. How did she do it? What happened to his uncle that robbed him of his fierceness and made him as docile as a lamb? What strange power did this child use that made her master over this man? These and other similar questions flashed into Darby's mind, but he did not find the answer until years later when he told me the story. Strangely, the story of this unusual experience was told to me in the old mill, on the very spot where the uncle took his whipping. Strangely, too, I had devoted nearly a quarter of a century to the study of that same power which enabled a small, illiterate sharecropper's child to conquer a powerful figure of authority.

As we stood there in that musty old mill, Mr. Darby repeated the story of the unusual conquest and finished by asking, "What can you make of it? What strange power did that child use that so completely whipped my uncle?"

The answer to his question will be found in the principles described in this book. The answer is full and complete. It contains details and instructions sufficient to enable anyone to understand

and apply the same force which the little child stumbled upon accidentally.

Keep your mind alert and you will observe exactly what strange power came to the rescue of the child. You will catch a glimpse of this power in the next chapter. Somewhere in this book you will find an idea that will quicken your receptive powers and place at your command, for your OWN benefit, this same irresistible power. The awareness of this power may come to you in the first chapter, or it may flash into your mind in some subsequent chapter. It may come in the form of a single idea. Or it may come in the nature of a plan or a purpose. Again, it may cause you to go back into your past experiences of failure or defeat and bring to the surface some lesson by which you can regain all that you "lost" through defeat.

After I had described to Mr. Darby the power unwittingly used by the little child, he quickly retraced his 30 years of experience as a life insurance salesman and frankly acknowledged that his success in that field was due in no small degree to the lesson he had learned from the child.

Mr. Darby pointed out: "Every time a prospect tried to bow me out without buying, I saw that child standing there in the old mill, her big eyes glaring in defiance, and I said to myself, 'I've *gotta* make this sale.' The better portion of all sales I have made were made after people had said 'NO.'" He recalled, too, his mistake in having stopped only three feet from gold, "but that experience," he said, "was a blessing in disguise. It taught me to *keep on keeping on* no matter how hard the going may be, a lesson I needed to learn before I could succeed in anything."

This story of Mr. Darby, his uncle, the child, and the gold mine doubtless will be read by hundreds of men and women who make their living in sales. To all of these, I wish to offer the suggestion that Darby owed to these two experiences his ability to sell more than a million dollars of life insurance every year—an incredible feat in his day.

Life is strange and often imponderable! Both its successes and its failures have their roots in simple experiences. Mr. Darby's experiences were commonplace and simple enough, yet they held the answer to his destiny in life, therefore, they were as important (to him) as life itself. He profited by these two dramatic experiences because *he analyzed them* and found the lesson they taught. But what of the person who has neither the time nor the inclination to study failure in search of knowledge that may lead to success? Where and how is that individual to learn the art of converting defeat into steppingstones to opportunity?

To answer these questions, this book was written. The answer calls for a description of 13 steps, or principles, but remember as you read, the answer you may be seeking to the questions which have caused you to ponder over the strangeness of life may be found *in your own mind* — which through some idea, plan, or purpose which may spring into your mind as you read.

One sound idea is all that one needs to achieve success. The principles described in this book contain the best and the most practical of all that is known concerning ways and means of creating useful ideas.

Before we go any further in our approach to the description of these principles, I believe you are entitled to receive this important suggestion: WHEN RICHES BEGIN TO COME, THEY COME SO QUICKLY, IN SUCH GREAT ABUNDANCE, THAT ONE WONDERS WHERE THEY HAVE BEEN HIDING DURING ALL THOSE LEAN YEARS. This is an astounding statement, and all the more so when we take into consideration the popular belief that riches come only to those who work hard and long.

When you begin to THINK AND GROW RICH, you will observe that riches begin with a state of mind — with definiteness of purpose and with little or no hard work. You and every other person ought to be interested in knowing how to acquire that state of mind which will attract riches. I spent 25 years in research, analyzing thousands of people, because I, too, wanted to know "how wealthy people become that way."

Without that research, this book could not have been written.

Here take notice of a very significant truth: The Great Depression started in 1929 and continued on to an all-time record of economic destruction until sometime after President Franklin D. Roosevelt entered office. Then the Depression began to fade into nothingness. Just as an usher in a theater raises the lights so gradually that darkness is "transmuted" into light before you realize it, so did the spell of *fear* in the minds of the people gradually fade away and become *faith*.

Observe closely that as soon as you master the principles of this philosophy and begin to follow the instructions for applying those principles, your financial status will begin to improve and everything you touch will begin to transmute itself into an asset for your benefit. Impossible? Not at all.

One of the main weaknesses of the human race is the average person's familiarity with the word "impossible." People know all the rules which will NOT work. They know all the things which CANNOT be done. This book was written for those who seek the rules which have made others successful and who are willing to *stake everything* on those rules.

A great many years ago I purchased a fine dictionary. The first thing I did with it was to turn to the word "impossible" and neatly clip it out of the book. That would not be an unwise thing for you to do.

Success comes to those who become SUCCESS-CONSCIOUS.

Failure comes to those who indifferently allow themselves to become FAILURE-CONSCIOUS.

The object of this book is to help all who seek it to learn the art of changing their minds from FAILURE CONSCIOUSNESS to SUCCESS CONSCIOUSNESS.

Another weakness found in altogether too many people is the habit of measuring everything and everyone by *their own* impressions and beliefs. Some who read this will believe that no one can THINK AND GROW RICH. They cannot think in terms of riches because their thought habits have been steeped in poverty, want, misery, failure, and defeat.

These unfortunate people remind me of a prominent Asian who came to America when he was a student to be educated in American ways. He attended the University of Chicago. One day President William Rainey Harper[6] met this young man on the campus, stopped to chat with him for a few minutes and asked what had impressed him as being the most noticeable characteristic of the American people.

"Why," the student exclaimed, "your eyes!"

What does the typical Caucasian say about people of Asian descent?

We refuse to believe, or we think odd, that which is not familiar or which we do not understand. We foolishly believe that our *own* limitations are the proper measure of limitations. Sure, another person's eyes may appear "different" BECAUSE THEY ARE NOT THE SAME AS OUR OWN.

Millions of people look at the achievements of highly successful entrepreneurs, such as Henry Ford, *after* they have arrived and envy them because of their good fortune, or luck, or genius, or whatever it is that they credit for the entrepreneurs' fortunes. Perhaps one person in every hundred thousand knows the secret of entrepreneurial success, and those who do know are too modest or too reluctant to speak of it *because of its simplicity*. A single event will illustrate the "secret" perfectly.

One day, Ford decided to produce his now famous V-8 automobile engine, one of the most successful developments in the history of the automobile industry. He chose to build an engine with the entire eight cylinders cast in one block, and he instructed his engineers to produce a design for the engine. The design was placed on paper, but the engineers agreed, to a man, that it was simply *impossible* to cast an eight-cylinder gas engine block in one piece.

Ford said, "Produce it anyway."

"But," they replied, "it's impossible!"

"Go ahead," Ford commanded, "and stay on the job until you succeed, no matter how much time is required."

The engineers went ahead. There was nothing else for them to do if they were to remain on the Ford staff. Six months went by; nothing happened. Another six months passed, and still nothing happened. The engineers tried every conceivable plan to carry out the orders, but the thing seemed out of the question – *"impossible!"*

At the end of the year, Ford checked with his engineers, and again they informed him they had found no way to carry out his orders.

"Go right ahead," said Ford. "I want it, and I'll have it."

They went ahead, and then, as if by a stroke of magic, the secret was discovered. The Ford DETERMINATION had won once more![7]

This story may not be described with minute accuracy, but the sum and substance of it is correct. Deduce from it, if you wish to THINK AND GROW RICH, the secret of the Ford millions. You'll not have to look very far.

Henry Ford was a success because he understood and *applied* the principles of success. One of these is DESIRE—knowing what you want. Remember this Ford story as you read, and pick out the lines in which the secret of his stupendous achievement has been described. If you can do this, if you can lay your finger on the particular group of principles which made Henry Ford rich, you can equal his achievements in almost any calling for which you are suited.

You are "the Master of Your Fate, the Captain of Your Soul"

When poet William Ernest Henley wrote the prophetic lines, "I am the Master of my Fate, I am the Captain of my Soul," he should have informed us that we are the Masters of our Fate, the Captains of our Souls, *because* we have the power to control our thoughts.

He should have told us that the universe in which this little earth floats, in which we move and have our being, is itself a form of energy, and it is filled with a form of universal power which ADAPTS itself to the nature of the thoughts we hold in our minds — and INFLUENCES us, in natural ways, to transmute our thoughts into their physical equivalent.

If the poet had told us of this great truth, we should know WHY IT IS that we are the Masters of our Fate, the Captains of our Souls. He should have told us, with great emphasis, that this power makes no attempt to discriminate between destructive thoughts and constructive thoughts, that it will urge us to translate into physical reality thoughts of poverty just as quickly as it will influence us to act upon thoughts of riches.

He should have told us, too, that our brains become "magnetized" with the dominating thoughts we hold in our minds. And that by means which no one fully understands, these dominating thoughts, like magnets, attract to us the forces, the people, the circumstances of life which harmonize with the nature of our *dominating* thoughts.

He should have told us that before we can accumulate riches in great abundance, we must magnetize our minds with intense DESIRE for riches, that we must become "money conscious" until the DESIRE for money drives us to create definite plans for acquiring it.

But, being a poet and not a philosopher, Henley contented himself by stating a great truth in poetic form, leaving those who followed him to interpret the philosophical meaning of his lines.

Little by little, the truth has unfolded itself, until it now appears certain that the principles described in this book hold the secret of mastery over our economic fate.

We are now almost ready to examine the first of *The 13 Steps to Riches* that underlie *The Think and Grow Rich Philosophy*. Maintain a spirit of open-mindedness, and remember as you read that these principles are the invention of no one individual. The principles were gathered from the life experiences of more than 500 people who actually accumulated riches in huge amounts—people who began in poverty, with but little education, without influence. The principles worked for these individuals. You can put them to work for your own enduring benefit.

You will find it easy, not hard, to do.

Before you read about *The First Step to Riches* in the next chapter, I want you to know that it conveys factual information that might easily change your entire financial destiny, just as it so definitely brought changes of stupendous proportions to two persons to be described.

I want you to know also that the relationship between these two individuals and myself is such that I could have taken no liberties with the facts even if I had wished to do so. One of them was my closest personal friend for more than a quarter of a century. The other is my own son. The unusual success of these two men, success which they generously accredit to the principle described in the next chapter, more than justifies this personal reference as a means of emphasizing the far-flung power of this principle.

Many years ago, I delivered the commencement address at Salem College in Salem, West Virginia.[8] I emphasized the principle described in the next chapter with so much intensity that one of the members of the graduating class definitely appropriated it and made it a part of his own philosophy. That young man went on to become a distinguished member of Congress and an important figure in the national government. Just before this book went to the publisher, this U. S. Senator wrote me a letter in which he so clearly stated his opinion of the principle outlined in the next chapter that I have chosen to publish his letter here as a "foreword" to that chapter. It gives you an idea of the rewards to come.

My dear Napoleon:

My service as a Member of Congress having given me an insight into the problems of men and women, I am writing to offer a suggestion which may become helpful to thousands of worthy people.

With apologies, I must state that the suggestion, if acted upon, will mean several years of labor and responsibility for you, but I am enheartened to make the suggestion, because I know your great love for rendering useful service.

You delivered the Commencement address at Salem College, when I was a member of the graduating class. In that address, you planted in my mind an idea which has been responsible for the opportunity I now have to serve the people of my State, and will be responsible, in a very large measure, for whatever success I may have in the future.

The suggestion I have in mind is that you put into a book the sum and substance of the address you delivered at

Salem College, and in that way give the people of America an opportunity to profit by your many years of experience and association with [those] who, by their greatness, have made America the richest nation on earth.

I recall, as though it were yesterday, the marvelous description you gave of the method by which Henry Ford, with but little schooling, without a dollar, with no influential friends, rose to great heights. I made up my mind then, even before you had finished your speech, that I would make a place for myself, no matter how many difficulties I had to surmount.

Thousands of young people will finish their schooling this year, and within the next few years. Every one of them will be seeking just such a message of practical encouragement as the one I received from you. They will want to know where to turn, what to do, to get started in life. You can tell them, because you have helped to solve the problems of so many, many people.

If there is any possible way that you can afford to render so great a service, may I offer the suggestion that you include with every book, one of your Personal Analysis Charts, in order that the purchaser of the book may have the benefit of a complete self-inventory, indicating, as you indicated to me years ago, exactly what is standing in the way of success.

Such a service as this, providing the readers of your book with a complete, unbiased picture of their faults and their virtues, would mean to them the difference between success and failure. The service would be priceless.

Millions of people are now facing the problem of staging a comeback,...and I speak from personal experience when I say, I know these earnest people would welcome the opportunity...to receive your suggestions for the solution.

You know the problems of those who face the necessity of beginning all over again. There are thousands of people in America today who would like to know how they can convert ideas into money, people who must start at scratch, without finances, and recoup their losses. If anyone can help them, you can.

If you publish the book, I would like to own the first copy that comes from the press, personally autographed by you.

With best wishes, believe me,
Cordially yours,
JENNINGS RANDOLPH [9]

What that commencement address had kindled in Senator Jennings Randolph as he was about to set out on adult life, was his first real understanding of the enormous power of DESIRE — *The First Step to Riches*.

A BURNING DESIRE TO BE AND TO DO
is the starting point from which the dreamer must take off. Dreams are not born of indifference, laziness, or lack of ambition.

Chapter 1

DESIRE

The Starting Point of All Achievement
The First Step to Riches

WHEN EDWIN C. BARNES climbed down from that freight train in Orange, N. J., he may have resembled a tramp, but his *thoughts* were those of a king!

As he made his way from the railroad tracks to Thomas Edison's office, his mind was at work. He saw himself *standing in Edison's presence*. He heard himself asking Mr. Edison for an opportunity to carry out the one CONSUMING OBSESSION OF HIS LIFE, a BURNING DESIRE to become the business associate of the great inventor.

Barnes' desire was not a *hope*! It was not a *wish*! It was a keen, pulsating DESIRE that transcended everything else. It was DEFINITE.

The desire was not new when he approached Edison. It had been Barnes' *dominating desire* for a long time. In the beginning, when the desire first appeared in his mind, it may have been, probably was, only a wish, but it was no mere wish when he appeared before Edison with it.

A few years later, Edwin C. Barnes again stood before Edison in the same office where he first met the inventor. This time his DESIRE had been translated into reality. *He was in business with Edison*. The dominating DREAM OF HIS LIFE had become a reality. People who later knew Barnes envied him because of the "break" that life had yielded him. They saw him in the days of his triumph, without taking the trouble to investigate the *cause* of his success.

Barnes succeeded because he chose a definite goal, placed all his energy, all his willpower, all his effort, everything back of that goal. He did not become the partner of Edison the day he arrived. He was content to start at the most menial work as long as it provided an opportunity to take even one step toward his cherished goal.

Five years passed before the chance he had been seeking made its appearance. During all those years, not one ray of hope, not one promise of attainment of his DESIRE, had been held out to him. To everyone except himself, he appeared to be only another cog in the Edison business wheel, but in his own mind HE WAS THE PARTNER OF EDISON EVERY MINUTE OF THE TIME from the very day that he first went to work there.

It is a remarkable illustration of the power of a DEFINITE DESIRE. Barnes won his goal because he wanted to be a business associate of Mr. Edison more than he wanted anything else. He created a plan by which to attain that purpose. But he BURNED ALL BRIDGES BEHIND HIM. He stood by his DESIRE until it became the dominating obsession of his life — and, finally, a fact.

When he went to Orange, he did not say to himself, "I will try to induce Edison to give me a job of some sort." He said, "I will see Edison and put him on notice that I have come to go into business with him." He did not say, "I will work there for a few months and if I get no encouragement, I will quit and get a job somewhere else." He did say, "I will start anywhere. I will do anything Edison tells me to do, but *before I am through*, I will be his associate."

He did not say, "I will keep my eyes open for another opportunity in case I fail to get what I want in the Edison organization." He said, "There is but ONE thing in this world that I am determined to have, and that is a business association with Thomas A. Edison. I will burn all bridges behind me and stake my ENTIRE FUTURE on my ability to get what I want."

He left himself no possible way of retreat. He had to win or perish!

That is all there is to the Barnes story of success!

A long while ago, a great warrior faced a situation which made it necessary for him to make a decision which ensured his success on the battlefield. He was about to send his armies against a powerful foe whose men outnumbered his own. He loaded his soldiers into boats, sailed to the enemy's country, unloaded soldiers and equipment, then gave the order to burn the ships that had carried them. Addressing his troops before the first battle, he said, "You see the boats going up in smoke. That means that we cannot leave these shores alive unless we win! We now have no choice. *We win — or we perish!*"

They won.

Those who would win in any undertaking must be willing to burn their ships and cut all sources of retreat. Only by so doing can one be sure of maintaining that state of mind known as a BURNING DESIRE TO WIN, essential to success.

The morning after the great Chicago Fire, a group of merchants stood on State Street looking at the smoking remains of what had been their stores.[1] They went into a conference to decide if they would try to rebuild or leave Chicago and start over in a more promising section of the country. They reached a decision — all except one — to leave Chicago.

The merchant who decided to stay and rebuild pointed a finger at the remains of his store and said, "Gentlemen, on that very spot I will build the world's greatest store, no matter how many times it may burn down."

That was in 1871. The store was built. It became a towering monument to the power of that state of mind known as BURNING DESIRE. The easy thing for Marshal Field to have done would have been exactly what his fellow merchants did. When the going was hard and the future looked dismal, they pulled up and went where the going seemed easier.[2]

Mark well this difference between Marshal Field and the other merchants because it is the same difference that distinguished Edwin C. Barnes from thousands of other young people who worked in the Edison organization. It is the same difference which distinguishes practically all who succeed from those who fail.

Every individual who reaches the age of understanding the purpose of money, wishes for it. *Wishing* will not bring riches. But *desiring* riches with a state of mind that becomes an obsession, then planning definite ways and means to acquire riches, and backing those plans with persistence *which does not recognize failure*, will bring riches.

The method by which DESIRE for riches can be transmuted into its financial equivalent consists of six definite, practical actions:

> *First.* Fix in your mind the *exact* amount of money you desire. It is not sufficient merely to say, "I want plenty of money." Be definite as to the amount. (There is a psychological reason for definiteness which will be described in a subsequent chapter.)
>
> *Second.* Determine exactly what you intend to give in return for the money you desire. (There is no such reality as "something for nothing.")
>
> *Third.* Establish a definite date when you intend to *possess* the money you desire.
>
> *Fourth.* Create a definite plan for carrying out your desire, and begin *at once*, whether you are ready or not, to put this plan into *action*.
>
> *Fifth.* Write out a clear, concise statement of the amount of money you intend to acquire, name the time limit for its acquisition, state what you intend to give in return for the money, and describe clearly the plan through which you intend to accumulate it.
>
> *Sixth.* Read your written statement aloud, twice daily, once just before retiring at night and once after arising in the morning. AS YOU READ, SEE AND FEEL AND BELIEVE YOURSELF ALREADY IN POSSESSION OF THE MONEY.

It is important that you follow the instructions described in these six actions. It is especially important that you observe and follow the instructions in the sixth. You may complain that it is impossible for you to "see yourself in possession of money" before you actually have it. Here is where a BURNING DESIRE will come to your aid. If you truly DESIRE money so keenly that your desire is an obsession, you will have no difficulty in convincing yourself that you will acquire it. The object is to want money and to become so determined to have it that you CONVINCE yourself you *will* have it.

Only those who become "money-conscious" ever accumulate great riches. Money-consciousness means that the mind has become so thoroughly saturated with the DESIRE for money that one can see one's self already in possession of it.

To the uninitiated, who have not been schooled in the working principles of the human mind, these instructions may appear impractical. It may be helpful to all who fail to recognize the soundness of the six actions to know that the information they convey was received from Andrew Carnegie, who began as an ordinary laborer in the steel mills, but managed, despite his humble beginnings, to make these principles yield him a fortune of considerably more than one hundred million dollars.[3] It may be of further help to know that the six actions here recommended were carefully scrutinized by Thomas A. Edison, who placed his stamp of approval upon them as being not only the steps essential for the accumulation of money, but necessary for the attainment of *any definite goal*.

The steps call for no "hard labor." They call for no "sacrifice." They do not require one to become ridiculous or unthinking. To apply them calls for no great amount of education. But the successful completion of these six actions does call for sufficient *imagination* to enable one to see, and to understand, that accumulation of money cannot be left to chance, good fortune, and luck. One must realize that all who have accumulated great fortunes first did a certain amount of dreaming, hoping, wishing, DESIRING, and PLANNING *before* they acquired money.

You may as well know, right here, that you can never have riches in great quantities UNLESS you can work yourself into a white heat of DESIRE for money and actually BELIEVE you will possess it.

You may as well know also that every great leader, from the dawn of civilization down to the present, was a dreamer. Christianity became one of the greatest powers in the world because its founder was an intense dreamer who had the vision and the imagination to see realities in their mental and spiritual form before they had been transmuted into physical form.

If you do not see great riches in your imagination, you will never see them in your bank balance.

Never in the history of America has there been so great an opportunity for practical dreamers as now exists. The hardships of these recent tough and unsettled economic times have put many people back at square one. A new race is about to be run. The stakes represent huge fortunes which will be accumulated within the next few years. The rules of the race have changed because we now live in a CHANGED WORLD that definitely favors those who have had little or no opportunity to win under the conditions existing recently, when fear often paralyzed personal and economic growth and development.

We who are in this race for riches should be encouraged to know that this changed world in which we live is demanding new ideas, new ways of doing things, new leaders, new inventions, new methods of teaching, new methods of marketing, new books, new literature, new features for the mass media, new ideas for entertainment. Back of all this demand for new and better things there is one quality which one must possess to win, and that is DEFINITENESS OF PURPOSE — the knowledge of what one wants and a burning DESIRE to possess it.

We have witnessed the death of one age and the birth of another. This changed world requires practical dreamers who can *and will* put their dreams into action. The practical dreamers have always been and always will be the pattern makers of civilization.

We who desire to accumulate riches should remember that the real leaders of the world always have been individuals who harnessed and put into practical use the intangible, unseen forces of unborn opportunity, and converted those forces (or impulses of thought) into skyscrapers, cities, factories, airplanes, automobiles, and every form of convenience that makes life more pleasant.

Tolerance and an open mind are practical necessities of the dreamer of today. Those who are afraid of new ideas are doomed before they start. Never has there been a time more favorable to pioneers than the present. True, there is no "Wild and Woolly West" to be conquered as in the days of the covered wagon. But there is a vast business, financial, and industrial world to be remolded and redirected along new and better lines.

In planning to acquire your share of the riches, let no one influence you to scorn the dreamer. To win the big stakes in this changed world, you must catch the spirit of the great pioneers of the past whose dreams have given to civilization all that it has of value. It is that spirit which serves as the lifeblood of America — the burning desire to take full advantage of the wonderful opportunity, yours and mine, to develop and market our talents in a free land.

Let us not forget, Columbus dreamed of an Unknown World, staked his life on the existence of such a world, and discovered it!

Copernicus, the great astronomer, dreamed of a multiplicity of worlds and revealed them! No one denounced him as "impractical" after he had triumphed. Instead, the world worshiped at his shrine, thus proving once more that "SUCCESS REQUIRES NO APOLOGIES, FAILURE PERMITS NO ALIBIS."

If the thing you wish to do is right and *you believe in it*, go ahead and do it! Put your dream across, and never mind what "they" say if you meet with temporary defeat, for "they" perhaps do not know that EVERY FAILURE BRINGS WITH IT THE SEED OF AN EQUIVALENT SUCCESS.

Henry Ford, poor and uneducated, dreamed of a "horseless carriage," went to work with what tools he possessed without waiting for opportunity to favor him, and now evidence of his dream belts the entire earth. He put more wheels into operation than anyone who ever lived — because he was not afraid to back his dreams.

Thomas Edison dreamed of a lamp that could be operated by electricity, began where he stood to put his dream into action, and despite more than 10,000 failures, he stood by that dream until he made it a physical reality. Practical dreamers DO NOT QUIT![4]

Lincoln dreamed of freedom for the slaves, put his dream into action, and barely missed living to see a united North and South translate his dream into reality.

The Wright brothers dreamed of a machine that would fly through the air. Now one may see evidence all over the world that they dreamed soundly.

Marconi dreamed of a system for harnessing the intangible forces of the electromagnetic spectrum.[5] Evidence that he did not dream in vain may be found in every radio and television set in the world. Moreover, Marconi's dream brought the humblest cabin and the stateliest manor house side by side. It has made the people of every nation on earth back-door neighbors. It gave the President of the United States the means by which to talk to all the people of America at one time and on short notice. It may interest you to know that Marconi's "friends" had him taken into custody and examined in a mental hospital when he announced he had discovered a principle through which he could send messages through the air, without the aid of wires or other direct physical means of communication. The dreamers of today fare better.

The world has become accustomed to new discoveries. It has shown a willingness to reward the dreamer who gives the world a new idea.

"The greatest achievement was at first and for a time a dream. The oak sleeps in the acorn; the bird waits in the egg; and in the highest vision of the soul a waking angel stirs. DREAMS ARE THE SEEDLINGS OF REALITIES."[6]

Awake, arise, and assert yourself, you dreamers of the world. Your star is in the ascendancy. Worldwide economic uncertainty has brought the opportunity you have been waiting for. It has taught many people humility, tolerance, and open-mindedness.

The world is filled with an abundance of OPPORTUNITY the dreamers of the past never knew.

A BURNING DESIRE TO BE, AND TO DO, is the starting point from which the dreamer must take off. Dreams are not born of indifference, laziness, or lack of ambition.

The world no longer scoffs at dreamers, nor calls them impractical. If you think it does, take a trip to Tennessee and visit the mighty dams and power plants of the Tennessee Valley Authority to witness what a "dreamer" President did in the way of harnessing and using the great water power of America. At one time, such a dream would have seemed like madness.[7]

You may have been disappointed, you may have suffered setbacks and defeat during hard economic times, you may have felt the great heart within you crushed until it bled. Take courage, for these experiences have tempered the spiritual metal of which you are made—they are assets of incomparable value.

Remember, too, that all who succeed in life get off to a bad start and pass through many heartbreaking struggles before they "arrive." The turning point in the lives of those who succeed usually comes at the moment of some crisis, through which they are introduced to their "other selves."

John Bunyan wrote *Pilgrim's Progress*, which is among the finest works in all of English literature, after he had been confined in prison and sorely punished because of his views on religion.

O. Henry discovered the genius which slept within his brain after he had met with great misfortune and was confined in a prison cell, in Columbus, Ohio. Being FORCED, through misfortune, to become acquainted with his "other self" and to use his IMAGINATION, he discovered himself to be a great author, instead of a miserable criminal and outcast.[8]

Strange and varied are the ways of life, and stranger are the ways of *Infinite Intelligence*,[9] through which human beings are sometimes forced to undergo all sorts of trouble and tribulation before discovering their own brains and their own capacity to create useful ideas through imagination.

Edison, the world's greatest inventor and scientist, started out as a "tramp" telegraph operator.[10] He failed innumerable times before he was driven finally to the discovery of the genius that slept within his brain.

Charles Dickens began by pasting labels on blacking pots. The tragedy of his first love penetrated the depths of his soul and converted him into one of the world's truly great authors. That tragedy produced, first, *David Copperfield*, then a succession of works that made this a richer and better world for all who read his books.[11] (Disappointment over love affairs can have the effect of driving many to drink and others to ruin—and this because most people never learn the art of transmuting their strongest emotions into dreams of a constructive nature. This power of "transmutation" will be dealt with in detail later.)

Helen Keller became deaf and blind shortly after birth and for years could not speak. Despite her misfortune, she wrote her name indelibly in the pages of the history of the great. Her entire life served as evidence *that no one ever is defeated until defeat has been accepted as a reality.*

Robert Burns was an illiterate country lad who was cursed by poverty and who grew up to be a drunkard in the bargain. The world was made better for his having lived because he clothed beautiful thoughts in poetry and thereby plucked a thorn and planted a rose in its place.

Booker T. Washington was born in slavery, handicapped by race and color in the society in which he lived. Because he was tolerant, had an open mind at all times and on all subjects, and was a DREAMER, he left his imprint for good on an entire nation.

Beethoven was deaf, Milton was blind, but their names will last as long as civilization endures because they dreamed and translated their dreams into organized thought.

Before passing to the next chapter, resolve yourself to kindle in your mind the fire of hope, faith, courage, and tolerance. Once you have these states of mind and a working knowledge of the principles described in this book, all else that you need will come to you—when you are READY for it.[12]

There is a difference between WISHING for a thing and being READY to receive it. You are never *ready* for a thing until you *believe* you can acquire it. The state of mind must be BELIEF, not mere hope or wish. Open-mindedness is essential for belief. Closed minds do not inspire faith, courage, and belief.

Remember—no more effort is required to aim high in life, to demand abundance and prosperity, than is required to accept misery and poverty. Jessie B. Rittenhouse has correctly stated this universal truth through these lines in his poem "My Wage":

> "I bargained with Life for a penny,
> And Life would pay no more,
> However I begged at evening
> When I counted my scanty store.
>
> "For Life is a just employer,
> He gives you what you ask,
> But once you have set the wages,
> Why, you must bear the task.
>
> "I worked for a menial's hire
> Only to learn, dismayed,
> That any wage I had asked of Life,
> Life would have willingly paid."

Desire Outwits Mother Nature

As a fitting conclusion to this chapter, I wish to introduce one of the most unusual persons I have ever known. I first saw him many years ago, a few minutes after he was born. He came into the world without any external, physical sign of ears, and the doctor admitted, when pressed for an opinion, that the child would likely be deaf and mute for life.*

I challenged the doctor's opinion. I had the right to do so. I was the child's father. I, too, reached a decision and rendered an opinion,

---

* This was long before the advent of the kind of reconstructive surgery that would be commonplace today.

but I expressed the opinion silently, in the secrecy of my own heart. I decided that my son would hear and speak. Nature could send me a child without normal organs of hearing, but Nature could not induce me to accept the reality of the affliction.

In my own mind, I knew that my son would hear and speak. How? I was sure there must be a way, and I knew I would find it. I thought of the words of the immortal Emerson: "The whole course of things goes to teach us faith. We need only obey. There is guidance for each of us, and by lowly listening, we shall hear *the right word.*"

The right word? DESIRE! More than anything else, I DESIRED that my son should not be deaf and mute. From that desire I never receded, not for a second.

Many years previously I had written, "Our only limitations are those we set up in our own minds." For the first time I wondered if that statement were true. Lying on the bed in front of me was a newborn child, without the natural equipment of hearing. Even though he might eventually hear and speak, he was obviously disfigured for life. Surely, this was a limitation which that child had not set up in his own mind.

What could I do about it? Somehow, I would find a way to transplant into that child's mind my own BURNING DESIRE for ways and means of conveying sound to his brain without the aid of ears.

As soon as the child was old enough to cooperate, I would fill his mind so completely with a BURNING DESIRE to hear that Nature would, by methods of her own, translate that desire into physical reality. All this thinking took place in my own mind, but I spoke of it to no one. Every day I renewed the pledge I had made to myself not to accept this disability for my son.

As he grew older and began to take notice of things around him, we observed that he had a slight degree of hearing. When he reached the age when children usually begin talking, he made no attempt to speak, but we could tell by his actions that he could hear certain sounds slightly. That was all I needed to know! I was convinced that if he could hear even slightly he might develop still greater hearing capacity. Then something happened which gave me hope. It came from an entirely unexpected source.

We bought a Victrola, an old fashioned phonograph. When the child heard the music for the first time, he went into ecstasies and promptly appropriated the machine. He soon showed a preference for certain records, among them "It's a Long Way to Tipperary." On one occasion, he played that piece over and over for almost two hours, standing in front of the Victrola *with his teeth clamped on the edge of the case.* The significance of this self-formed habit of his did not become clear to us until years afterward, for we had never heard of the principle of "bone conduction" of sound at that time.

Shortly after he appropriated the Victrola, I discovered that he could hear me quite clearly when I spoke with my lips touching his mastoid bone, at his jawbone near where his ear canal would have been. These discoveries placed into my possession the necessary means by which I began to translate into reality my BURNING DESIRE to help my son develop hearing and speech. By that time he was making stabs at speaking certain words. The outlook was far from encouraging, but DESIRE BACKED BY FAITH knows no such word as impossible.

Having determined that he could hear the sound of my voice plainly, I began immediately to transfer to his mind the desire to hear and speak. I soon discovered that the child enjoyed bedtime stories, so I went to work creating stories designed to develop in him self-reliance, imagination, and a *keen desire to hear.*

There was one story in particular which I emphasized by giving it some new and dramatic coloring each time it was told. It was designed to plant in his mind the thought that his disability was not a liability, but an asset of great value. Despite the fact that all the philosophy I had examined clearly indicated that EVERY ADVERSITY BRINGS WITH IT THE SEED OF AN EQUIVALENT ADVANTAGE, I must confess that I had not the slightest idea *how* this affliction could ever become an asset. However, I continued my practice of wrapping that philosophy in bedtime stories, hoping the time would come when he would find some plan by which his disability could be made to serve some useful purpose.

Reason told me plainly that there was no adequate compensation for the lack of ears and natural hearing equipment. DESIRE, backed by FAITH, pushed reason aside and inspired me to carry on.

As I analyze the experience in retrospect, I can see now that my son's *faith in me* had much to do with the astounding results. He did not question anything I told him. I sold him the idea that he had a distinct *advantage* over his older brother and that this advantage would reflect itself in many ways.[13]

We could notice that the child's hearing was gradually improving. Moreover, he had not the slightest tendency to be self-conscious because of his affliction. When he was about seven, he showed the first evidence that our method of servicing his mind was bearing fruit. For several months he begged for the privilege of selling newspapers, but his mother would not give her consent. She was afraid that his deafness made it unsafe for him to go out on the street alone.

Finally, he took matters into his own hands. One afternoon when he was left at home with the servants, he climbed through the kitchen window, shinnied to the ground, and set out on his own. He borrowed six cents in capital from the neighborhood shoemaker, invested it in papers, sold out, reinvested, and kept repeating this process until late in the evening. After balancing his accounts and paying back the six cents he had borrowed from his "banker," he had a net profit of 42 cents. When we got home that night, we found him in bed asleep with the money tightly clenched in his little hand.

His mother opened his hand, removed the coins, and cried. Of all things! Crying over her son's first victory seemed so inappropriate. My reaction was the reverse. I laughed heartily, for I knew that my endeavor to plant in the child's mind an attitude of faith in himself had been successful.

His mother saw in his first business venture a little deaf boy who had gone out in the streets and risked his life to earn money. I saw a brave, ambitious, self-reliant little businessman whose stock in himself had been increased a hundred percent because he had gone into business on his own initiative and had won. The transaction pleased me because I knew that he had given evidence of a trait of resourcefulness that would go with him all through life. Later events proved this to be true. When his older brother wanted something, he would lie down on the floor, kick his feet in the air, cry for it — and get it. When the "little deaf boy" wanted something, he would plan a way to earn the money, then buy it for himself. He would follow that pattern throughout adult life.

Truly, my own son taught me that disabilities can be converted into steppingstones on which one may climb toward some worthy goal — *unless* they are accepted as obstacles and used as alibis.

The little deaf boy went through grade school, high school, and college without being able to hear his teachers, except when they shouted loudly at close range. He did not go to a special school.[14] We were determined that he should live as normal a life as possible and associate with children with hearing, and we stood by that decision although it cost us many heated debates with school officials.

While he was in high school, he tried a hearing aid, but it was of no value to him. During his last week in college, something happened which marked the most important turning point of his life. Through what seemed to be mere chance, he came into possession of another hearing aid device, which was sent to him on trial. He was slow about testing it because of his disappointment with the earlier device. Finally he picked the instrument up and more or less carelessly placed it on his head, hooked up the battery, and lo! — as if by a stroke of magic — his lifelong DESIRE FOR NORMAL HEARING BECAME A REALITY! For the first time in his life, he could hear practically as well as any person with normal hearing.[15]

Overjoyed because of the "Changed World" which had been brought to him through his hearing device, he rushed to the telephone, called his mother, and heard her voice perfectly. The next day he plainly heard the voices of his professors in class for the first time in his life! Previously he could hear them only when they shouted at short range. He heard the radio. He heard the movies. For the first time in his life he could converse freely with other people without the necessity of their having to speak loudly. Truly, he had come into possession of a Changed World. We had refused to accept Nature's error, and, by PERSISTENT DESIRE, we had induced Nature to correct that error through the only practical means available.

DESIRE had commenced to pay dividends, but the victory was not yet complete. The boy still had to find a definite and practical way to convert his disability into an *equivalent asset.*

Hardly realizing the significance of what had already been accomplished, but intoxicated with the joy of his newly discovered world of sound, he wrote a letter to the manufacturer of the hearing aid, enthusiastically describing his experience. Something in his letter—something, perhaps, which was not written *on* the lines, but *back* of them—caused the company to invite him to New York. When he arrived, he was escorted through the factory and while talking with the chief engineer, telling him about his Changed World, a hunch, an idea, or an inspiration—call it what you wish—flashed into his mind. It was this impulse of thought which converted his affliction into an asset destined to pay dividends in both money and happiness to thousands of other people.

The sum and substance of that impulse of thought was this: It occurred to him that he might be of help to the millions of deaf people who go through life without the benefit of hearing aids, if he could find a way to tell them the story of his Changed World. Then and there he reached a decision to devote the remainder of his life to rendering useful service to the hard of hearing.

For an entire month he did intensive research during which he analyzed the entire marketing system of the manufacturer of the hearing device. He figured out possible ways and means to communicate with hearing-impaired people all over the world for the purpose of sharing with them his newly discovered "Changed World." When this was done, he put in writing a two-year plan based upon his findings. When he presented the plan to the company, he was instantly given a position for the purpose of carrying out his ambition.

Little did he dream when he went to work that he was destined to bring hope and practical relief to thousands of people who without his help would never have overcome their hearing disability.

Shortly after he became associated with the manufacturer of his hearing aid, he invited me to attend a class conducted by his company to teach deaf people to hear and to speak. I had never heard of such a form of education; therefore, I visited the class, skeptical but hopeful that my time would not be entirely wasted. Here I saw a demonstration which gave me a greatly enlarged vision of what I had done to arouse and keep alive in my son's mind the DESIRE for normal hearing. I saw deaf people actually being taught to hear and to speak through application of the self-same principle I had used more than 20 years previously with my son, Blair.

There is no doubt in my mind that Blair would have been unable to hear or speak for all his life if his mother and I had not managed to shape his mind as we did. The doctor who attended at his birth told us the child might never hear a sound or say a word. Later, Dr. Irving Voorhees, a noted specialist on such cases, examined Blair thoroughly. He was astounded when he learned how well my son could hear and speak, and he said his examination indicated that "theoretically, the boy should not be able to hear at all."

When I planted in Blair's mind the DESIRE to hear and talk and live normally, there went with that impulse some strange influence which caused Nature to become "bridge-builder" and to span the gulf of silence between his brain and the outer world— by some means which the keenest medical specialists were not able to interpret. It would be sacrilege for me even to pretend I fully understand how Nature performed this miracle. It would be unforgivable if I neglected to tell the world as much as I know of the humble part I assumed in the strange experience. It is my duty and a privilege to say I believe, and not without reason, that *nothing is impossible to the person who backs DESIRE with enduring FAITH.*

A BURNING DESIRE has devious ways of transmuting itself into its physical equivalent. Blair DESIRED normal hearing. And he received it! He was born with a disability which might easily have sent one with a less defined DESIRE to the street with a bundle of pencils and a tin cup. That disability served as the medium by which he would go on to render useful service to many thousands of hearing-impaired people, and it gave him useful employment at adequate financial compensation for years.

The little "white lie" I planted in his mind when he was a child — by leading him to BELIEVE his affliction would become a great asset which he could capitalize on — justified itself. Verily, there is nothing, right or wrong, that BELIEF plus BURNING DESIRE cannot make real. These qualities are free to everyone.

In all my experience in dealing with men and women with personal problems, I never handled a single case which more definitely demonstrated the power of DESIRE. Authors sometimes make the mistake of writing of subjects of which they have but superficial or very elementary knowledge. It has been my good fortune to have had the privilege of testing the soundness of the POWER OF DESIRE through the affliction of my own son. Perhaps it was providential that the experience came as it did, for surely no one was better prepared than he to serve as an example of what happens when DESIRE is put to the test. *If Mother Nature bends to the will of a burning desire, is it logical to think that mere human beings can defeat one?*

Strange and imponderable is the power of the human mind! We do not understand the method by which it uses every circumstance, every individual, every physical thing within its reach as a means of transmuting DESIRE into its physical counterpart. Perhaps science will one day uncover this secret.

I planted in my son's mind the DESIRE to hear and to speak as any other person hears and speaks. That DESIRE became a reality. I planted in his mind the DESIRE to convert his greatest disability into his greatest asset. That DESIRE was realized. The method by which this astounding result was achieved is not hard to describe. It consisted of three very definite acts: First, I MIXED FAITH with the DESIRE for normal hearing, which I passed on to my son. Second, I communicated my desire to him in every conceivable way available through persistent, continuous effort, over a period of years. Third, HE BELIEVED ME!

As this chapter was being completed, news came of the death of Mme. Schuman-Heink.[16] One short paragraph in the news dispatch about her death gives the clue to this unusual woman's stupendous success as a singer. I quote portions of the paragraph because the clue it contains is none other than DESIRE.

Early in her career, Mme. Schuman-Heink visited the director of the Vienna Court Opera to audition for him. But he did not grant the audition. After taking one look at the awkward and poorly dressed girl, he exclaimed, none too gently, "With such a face, and with no personality at all, how can you ever expect to succeed in opera? My good child, give up the idea. Buy a sewing machine, and go to work. YOU CAN NEVER BE A SINGER."

Never is a long time! The director of the Vienna Court Opera knew much about the technique of singing. He knew little about the power of desire when it assumes the proportion of an obsession. If he had known more about that power, he would not have made the mistake of condemning genius without giving it an opportunity.

Several years ago, one of my business associates became seriously ill. He became worse as time went on and finally was taken to the hospital for surgery. Just before he was wheeled into the operating room, I took a look at him and wondered how anyone as thin and emaciated as he could possibly go through such a major operation successfully. The surgeon warned me that there was little if any chance of my ever seeing him alive again. But that was the DOCTOR'S OPINION. It was not the opinion of the patient. Just before he was wheeled away, he whispered feebly, "Do not be disturbed, Chief, I will be out of here in a few days." The attending nurse looked at me with pity. But the patient did come through safely. After it was all over, his physician said, "Nothing but his own desire to live saved him. He never would have pulled through if he had not refused to accept the possibility of death."

I believe in the power of DESIRE backed by FAITH because I have seen this power lift people from lowly beginnings to places of power and wealth. I have seen it rob the grave of its victims. I have seen it serve as the medium by which individuals staged a comeback after having been defeated in a hundred different ways. I have seen it provide my own son with a normal, happy, successful life despite Nature's having sent him into the world severely disabled.

How can one harness and use the power of DESIRE? This question is answered through this and the subsequent chapters of this book. This message is going out to the world at the end of one of the most devastating economic upheavals America has ever known. It is reasonable to presume that the message may come to the attention of many who have been wounded by personal economic calamity, those who have lost their fortunes, others who have lost their positions, and great numbers who must reorganize their plans and stage a comeback. To all these, I wish to convey this thought: All achievement, no matter what may be its nature or its purpose, must begin with an intense, BURNING DESIRE for something definite.

Through some strange and powerful principle of "mental chemistry" which she has never divulged, Nature wraps up in the impulse of STRONG DESIRE that "something" which recognizes no such word as "impossible" and accepts no such reality as failure.

Fortunately, Nature has also given us the way to channel DESIRE unwaveringly toward the goals we name and seek. It is the way of FAITH — *The Second Step to Riches.*

FAITH IS A STATE OF MIND WHICH MAY BE INDUCED BY AUTOSUGGESTION.

Chapter 2

FAITH

Visualization and Belief in the Attainment of Desire
The Second Step to Riches

FAITH IS the head chemist of the mind. When FAITH is blended with the "vibration of thought," the subconscious mind instantly picks up the vibration, translates it into its spiritual equivalent, and transmits it to Infinite Intelligence, as in the case of prayer. [1]

The emotions of FAITH, LOVE, and SEX are the most powerful of all the major positive emotions. When the three are blended, they have the effect of "coloring" the vibration of thought in such a way that it instantly reaches the subconscious mind, where it is changed into its spiritual equivalent — the only form that induces a response from Infinite Intelligence.

Love and faith are psychic, related to the spiritual side of humanity. Sex is purely biological and related only to the physical. The mixing, or blending, of these three emotions has the effect of opening a direct line of communication between the finite, thinking human mind and Infinite Intelligence.

How to Develop Faith

There comes now a statement which will give a better understanding of the importance the *principle of autosuggestion* assumes in the transmutation of desire into its physical, or monetary, equivalent: *FAITH is a state of mind which may be induced, or created, by affirmations or repeated instructions to the subconscious mind, through the principle of autosuggestion.*

As an illustration, consider one main purpose for which, presumably, you are reading this book. The object is, naturally, to acquire the ability to transmute the intangible thought impulse of DESIRE into its physical counterpart — money. By following the instructions laid down in the chapters on autosuggestion (Chapter 3) and the subconscious mind (Chapter 11), as summarized in the chapter on autosuggestion, you can CONVINCE your subconscious mind that you *believe* you will receive that for which you ask. Your subconscious mind will act upon that belief, then pass it back to you in the form of FAITH, followed by definite plans for procuring that which you desire.

The method by which one develops FAITH where it does not already exist is extremely difficult to describe, almost as difficult, in fact, as it would be to describe the color of red to a blind person who has never seen color and has nothing with which to compare what you describe. Faith is a state of mind which you can develop *at will* after you have mastered the 13 principles in this book — because it is a state of mind which develops through voluntary application and use of these principles.

Repetition or affirmation of orders to your subconscious mind is the only method of voluntary development of the emotion of faith.

Perhaps the meaning will be made clearer through the following explanation of how individuals sometimes become criminals. Stated in the words of a famous criminologist, "When people first come into contact with crime, they abhor it. If they remain in contact with crime for a time, they become accustomed to it and endure it. If they remain in contact with it long enough, they finally embrace it and become influenced by it."

This is the equivalent of saying that any impulse of thought which is repeatedly passed on to the subconscious mind is finally accepted and acted upon by the subconscious mind, which proceeds to translate that impulse into its physical equivalent, by the most practical procedure available.

In connection with this, consider again the statement ALL THOUGHTS WHICH HAVE BEEN EMOTIONALIZED (given feeling) AND MIXED WITH FAITH begin immediately to translate themselves into their physical equivalent or counterpart.

The emotions, or the "feeling" portion of thoughts, are the factors which give thoughts vitality, life, and action. The emotions of faith, love, and sex, when mixed together with any thought impulse, give it greater action than any of these emotions can do singly.

It is not only those thought impulses which have been mixed with FAITH, but those which have been mixed with any of the positive emotions, or any of the negative emotions, that can reach and influence the subconscious mind.

From this statement you will understand that the subconscious mind will translate into its *physical equivalent* a thought impulse of a negative or destructive nature just as readily as it will act upon thought impulses of a positive or constructive nature. This accounts for the strange phenomenon, which so many millions of people experience, referred to as "misfortune" or "bad luck."

There are millions of people who BELIEVE themselves "doomed" to poverty and failure because of some strange force over which they BELIEVE they have no control. They are the creators of their own misfortunes because of this negative BELIEF, which is picked up by their subconscious mind and translated into its physical equivalent.

This is an appropriate place at which to suggest again that *you may benefit, by passing on to your subconscious mind, any DESIRE which you wish translated into its physical or monetary equivalent, in a state of expectancy or BELIEF that the transmutation will actually take place.* Your BELIEF, or FAITH, is the element which determines the action of your subconscious mind. There is nothing to hinder you from "deceiving" your subconscious mind when giving it instructions through autosuggestion, as I deceived my son's subconscious mind.

To make this "deceit" more realistic, conduct yourself when you call upon your subconscious mind just as you would if you were ALREADY IN POSSESSION OF THE MATERIAL THING WHICH YOU ARE DEMANDING.

The subconscious mind will transmute into its physical equivalent, by the most direct and practical media available, *any* order which is given to it in a state of BELIEF, or FAITH, that the order will be carried out.

Surely, enough has been stated by now to give you a starting point from which you may, through experiment and practice, acquire the ability to mix FAITH with any order given to your subconscious mind. Perfection will come through practice. It cannot come by merely reading instructions.

If it be true that one may become a criminal by association with crime (and this is a known fact), it is equally true that one may develop faith by voluntarily suggesting to the subconscious mind that one has faith. The mind comes, finally, to take on the nature of the influences which dominate it. Understand this truth, and you will know why it is essential for you to encourage the *positive emotions* as dominating forces of your mind and to discourage— and *eliminate*—negative emotions.[2]

A mind dominated by positive emotions, or "positive mental attitude," becomes a favorable abode for the state of mind known as faith. A mind so dominated may, at will, give the subconscious mind instructions which it will accept and act upon immediately.

Faith Is a State of Mind Which May Be Induced by Autosuggestion

All down the ages, the religionists[3] have admonished struggling humanity to "have faith" in this, that, and the other dogma or creed, but they have failed to tell people HOW to have faith. They have not stated that "faith is a state of mind and that it may be induced by self-suggestion."

In language which any normal human being can understand, this book will describe all that is known about the principle through which FAITH can be developed where it does not already exist.

Have faith in yourself; faith in the Infinite.

Before we begin, you should be reminded again that: FAITH is the "eternal elixir" which gives life, power, and action to the impulse of thought!

The foregoing sentence is worth reading a second time, and a third, and a fourth. It is worth reading aloud!

FAITH is the starting point of all accumulation of riches!

FAITH is the basis of all "miracles" and all mysteries which cannot be analyzed by the rules of science!

FAITH is the only known antidote for FAILURE!

FAITH is the element, the "chemical" which when mixed with prayer gives one direct communication with Infinite Intelligence.

FAITH is the element which transforms the ordinary "vibration of thought," created by the finite human mind, into its spiritual equivalent.

FAITH is the only agency through which the cosmic force of Infinite Intelligence can be harnessed and used by humanity.

EVERY ONE OF THE FOREGOING STATEMENTS IS CAPABLE OF PROOF!

The proof is simple and easily demonstrated. It is wrapped up in the principle of autosuggestion. Let us center our attention, therefore, on the subject of self-suggestion and find out what it is and what it is capable of achieving.

It is a well-known fact that one comes finally to BELIEVE whatever one repeats to one's self, *whether the statement be true or false*. If we repeat a lie over and over, we will eventually accept the lie as truth. Moreover, we will BELIEVE it to be the truth. Each of us is what we are because of the DOMINATING THOUGHTS which we permit to occupy our mind. Thoughts which we deliberately place in our own mind, and encourage with sympathy, and with which we mix any one or more of the emotions, constitute the motivating forces which direct and control our every movement, act, and deed!

Comes, now, a very significant statement of truth:

THOUGHTS WHICH ARE MIXED WITH ANY OF THE FEELINGS OF EMOTIONS CONSTITUTE A "MAGNETIC" FORCE WHICH ATTRACTS OTHER SIMILAR, OR RELATED THOUGHTS.

A thought thus "magnetized" with emotion may be compared to a seed which, when planted in fertile soil, germinates, grows, and multiplies itself over and over again until that which was originally one small seed becomes countless millions of seeds of the SAME KIND!

All human experience, and all human thinking, occurs in an environment—in a *universe*—saturated with radiated energy and "signals." From gravity to magnetism, from cosmic rays to X- rays, infrared rays, visible light, sound waves, radar, shortwaves, radio and television signals—we live in a world constantly bombarded by "vibrations" of energy, though we can perceive directly only the tiniest portion of them.

Likewise, thought impulses are "vibrations" of energy trans- mitted in some deeply mysterious, and as yet uncomprehended, way as electrical and chemical currents among brain cells. While we do not yet understand and cannot describe scientifically the how of the process, it is clear that thought impulses, like electromagnetic radiation, also are "out there" somehow—as some experiments with extrasensory perception, or ESP, seem clearly to indicate.

Human experience, like the cosmos itself, teems with thought vibrations or "influences"—both destructive and constructive. It is characterized, at all times, by vibrations of fear, poverty, disease, failure, misery, and vibrations of prosperity, health, success, and happiness—just as surely as the atmosphere carries the sound of hundreds of orchestrations of music, and hundreds of human voices, all of which maintain their own individuality, and means of identification, through the medium of television or radio.

From this great "storehouse" of experience, the human mind is constantly attracting vibrations which harmonize with that which DOMINATES the mind. Any thought, idea, plan, or purpose which one holds in one's mind attracts from the "thought vibrations of existence" a host of its relatives, adds these relatives to its own force, and grows until it becomes the dominating, MOTIVATING MASTER of the individual in whose mind it has been housed.

Now, let us go back to the starting point and become informed as to how the original seed of an idea, plan, or purpose may be planted in the mind. The information is easily conveyed: Any idea, plan, or purpose may be placed in the mind *through repetition of thought.* This is why you are asked in the next few pages to write out a statement of your major purpose, or Definite Chief Aim, commit it to memory, and repeat it *out loud* day after day until these vibrations of sound have reached your subconscious mind.

We are what we are because of the vibrations of thought which we pick up and register through the stimuli of our daily environment.

Resolve to throw off the influences of any unfortunate environment you may have grown up in or now find yourself living in, and to build your own life to ORDER. Taking inventory of mental assets and abilities, you will discover that your greatest weakness is lack of self-confidence. This handicap can be surmounted, and timidity translated into courage, through the aid of the principle of autosuggestion. The application of this principle may be made through a simple arrangement of positive thought impulses stated in writing, memorized, and repeated until they become a part of the working equipment of your subconscious mind.

Self-Confidence Formula

First. I know that I have the ability to achieve the object of my Definite Purpose in life; therefore, I DEMAND of myself persistent, continuous action toward its attainment, and I here and now promise to render such action.

Second. I realize that the dominating thoughts of my mind will eventually reproduce themselves in outward, physical action, and gradually transform themselves into physical reality; therefore, I will concentrate my thoughts for 30 minutes daily upon the task of thinking of *the person I intend to become*, thereby creating in my mind a clear mental picture of that person.

Third. I know that through the principle of autosuggestion any desire that I persistently hold in my mind will eventually seek expression through some practical means of attaining the object back of it; therefore, I will devote ten minutes daily to demanding of myself the development of SELF-CONFIDENCE.

Fourth. I have clearly written down a description of my DEFINITE CHIEF AIM in life, and I will never stop trying until I shall have developed sufficient self-confidence for its attainment.[4]

Fifth. I fully realize that no wealth or position can long endure unless built upon truth and justice; therefore, I will engage in no transaction that does not benefit all whom it affects. I will succeed by attracting to myself the forces I wish to use and the cooperation of other people. I will induce others to serve me because of my willingness to serve others. I will eliminate hatred, envy, jealousy, selfishness, and cynicism by developing love for all humanity — because I know that a negative attitude toward others can never bring me success. I will cause others to believe in me because I will believe in them and in myself.

Sixth. I will sign my name to this formula, commit it to memory, and repeat it aloud once a day, with full FAITH that it will gradually influence my THOUGHTS and ACTIONS so that I will become a self-reliant and successful person.

Back of this formula is a law of Nature which no one has yet been able to explain. It has baffled the scientists of all ages. The psychologists have named this the "Law of Autosuggestion" and let it go at that.

The name by which one calls this law is of little importance. The important fact about it is — it WORKS for the glory and success of mankind, IF it is used constructively. On the other hand, if used destructively, it will destroy just as readily. In this statement may be found a very significant truth, namely, that those who go down in defeat and end their lives in poverty, misery, and distress do so because of negative application of the principle of autosuggestion. The cause may be found in the fact that ALL IMPULSES OF THOUGHT HAVE A TENDENCY TO CLOTHE THEMSELVES IN THEIR PHYSICAL EQUIVALENT.

The subconscious mind (the "chemical laboratory" in which all thought impulses are combined and made ready for translation into physical reality) makes no distinction between constructive and destructive thought impulses. It works with the material we feed it through our thought impulses. The subconscious mind will translate into reality a thought driven by FEAR just as readily as it will translate into reality a thought driven by COURAGE or FAITH.

The pages of medical history are rich with illustrations of cases of "suggestive suicide." A person may commit suicide through negative suggestion just as effectively as by any other means. In a Midwestern city, a man by the name of Joseph Grant, a bank official, "borrowed" a large sum of the bank's money without the consent of the directors. He lost the money through gambling. One afternoon, the bank examiner came and began to check the accounts. Grant left the bank, took a room in a local hotel, and when they found him three days later, he was lying in bed, wailing and moaning, repeating over and over these words, "My God, this will kill me! I cannot stand the disgrace." In a short time he was dead. The doctors pronounced the case one of "mental suicide."

Just as electricity turns the wheels of industry and renders useful service if used constructively, or can snuff out life if used improperly, so will the Law of Autosuggestion lead you to peace and prosperity or down into the valley of misery, failure, and death, according to your degree of understanding and application of it.

If you fill your mind with FEAR, DOUBT, AND UNBELIEF in your ability to connect with and use the forces of Infinite Intelligence, then the Law of Autosuggestion will take this spirit of unbelief and use it as a pattern by which your subconscious mind will translate it into its physical equivalent.

THIS STATEMENT IS AS TRUE AS THE STATEMENT THAT TWO AND TWO EQUALS FOUR!

Like the wind which carries one ship East and another West, the Law of Autosuggestion will lift you up or pull you down, according to the way you set your sails of THOUGHT.

The Law of Autosuggestion, through which any person may rise to altitudes of achievement which stagger the imagination, is well described in the following verse:

"If you *think* you are beaten, you are,
If you *think* you dare not, you don't.
If you like to win, but you *think* you can't,
It is almost certain you won't.

"If you *think* you'll lose, you're lost,
For out of the world we find,
Success begins with a fellow's will --
It's all in the *state of mind*.

"If you *think* you are outclassed, you are,
You've got to *think* high to rise,
You've got to be *sure of yourself* before
You can ever win a prize.

"Life's battles don't always go
To the stronger or faster man,
But soon or late the man who wins
Is the man WHO THINKS HE CAN!"

Observe the words which have been emphasized and you will catch the deep meaning the poet[5] had in mind.

Somewhere in your makeup (perhaps in the cells of your brain) there lies sleeping the seed of achievement which, if aroused and put into action, would carry you to heights such as you may never have hoped to attain.

Just as a master musician may cause the most beautiful strains of music to pour forth from the strings of a violin, so may you arouse the genius which lies asleep in your brain and cause it to drive you upward to whatever goal you may wish to achieve.

Abraham Lincoln was a failure at everything he tried until he was well past the age of 40. He was a Mr. Nobody from Nowhere until a great experience came into his life, aroused the sleeping genius within his heart and brain, and gave the world one of its truly great men. That experience was mixed with the emotions of sorrow and LOVE. It came to him through Anne Rutledge, the only woman he ever truly loved.

It is a known fact that the emotion of LOVE is closely akin to the state of mind known as FAITH because love comes very near to translating one's thought impulses into their spiritual equivalent. During my long years of research, I discovered from the analysis of the life work and achievements of hundreds of people of outstanding accomplishment that there was the influence of a spouse's love back of nearly EVERY ONE OF THEM.

If you wish evidence of the power of FAITH, study the achievements of men and women who have employed it. At the head of the list comes the Nazarene. Christianity is one of the greatest single forces ever to influence the minds of people. The basis of Christianity is FAITH, no matter how many people may have perverted or misinterpreted the meaning of this great force, and no matter how many dogmas and creeds have been created in its name which do not reflect its tenets.

The sum and substance of the teachings and the achievements of Christ, which have been interpreted as miracles, were nothing more nor less than FAITH. If there are any such phenomena as miracles, they are produced only through the state of mind known as FAITH! Some teachers of religion and many who call themselves Christians neither understand nor practice FAITH.

FAITH is the cornerstone of every great religion. The Old Testament psalmist has written, "O love the LORD, all ye his saints: for the LORD preserveth the FAITHFUL, and plentifully rewardeth the proud doer." The apostle Luke tells us, "And Stephen, full of FAITH and power, did great wonders and miracles among the people," and Mark reports Jesus as saying, "Daughter, thy FAITH hath made thee whole; go in peace, and be whole of thy plague."

The prophet says in the *Qur'an*, "Surely those who believe and do good, their Lord will guide them by their FAITH; there shall flow from beneath them rivers in gardens of bliss." In the *Analects of Confucius*, the master says, "Hold FAITHFULNESS and sincerity as first principles, and be moving continually to what is right. This is the way to exalt one's virtue."

In the *Bhagavad-Gita* we find, "The FAITH of each is in accordance with one's own nature....A person is known by the faith. One can become whatever one wants to be (if one constantly contemplates on the object of desire with FAITH)." And again, "The one who has FAITH, and is sincere, and has mastery over the senses, gains...knowledge. Having gained this, one at once attains the supreme peace. But the ignorant, who has no faith and is full of doubt...perishes. There is neither this world nor the world beyond nor happiness for the one who doubts."

Let us consider the power of FAITH as it was demonstrated by Mahatma Gandhi of India,[6] who exhorted his followers to "Be the change you want to see in the world." In this man the world had one of the most astounding examples known to civilization of the possibilities of FAITH. Gandhi wielded more power than any other person living in his time, and, yet, he had none of the orthodox tools of power such as money, battleships, soldiers, and materials of warfare. Gandhi had no money, he had no home, he did not own a suit of clothes, but HE DID HAVE POWER. How did he come by that power?

HE CREATED IT OUT OF HIS UNDERSTANDING OF THE PRINCIPLE OF FAITH AND THROUGH HIS ABILITY TO TRANSPLANT THAT FAITH INTO THE MINDS OF TWO HUNDRED MILLION PEOPLE.

Gandhi accomplished through the influence of FAITH that which the strongest military power on earth could not then — and never will — accomplish through soldiers and military equipment. He accomplished the astounding feat of INFLUENCING two hundred million minds to COALESCE AND MOVE IN UNISON, AS A SINGLE MIND.

What other force on earth except FAITH could do as much?

There will come a day when employees, as well as employers, will discover the possibilities of FAITH. That day is dawning. The whole world has had ample opportunity during the recent worldwide economic downturn to witness what the LACK OF FAITH will do to business.

Surely, civilization has produced a sufficient number of intelligent human beings to make use of this great lesson which has been taught the world. During this time of difficulty, the world had evidence in abundance that widespread FEAR can paralyze the wheels of industry and business. Out of this experience will arise leaders in business and industry who will profit by the example which Gandhi set for the world, and they will apply to business the same tactics which he used in building the greatest following known in the history of the world. These leaders will come from the rank and file of the "unknown" who now labor in the steel plants, the coal mines, the factories, and in the small towns and cities of America.

Business is due for a reform, make no mistake about this! The methods of the past, based upon economic combinations of FORCE and FEAR, will be supplanted by the better principles of FAITH and cooperation. People who labor will receive more than daily wages. They will share more and more in profits from the business, the same as those who supply the capital for business. But first they must GIVE MORE TO THEIR EMPLOYERS and stop bickering and bargaining by force, at the expense of the public. *They must earn the right to profit-sharing!*

Moreover—and this is the most important thing of all—THEY WILL BE LED BY LEADERS WHO WILL UNDERSTAND AND APPLY THE PRINCIPLES EMPLOYED BY GANDHI. Only in this way can leaders get from their followers the spirit of FULL cooperation which constitutes power in its highest and most enduring form.[7]

This stupendous age in which we live and from which we are just emerging has taken the soul out of people. Its leaders have driven workers as though they were pieces of cold machinery; they were forced to do so by the employees who bargained, at the expense of all concerned, to *get* and not to *give*. The watchword of the future will be HUMAN HAPPINESS AND CONTENTMENT, and when this state of mind shall have been attained, the production will take care of itself more effectively than anything that has ever been accomplished where workers did not, and could not, mix FAITH and individual interest with their labor.

Because of the need for faith and cooperation in operating business and industry, it is both interesting and profitable to analyze an event which provides an excellent understanding of the method by which industrialists and business people accumulate great fortunes — by *giving* before they try to *get.*

The event chosen for this illustration dates back to 1900, when the United States Steel Corporation was being formed. As you read the story, keep in mind these fundamental facts and you will understand how IDEAS have been converted into huge fortunes:

First, the huge United States Steel Corporation was born in the mind of Charles M. Schwab in the form of an IDEA he created through his IMAGINATION!

Second, he mixed FAITH with his IDEA.

Third, he formulated a PLAN for the transformation of his IDEA into physical and financial reality.

Fourth, he put his plan into action with his famous speech at the University Club.

Fifth, he applied and followed through on his PLAN with PERSISTENCE and backed it with firm DECISION until it had been fully carried out.

Sixth, he prepared the way for success by a BURNING DESIRE for success.

If you are one of those who often wonder how great fortunes are accumulated, this story of the creation of the United States Steel Corporation will be enlightening. If you have any doubt that individuals can THINK AND GROW RICH, this story should dispel that doubt because you can plainly see in the story of   U.S. Steel the application of a major portion of *The 13 Steps to Riches*[8] described in this book.

This astounding description of the power of an IDEA was dramatically told by John Lowell in the *New York World-Telegram,* with whose courtesy it is here reprinted.

A PRETTY AFTER-DINNER SPEECH
FOR A BILLION DOLLARS

When, on the evening of December 12, 1900, some eighty of the nation's financial nobility gathered in the banquet hall of the University Club on Fifth Avenue to do honor to a young man from out of the West, not half a dozen of the guests realized they were to witness the most significant episode in American industrial history.

J. Edward Simmons and Charles Stewart Smith, their hearts full of gratitude for the lavish hospitality bestowed on them by Charles M. Schwab during a recent visit to Pittsburgh, had arranged the dinner to introduce the thirty-eight-year-old steel man to eastern banking society. But they didn't expect him to stampede the convention. They warned him, in fact, that the bosoms within New York's stuffed shirts would not be responsive to oratory, and that, if he didn't want to bore the Stillmans and Harrimans and Vanderbilts, he had better limit himself to fifteen or twenty minutes of polite vaporings and let it go at that.

Even John Pierpont Morgan,[9] sitting on the right hand of Schwab as became his imperial dignity, intended to grace the banquet table with his presence only briefly. And so far as the press and public were concerned, the whole affair was of so little moment that no mention of it found its way into print the next day.

So the two hosts and their distinguished guests ate their way through the usual seven or eight courses. There was little conversation and what there was of it was restrained. Few of the bankers and brokers had met Schwab, whose career had flowered along the banks of the Monongahela, and none knew him well. But before the evening was over, they -- and with them Money Master Morgan -- were to be swept off their feet, and a billion-dollar baby, the United States Steel Corporation, was to be conceived.

It is perhaps unfortunate, for the sake of history, that no record of Charlie Schwab's speech at the dinner ever was made. He repeated some parts of it at a later date during a similar meeting of Chicago bankers. And still later, when the Government brought suit to dissolve the Steel Trust, he gave his own version, from the witness stand, of the remarks that stimulated Morgan into a frenzy of financial activity.[10]

It is probable, however, that it was a "homely" speech, somewhat ungrammatical (for the niceties of language never bothered Schwab), full of epigram and threaded with wit. But aside from that it had a galvanic force and effect upon the five billions of estimated capital that was represented by the diners. After it was over and the gathering was still under its spell, although Schwab had talked for ninety minutes, Morgan led the orator to a recessed window where, dangling their legs from the high, uncomfortable seat, they talked for an hour more.

The magic of the Schwab personality had been turned on, full force, but what was more important and lasting was the full-fledged, clear-cut program he laid down for the aggrandizement of Steel. Many other men had tried to interest Morgan in slapping together a steel trust after the pattern of the biscuit, wire and hoop, sugar, rubber, whisky, oil or chewing gum combinations. John W. Gates, the gambler, had urged it, but Morgan distrusted him. The Moore boys, Bill and Jim, Chicago stockjobbers who had glued together a match trust and a cracker corporation, had urged it and failed. Elbert H. Gary, the sanctimonious country lawyer, wanted to foster it, but he wasn't big enough to be impressive. Until Schwab's eloquence took J. P. Morgan to the heights from which he could visualize the solid results of the most daring financial undertaking ever conceived, the project was regarded as a delirious dream of easy-money crackpots.

The financial magnetism that began a generation ago to attract thousands of small and sometimes inefficiently managed companies into large and competition-crushing combinations, had become operative in the steel world through the devices of that jovial business pirate, John W. Gates. Gates already had formed the American Steel and Wire Company out of a chain of small concerns, and together with Morgan had created the Federal Steel Company. The National Tube and American Bridge companies were two more Morgan concerns, and the Moore Brothers had forsaken the match and cookie business to form the "American group" — Tin Plate, Steel Hoop, Sheet Steel — and the National Steel Company.

But by the side of Andrew Carnegie's gigantic vertical trust, a trust owned and operated by fifty-three partners, those other combinations were picayune. They might combine to their heart's content but the whole lot of them couldn't make a dent in the Carnegie organization, and Morgan knew it.

The eccentric old Scot knew it, too. From the magnificent heights of Skibo* Castle he had viewed, first with amusement and then with resentment, the attempts of Morgan's smaller companies to cut into his business. When the attempts became too bold, Carnegie's temper was translated into anger and retaliation. He decided to duplicate every mill owned by his rivals. Hitherto, he hadn't been interested in wire, pipe, hoops, or sheet. Instead, he was content to sell such companies the raw steel and let them work it into whatever shape they wanted. Now, with Schwab as his chief and able lieutenant, he planned to drive his enemies to the wall. So it was that in the speech of Charles M. Schwab, Morgan saw the answer to his problem of combination. A trust without Carnegie — giant of them all — would be no trust at all, a plum pudding, as one writer said, without the plums.

---

* Skibo was a splendid castle Carnegie built for his family on Dornoch Firth in Scotland.

Schwab's speech on the night of December 12, 1900, undoubtedly carried the inference, though not the pledge, that the vast Carnegie enterprise could be brought under the Morgan tent. He talked of the world future for steel, of reorganization for efficiency, of specialization, of the scrapping of unsuccessful mills and concentration of effort on the flourishing properties, of economies in the ore traffic, of economies in overhead and administrative departments, of capturing foreign markets.

More than that, he told the buccaneers among them wherein lay the errors of their customary piracy. Their purposes, he inferred, had been to create monopolies, raise prices, and pay themselves fat dividends out of privilege. Schwab condemned the system in his heartiest manner. The shortsightedness of such a policy, he told his hearers, lay in the fact that it restricted the market in an era when everything cried for expansion. By cheapening the cost of steel, he argued, an ever- expanding market would be created; more uses for steel would be devised, and a goodly portion of the world trade could be captured. Actually, though he did not know it, Schwab was an apostle of modern mass production.

So the dinner at the University Club came to an end. Morgan went home, to think about Schwab's rosy predictions. Schwab went back to Pittsburgh to run the steel business for "Wee Andra Carnegie," while Gary and the rest went back to their stock tickers, to fiddle around in anticipation of the next move.

It was not long coming. It took Morgan about one week to digest the feast of reason Schwab had placed before him. When he had assured himself that no financial indigestion was to result, he sent for Schwab—and found that young man rather coy. Mr. Carnegie, Schwab indicated, might not like it if he found his trusted company president had been flirting with the Emperor of Wall Street, the Street upon which Carnegie was resolved never to tread. Then it was suggested by John W. Gates the go-between, that if Schwab "happened" to be in the Bellevue Hotel in Philadelphia, J. P. Morgan might also "happen" to be there. When Schwab arrived, however, Morgan was inconveniently ill at his New York home, and so, on the elder man's pressing invitation, Schwab went to New York and presented himself at the door of the financier's library.

Now certain economic historians have professed the belief that from the beginning to the end of the drama, the stage was set by Andrew Carnegie that the dinner to Schwab, the famous speech, the Sunday night conference between Schwab and the Money King, were events arranged by the canny Scot. The truth is exactly the opposite. When Schwab was called in to consummate the deal, he didn't even know whether "the little boss," as Andrew was called, would so much as listen to an offer to sell, particularly to a group of men whom Andrew regarded as being endowed with something less than holiness. But Schwab did take into the conference with him, in his own handwriting, six sheets of copper-plate figures, representing to his mind the physical worth and the potential earning capacity of every steel company he regarded as an essential star in the new metal firmament.

Four men pondered over these figures all night. The chief, of course, was Morgan, steadfast in his belief in the Divine Right of Money. With him was his aristocratic partner, Robert Bacon, a scholar and a gentleman. The third was John W. Gates, whom Morgan scorned as a gambler and used as a tool. The fourth was Schwab, who knew more about the processes of making and selling steel than any whole group of men then living. Throughout that conference, the Pittsburgher's figures were never questioned. If he said a company was worth so much, then it was worth that much and no more. He was insistent, too, upon including in the combination only those concerns he nominated. He had conceived a corporation in which there would be no duplication, not even to satisfy the greed of friends who wanted to unload their companies upon the broad Morgan shoulders. Thus he left out, by design, a number of the larger concerns upon which the Walruses and Carpenters of Wall Street had cast hungry eyes.

When dawn came, Morgan rose and straightened his back. Only one question remained.

"Do you think you can persuade Andrew Carnegie to sell?" he asked.

"I can try," said Schwab.

"If you can get him to sell, I will undertake the matter," said Morgan.

So far so good. But would Carnegie sell? How much would he demand? (Schwab thought about $320,000,000). What would he take payment in? Common or preferred stocks? Bonds? Cash? Nobody could raise a third of a billion dollars in cash.

There was a golf game in January on the frost-cracking heath of the St. Andrews links in Westchester, with Andrew bundled up in sweaters against the cold, and Charlie talking volubly, as usual, to keep his spirits up. But no word of business was mentioned until the pair sat down in the cozy warmth of the Carnegie cottage hard by. Then, with the same persuasiveness that had hypnotized eighty millionaires at the University Club, Schwab poured out the glittering promises of retirement in comfort, of untold millions to satisfy the old man's social caprices. Carnegie capitulated, wrote a figure on a slip of paper, handed it to Schwab and said, "All right, that's what we'll sell for."

The figure was approximately $400,000,000, and was reached by taking the $320,000,000 mentioned by Schwab as a basic figure, and adding to it $80,000,000 to represent the increased capital value over the previous two years. Later, on the deck of a trans-Atlantic liner, the Scotsman said ruefully to Morgan, "I wish I had asked you for $100,000,000 more."

"If you had asked for it, you'd have gotten it," Morgan told him cheerfully.[11]

*　　*　　*　　*　　*　　*　　*　　*

There was an uproar, of course. A British correspondent cabled that the foreign steel world was "appalled" by the gigantic combination. President Hadley, of Yale, declared that unless trusts were regulated the country might expect "an emperor in Washington within the next twenty-five years." But that able stock manipulator, Keene, went at his work of shoving the new stock at the public so vigorously that all the excess water — estimated by some at nearly $600,000,000 — was absorbed in a twinkling. So Carnegie had his millions, and the Morgan syndicate had $62,000,000 for all its "trouble," and all the "boys," from Gates to Gary, had their millions.

*　　*　　*　　*　　*　　*　　*　　*

The thirty-eight-year-old Schwab had his reward. He was made president of the new corporation and remained in control until 1930.

The dramatic story of "Big Business" which you have just finished was included in this book because it is a perfect illustration of the method by which *DESIRE CAN BE TRANSMUTED INTO ITS PHYSICAL EQUIVALENT!*

I imagine some readers will question the statement that a mere intangible DESIRE can be converted into its physical equivalent. Doubtless some will say, "You cannot convert NOTHING into SOMETHING!" The answer is in the story of United States Steel.

That giant organization was created in the mind of one man. The plan by which the organization was provided with the steel mills that gave it financial stability was created in the mind of the same man. His FAITH, his DESIRE, his IMAGINATION, his PERSISTENCE were the real ingredients that went into United States Steel. The steel mills and mechanical equipment acquired by the corporation AFTER IT HAD BEEN BROUGHT INTO LEGAL EXISTENCE were incidental, but careful analysis will disclose the fact that the appraised value of the properties acquired by the corporation increased in value by an estimated SIX HUNDRED MILLION DOLLARS[12] by the mere transaction which consolidated them under one management.

In other words, Charles M. Schwab's IDEA, plus the FAITH with which he conveyed it to the minds of J. P. Morgan and the others, was marketed for a profit of approximately $600,000,000. Not an insignificant sum for a single IDEA!

What happened to some of those who took their share of the millions of dollars of profit made by this transaction is a matter with which we are not now concerned. The important feature of the astounding achievement is that it serves as unquestionable evidence of the soundness of the philosophy described in this book — because this philosophy was the warp and the woof of the entire transaction. Moreover, the practicability of the philosophy has been established by the fact that the United States Steel Corporation prospered and became one of the richest and most powerful corporations in America, employing thousands of people, developing new uses for steel, and opening new markets — thus proving that the $600,000,000 in profit which the Schwab IDEA produced was earned.

RICHES begin in the form of THOUGHT!

The amount is limited only by the person in whose mind the THOUGHT is put into motion. FAITH removes limitations! Remember this when you are ready to bargain with Life for whatever it is that you ask as your price for having passed this way.

Remember, also, that the man who created the United States Steel Corporation was practically unknown at the time. He was merely Andrew Carnegie's "Man Friday" until he gave birth to his famous IDEA. After that he quickly rose to a position of power, fame, and riches.

And he rose, like all great achievers, on the wings of FAITH, which can be created by a powerful force known as AUTO-SUGGESTION.

Chapter 3

AUTOSUGGESTION
The Medium for Influencing the Subconscious Mind
The Third Step to Riches

AUTOSUGGESTION is a term which applies to all suggestions and all self-administered stimuli which reach one's mind through the five senses. Stated in another way, autosuggestion is *self-suggestion*. It is the agency of communication between that part of the mind where conscious thought takes place and that which serves as the seat of action for the subconscious mind.

The dominating thoughts which one *permits* to remain in the conscious mind (whether these thoughts be negative or positive is immaterial) will *reach and influence* the subconscious mind, through the Law of Autosuggestion.

NO THOUGHT, whether it be negative or positive, CAN ENTER THE SUBCONSCIOUS MIND WITHOUT THE AID OF THE PRINCIPLE OF AUTOSUGGESTION, with the exception of those thoughts picked up as "flashes of insight or inspiration." Stated differently, all sense impressions which are perceived through the five senses are captured and processed by the *conscious* thinking mind and may be either passed on to the *subconscious* mind or rejected, at will. The conscious faculty serves, therefore, as an outer guard at the approach to the subconscious.

Nature has so "wired" human beings that they have ABSOLUTE CONTROL over the material which reaches their subconscious mind through the five senses, although this is not meant to be construed as a statement that individuals always EXERCISE this control. In the great majority of instances, they do NOT exercise it, which explains why so many people go through life in poverty.

Recall what has been said about the subconscious mind resembling a fertile garden in which weeds will grow in abundance if the seeds of more desirable crops are not sown therein. Autosuggestion is the agency of control through which an individual may voluntarily feed his or her subconscious mind on thoughts of a creative nature, or, by neglect, permit thoughts of a destructive nature to find their way into this rich garden of the mind.

You were instructed in the last of the six action steps described in Chapter 1 to read ALOUD twice daily the WRITTEN statement of your DESIRE FOR MONEY, and to SEE AND FEEL yourself ALREADY in possession of the money! By following these instructions, you communicate the object of your DESIRE directly to your SUBCONSCIOUS mind in a spirit of absolute FAITH. Through repetition of this procedure, you voluntarily create thought habits which are favorable to your efforts to transmute desire into its monetary equivalent. (This procedure is NOT restricted to monetary gain alone. It can be used to help you achieve WHATEVER IT IS that you DESIRE STRONGLY, so long as it does not violate the laws of God or the rights of others.)

Go back to these six actions described in Chapter 1 and read them again very carefully before you proceed further. Then skip ahead for a moment and read very carefully the four instructions for the organization of your Master Mind Group which are described in Chapter 6 on Organized Planning. By comparing these two sets of instructions with those that will be stated in this chapter on autosuggestion, you will see that all of these instructions involve the application of the Law of Autosuggestion.

Remember, therefore, when reading aloud the statement of your desire (through which you are endeavoring to develop a "money consciousness" or any other "success consciousness") that the mere reading of the words is of NO CONSEQUENCE—UNLESS you mix emotion, or feeling, with your words. If you repeat a million times the famous Emile Coue[1] formula, "Day by day, in every way, I am getting better and better," without mixing emotion and FAITH with your words, you will experience no desirable results. Your subconscious mind recognizes and acts ONLY upon thoughts which have been well-mixed with emotion or feeling.

This is a fact of such importance as to warrant repetition in practically every chapter of this book because the lack of understanding of this truth is the main reason why the majority of people who try to apply the Law of Autosuggestion get no desirable results.

Plain, unemotional words do not influence the subconscious mind. You will get no appreciable results until you learn to reach your subconscious mind with thoughts or spoken words which have been *well emotionalized* with BELIEF.

Do not become discouraged if you cannot control and direct your emotions the first time you try to do so. Remember, there is no such possibility as SOMETHING FOR NOTHING. The ability to reach and influence your subconscious mind has its price, and you MUST PAY THAT PRICE. You cannot cheat, even if you desire to do so. The price of ability to influence your subconscious mind is everlasting PERSISTENCE in applying the principles described here. You cannot develop the desired ability for a lower price. You, and YOU ALONE, must decide whether or not the reward for which you are striving (money consciousness) is worth the price you must pay for it in effort.

Wisdom and cleverness alone will not attract and retain money except in a few very rare instances where the law of averages favors the attraction of money through such means. However, the method of attracting money described here does *not* depend upon the law of averages. Moreover, the method plays no favorites. It will work for one person as effectively as it will for another. Where failure is experienced, it is the individual, *not the method*, which has failed. If you try and fail, make another effort, and still another, until you succeed.

Your ability to use the Law of Autosuggestion will depend very largely upon your capacity to CONCENTRATE upon a given

DESIRE until that desire becomes a BURNING OBSESSION.

When you begin to carry out the instructions in connection with the six action steps described in Chapter 1, it will be necessary for you to make use of the principle of CONCENTRATION.

Let us here offer suggestions for the effective use of concentration. When you begin to carry out the first of the six actions (which instructs you to "fix in your own mind the EXACT amount of money you desire"), hold your thoughts on that amount of money by CONCENTRATION, or fixation of attention, with your eyes closed, until you can ACTUALLY SEE the physical appearance of the money. Do this at least once each day. As you go through these exercises, follow the instructions given in Chapter 2 on FAITH and see yourself actually IN POSSESSION OF THE MONEY!

Here is a most significant fact—the subconscious mind takes any orders given it in a spirit of absolute FAITH, and acts upon those orders, although the orders often have to be presented *over and over again*, through repetition, before they are interpreted by the subconscious mind. Consider the possibility of playing a perfectly legitimate trick on your subconscious mind by making it believe, *because you believe it*, that you must have the amount of money you are visualizing, that this money is already awaiting your claim, that the subconscious mind MUST hand over to you practical plans for acquiring the money which is yours.

Hand over the thought suggested in the preceding paragraph to your IMAGINATION and see what your imagination can, or will do, to create practical plans for the accumulation of money through transmutation of your desire.

DO NOT WAIT for a definite plan through which you intend to exchange services or merchandise in return for the money you are visualizing, but begin at once to see yourself in possession of the money, DEMANDING and EXPECTING meanwhile that your subconscious mind will hand over the plan or plans you need. Be on the alert for these plans, and when they appear, put them into ACTION IMMEDIATELY. When the plans appear, they will probably flash into your mind through the sixth sense, in the form of an inspiration. This inspiration may be considered a direct "telegram" or "message" from Infinite Intelligence. Treat it with respect, and act upon it as soon as you receive it. Failure to do this will be FATAL to your success.

In the fourth of the six action steps you were instructed to "Create a definite plan for carrying out your desire, and begin at once to put this plan into action." You should follow this instruction in the manner described in the preceding paragraph. Do not trust to your reason when creating your plan for accumulating money through the transmutation of desire. Your reason is faulty. Moreover, your reasoning faculty may be lazy, and if you depend entirely upon it to serve you, it may disappoint you.

When visualizing (with closed eyes) the money you intend to accumulate, *see yourself rendering the service or delivering the merchandise you intend to give in return for this money. This is important![2]*

Summary of Instructions

The fact that you are reading this book is an indication that you earnestly seek knowledge. It is also an indication that you are a student of this subject. If you are only a student, there is a chance you may learn much that you did not know, but you will learn only by assuming an attitude of humility. If you choose to follow some of the instructions, but neglect or refuse to follow others—*you will fail!* To get satisfactory results, you must follow ALL instructions in a spirit of FAITH.

The instructions given in connection with the six action steps in Chapter 1 will now be summarized and blended with the principles covered by this chapter. If your DEFINITE CHIEF AIM involves money and the attainment of wealth:

First. Go into some quiet spot (preferably in bed at night) where you will not be disturbed or interrupted, close your eyes, and repeat aloud (so you may hear your own words) the written statement of the amount of money you intend to accumulate, the time limit for its accumulation, and a description of the service or merchandise you intend to give in return for the money.

As you carry out these instructions, SEE YOURSELF ALREADY IN POSSESSION OF THE MONEY.

For example, suppose that you intend to accumulate $500,000 by the first of January, five years hence, that you intend to give personal services in return for the money in the capacity of a sales representative. Your written statement of your purpose should be similar to the following:

"By the first day of January, [here state the year], I will have in my possession $500,000, which will come to me in various amounts from time to time during the interim.

"In return for this money I will give the most efficient service of which I am capable, rendering the fullest possible quantity, and the best possible quality of service in the capacity of selling.... (describe the service or merchandise you intend to sell).

"I believe that I will have this money in my possession. My faith is so strong that I can now see this money before my eyes. I can touch it with my hands. It is now awaiting transfer to me at the time and in the proportion that I deliver the service I intend to render in return for it. I am awaiting a plan by which to accumulate this money, and I will follow that plan when it is received."

Second. Repeat this program night and morning until you can clearly visualize (in your imagination) the money you intend to accumulate.

Third. Place a written copy of your statement where you can see it night and morning, and read it just before retiring and upon arising until it has been memorized.[3]

Remember as you carry out these instructions that you are applying the Law of Autosuggestion for the purpose of giving orders to your subconscious mind. Remember that these instructions apply particularly to the desire for money, but also to any other object you desire or goal you seek. Remember also that your subconscious mind will act ONLY upon instructions which are emotionalized and handed over to it with feeling. FAITH is the strongest and most productive of the emotions. Follow the instructions given in Chapter 2.

These instructions may at first seem abstract. Do not let this disturb you. Follow the instructions no matter how abstract or impractical they may at first appear to be. The time will soon come, if you do as you have been instructed, *in spirit as well as in fact*, when a whole new universe of power will unfold to you.

Skepticism, in connection with ALL new ideas, is characteristic of all human beings. But if you follow the instructions outlined, your skepticism will soon be replaced by belief, and this in turn will soon become crystallized into ABSOLUTE FAITH. Then you will have arrived at the point where you may truly say, "I am the Master of my Fate, I am the Captain of my Soul!"

Many philosophers have made the statement that each person is the master of his or her own earthly destiny, but most of them have failed to say why this is so. The reason that we may be the master of our own earthly status, and especially our financial status, is thoroughly explained in this chapter. We may become the master of ourselves, and of our environment, because we have the POWER TO INFLUENCE OUR OWN SUBCONSCIOUS MIND, and through it, to gain the cooperation of Infinite Intelligence.

The chapter you are now reading represents the keystone in the arch of *The Think and Grow Rich Philosophy*. The instructions contained in this chapter must be understood and APPLIED WITH PERSISTENCE if you are to succeed in transmuting desire into money or any other result you seek.

The actual performance of transmuting DESIRE into money involves the use of autosuggestion as an agency by which you may reach and influence the subconscious mind. The other principles are simply tools with which to apply autosuggestion. Keep this thought in mind, and you will at all times be conscious of the important part that the Law of Autosuggestion is to play in your efforts to accumulate money through the methods described in this book.

Carry out these instructions as though you were a small child. Inject into your efforts something of the FAITH of a child. I have been most careful to see that no impractical instructions are included because of my sincere desire to be helpful.

After you have read the entire book, come back to this chapter and follow in spirit, and in action, this instruction:

READ THIS ENTIRE CHAPTER ALOUD ONCE EVERY NIGHT UNTIL YOU BECOME THOROUGHLY CONVINCED THAT THE PRINCIPLE OF AUTOSUGGESTION IS SOUND, THAT IT WILL ACCOMPLISH FOR YOU ALL THAT HAS BEEN CLAIMED FOR IT. AS YOU READ, *UNDERSCORE WITH A PENCIL* EVERY SENTENCE WHICH IMPRESSES YOU FAVORABLY.

Follow the foregoing instructions to the letter and it will open the way for a complete understanding and mastery of all the principles of success, including the one to which we now turn—SPECIALIZED KNOWLEDGE, *The Fourth Step to Riches.*

I BELIEVE THAT CLOSE ASSOCIATION WITH ONE WHO REFUSES TO COMPROMISE WITH CIRCUMSTANCES HE OR SHE DOES NOT LIKE IS AN ASSET THAT CAN NEVER BE MEASURED IN TERMS OF MONEY.

Chapter 4

SPECIALIZED KNOWLEDGE
Personal Experiences or Observations
The Fourth Step to Riches

THERE ARE two kinds of knowledge. One is general; the other, specialized. General knowledge, no matter how great in quantity or variety it may be, is of but little use in the accumulation of money. The faculties of the great universities possess, in the aggregate, practically every form of general knowledge known to civilization. *Most of the professors have not amassed great wealth!* They specialize in *teaching* knowledge, but they do not specialize in the organization or the *use* of knowledge for the accumulation of money.

KNOWLEDGE will not attract money (or any other kind of success) unless it is organized and intelligently directed, through practical PLANS OF ACTION, to the DEFINITE END of accumulating money. Lack of understanding of this fact has been the source of confusion to millions of people who falsely believe that "knowledge is power." It is nothing of the sort! Knowledge is only *potential* power. It becomes power only when, and if, it is organized into definite plans of action and directed to a definite end.

This "missing link" in all systems of education known to civilization today may be found in the failure of educational institutions to teach their students HOW TO ORGANIZE AND USE KNOWLEDGE AFTER THEY ACQUIRE IT.

Many people make the mistake of assuming that because Henry Ford had but little schooling, he was not educated. Those who make this mistake did not know Henry Ford, nor do they understand the real meaning of the word "educate." The word is derived from the Latin word *educo*, meaning to educe, to draw out, to DEVELOP FROM WITHIN.

An educated person is not necessarily one who has an abundance of general or specialized knowledge. To be truly educated is to have so developed the faculties of mind that one may acquire anything one wishes, or its equivalent, without violating the rights of others. Henry Ford comes well within the meaning of this definition.

During World War I, a Chicago newspaper published certain editorials in which, among other statements, Henry Ford was called "an ignorant pacifist." Mr. Ford objected to the statements and brought suit against the paper for libeling him. When the suit was tried in the courts, the attorneys for the paper pleaded justification and placed Mr. Ford himself on the witness stand for the purpose of proving to the jury that he was ignorant. The attorneys asked Mr. Ford a great variety of questions, all of them intended to prove by his own evidence that, while he might possess considerable specialized knowledge pertaining to the manufacture of automobiles, he was, in the main, ignorant.

Mr. Ford was plied with such questions as the following: "Who was Benedict Arnold?" and "How many soldiers did the British send over to America to put down the Rebellion of 1776?" In answer to the last question, Mr. Ford replied, "I do not know the exact number of soldiers the British sent over, but I have heard that it was a considerably larger number than ever went back."

Finally, Mr. Ford became tired of this line of questioning, and in reply to a particularly offensive question, he leaned over, pointed his finger at the lawyer who had asked the question, and said, "If I should really WANT to answer the foolish question you have just asked or any of the other questions you have been asking me, let me remind you that I have a row of electric push-buttons on my desk, and by pushing the right button, I can summon to my aid men who can answer ANY question I desire to ask concerning the business to which I am devoting most of my efforts. Now, will you kindly tell me WHY I should clutter up my mind with general knowledge for the purpose of being able to answer questions when I have men around me who can supply any knowledge I require?"

There certainly was good logic to that reply. The answer floored the lawyer. Every person in the courtroom realized it was the answer not of an ignorant man, but of a man of EDUCATION. Any person is educated who knows where to get knowledge when it is needed and how to organize that knowledge into definite plans of action. Through the assistance of his Master Mind Group, Henry Ford had at his command all the specialized knowledge he needed to enable him to become one of the wealthiest individuals in America. *It was not essential that he have this knowledge in his own mind.* Surely no person who has sufficient inclination and intelligence to read a book of this nature can possibly miss the significance of this illustration.

Before you can be sure of your ability to transmute DESIRE into its monetary equivalent, you will require SPECIALIZED KNOWLEDGE of the service, merchandise, or profession which you intend to offer in return for fortune. Perhaps you may need much more specialized knowledge than you have the ability or the inclination to acquire, and if this should be true, you may bridge your weakness through the aid of your Master Mind Group.

Andrew Carnegie stated that he personally knew nothing about the technical end of the steel business. Moreover, he did not particularly care to know anything about it. The specialized knowledge which he required for the manufacture and marketing of steel he found available through the individual units of his MASTER MIND GROUP.

The accumulation of great fortunes calls for POWER, and power is acquired through highly organized and intelligently directed specialized knowledge, but that knowledge does not necessarily have to be in the possession of the person who accumulates the fortune.

The preceding paragraph should give hope and encouragement to the person who has ambition to accumulate a fortune, but who does not have the necessary education to supply such specialized knowledge as may be required. People sometimes go through life suffering from inferiority complexes because they are not "well educated." Yet, the individual who can organize and direct a Master Mind Group of people who possess knowledge useful in the accumulation of money is just as educated as anyone in the group. REMEMBER THAT if you suffer from a feeling of inferiority because your schooling has been limited.

Thomas A. Edison had only three months of formal education during his entire life. Yet he did not lack education, nor did he die poor.

Henry Ford had less than a sixth grade schooling, but he managed to do pretty well by himself financially.

SPECIALIZED KNOWLEDGE is among the most plentiful and the cheapest forms of service which may be had! If you doubt this, consult the payroll of any college or university.

It Pays to Know How to Purchase Knowledge

First of all, decide the sort of specialized knowledge you require and the purpose for which it is needed. To a large extent, your major purpose in life, the goal toward which you are working, will help determine what knowledge you need. With this question settled, your next move requires that you have accurate information concerning dependable sources of knowledge. The more important of these are:

(a) your own experience and education
(b) experience and education available through cooperation of others (Master Mind Alliance)
(c) colleges and universities
(d) public libraries (through books and periodicals in which may be found all the knowledge organized by civilization)
(e) special training courses (through night schools and home study materials in particular)

As knowledge is acquired, it must be organized and put into use, for a definite purpose, through practical plans. Knowledge has no value except that which can be gained from its application toward some worthy end. This is one reason why a college degree in itself is not valued more highly. It often represents nothing but miscellaneous knowledge.

If you contemplate pursuing additional formal education, first determine the purpose for which you want the knowledge you are seeking, then learn where this particular sort of knowledge can be obtained from reliable sources.

Successful people, in all callings, never stop acquiring specialized knowledge related to their major purpose, business, or profession. Those who are not successful usually make the mistake of believing that the "knowledge-acquiring" period ends when one finishes school. The truth is that formal education does but little more than to put one in the way of learning how to acquire practical knowledge.

We find ourselves in a Changed World today, and we have also seen some astounding changes in educational requirements. The order of the day is SPECIALIZATION. This truth was emphasized by Robert P. Moore, quoted in a piece written when he was an administrator at Columbia University:

SPECIALISTS MOST SOUGHT

Particularly sought after by employing companies are candidates who have specialized in some field — business school graduates with training in accounting and statistics, engineers of all varieties, journalists, architects, chemists, and also outstanding leaders...of the senior class.

The [graduate] who has been active on the campus, whose personality is such that he or she gets along with all kinds of people and who has done an adequate job with studies has a most decided edge over the strictly academic student. Some of these, because of their all-around qualifications, have received several offers of positions, a few of them as many as six.

In departing from the conception that the 'straight A' student was invariably the one to get the choice of the better jobs, Mr. Moore said that most companies look not only to academic records but to activity records and personalities of the students.

One of the largest industrial companies, the leader in its field, in writing to Mr. Moore concerning prospective seniors at the college, said:

"We are interested primarily in finding people who can make exceptional progress in management work. For this reason we emphasize qualities of character, intelligence and personality far more than specific educational background."

APPRENTICESHIP PROPOSED

Proposing a system of "apprenticing" students in offices, stores and industrial occupations during the summer vacation, Mr. Moore asserts that after the first two or three years of college, every student should be asked "to choose a definite future course and to call a halt if the student has been merely pleasantly drifting without purpose through an unspecialized academic curriculum.

"Colleges and universities must face the practical consideration that all professions and occupations now demand specialists," he said, urging that educational institutions accept more direct responsibility for vocational guidance.[1]

One of the most reliable and practical sources of knowledge available to those who need specialized training is the night schools operated in most large cities. And correspondence schools give specialized training anywhere the U. S. mails go, on all subjects that can be taught by the extension method. America is also blessed with an abundance of self-study books, courses, and other materials which one may use to acquire specialized training and knowledge. One advantage, in particular, of self-study training is the flexibility of the study program which permits one to study during spare time, during work breaks, or during travel.[2]

Anything acquired without effort and without cost is generally unappreciated, often discredited. Perhaps this is why we get so little from our marvelous opportunity in public schools. The SELF-DISCIPLINE one receives from a definite program of specialized study makes up, to some extent, for the wasted opportunity when knowledge was available without cost.[3]

I learned this from experience early in my career. I enrolled for a home study course in advertising. After completing eight or ten lessons I stopped studying, but the school did not stop sending me bills. Moreover, it insisted upon payment whether I kept up my studies or not. I decided that if I had to pay for the course (which I had legally obligated myself to do), I should complete the lessons and get my money's worth. I felt at the time that the collection system of the school was somewhat too well organized, but I learned later in life that it was a valuable part of my training for which no charge had been made. Being forced to pay, I went ahead and completed the course. Later in life I discovered that the efficient collection system of that school had been worth much to me in the form of money I would later earn because of the training in advertising I had so reluctantly taken.

We have in this country the greatest public school system in the world. We have invested fabulous sums for fine buildings. We have provided convenient transportation for children living in rural and other areas. But there is one astounding weakness to this marvelous system—IT IS FREE! One of the strange things about human beings is that they value only that which has a price. The free schools of America and the free public libraries do not impress people *because they are free* (or appear to be so). This is the major reason why so many people find it necessary to acquire additional training after they quit school and go to work. It is also one of the major reasons why EMPLOYERS GIVE GREATER CONSIDERATION TO EMPLOYEES WHO PARTICIPATE REGULARLY IN SELF-STUDY COURSES AND OTHER FORMS OF PROFESSIONAL DEVELOPMENT. They have learned from experience that any person who has the ambition to give up a part of his or her spare time, or to use slack time at work, for professional development, has those qualities which make for leadership. This recognition is not a charitable gesture. It is sound business judgment upon the part of the employers.

There is one weakness in people for which there is no remedy. It is the universal weakness of LACK OF AMBITION! People, especially those on salary, who schedule their spare time and slack time to provide for self-improvement seldom remain at the bottom very long. Their action opens the way for the upward climb, removes many obstacles from their path, and gains the friendly interest of those who have the power to put them in the way of OPPORTUNITY.

The self-improvement or "home study" method of training is especially suited to the needs of employed people who find, after leaving school, that they must acquire additional specialized knowledge, but cannot spare the time to go back to school.

The changed economic conditions that now prevail have made it necessary for thousands of people to find additional or new sources of income. For the majority of these, the solution to their problem may be found only by acquiring specialized knowledge. Many will be forced to change their occupation entirely. When merchants find that a certain line of merchandise is not selling, they usually supplant it with another that is in demand. The person whose business is that of marketing personal services must also be an efficient merchant. If the services do not bring adequate returns in one occupation, the individual must change to another, where broader opportunities are available.

Stuart Austin Wier prepared himself as a construction engineer and followed this line of work until the Depression limited his market to where it did not give him the income he required. He took inventory of himself, decided to change his profession to law, went back to school, and took special courses by which he prepared himself as a corporation lawyer. Despite the fact the Depression had not ended, he completed his training, passed the bar examination, and quickly built a lucrative law practice in Dallas, Texas. He actually had to turn away clients.

Just to keep the record straight and to anticipate the alibis of those who will say, "I couldn't go to school because I have a family to support" or "I'm too old," I will add that Mr. Wier was past 40 and married when he went back to school. Moreover, by carefully selecting highly specialized courses, in colleges best prepared to teach the subjects chosen, Mr. Wier completed in two years the work for which the majority of law students require four years. IT PAYS TO KNOW HOW TO PURCHASE KNOWLEDGE!

The person who stops studying merely because he or she has finished school is forever hopelessly doomed to mediocrity, no matter what that person's calling. The way of success is the way of *continuous pursuit of knowledge.*

Let us consider a specific instance.

During the Depression a salesman in a grocery store found himself without a position. Having had some bookkeeping experience, he took a special course in accounting, familiarized himself with all the latest bookkeeping and office equipment, and went into business for himself. Starting with the grocer for whom he had formerly worked, he made contracts with more than 100 small merchants to keep their books, at a very nominal monthly fee. His idea was so practical that he soon found it necessary to set up a portable office in a light delivery truck, which he equipped with modern bookkeeping equipment. He went on to create a fleet of these bookkeeping "offices on wheels," and he employed a large staff of assistants, thus providing small merchants with accounting service equal to the best that money could buy, at very nominal cost.

Specialized knowledge, plus imagination, were the ingredients that went into this unique and successful business. In only a short time, the owner of that business was paying an income tax of almost ten times as much as was paid by the merchant for whom he worked, when the Depression forced upon him a temporary adversity which proved to be a blessing in disguise.

The beginning of this successful business was an IDEA!

Inasmuch as I had the privilege of supplying the unemployed salesman with that idea, I now assume the further privilege of suggesting another idea which has within it the possibility of significant income, as well as the possibility of rendering useful service to thousands of people who badly need that service.

The idea was initially suggested by the salesman who gave up selling and went into the business of keeping books on a wholesale basis. When that plan was suggested as a solution to his unemployment problem, he quickly exclaimed, "I like the idea, but I would not know how to turn it into cash." In other words, he complained he would not know how to *market* his bookkeeping knowledge *after he acquired it.*

So that brought up another problem which had to be solved. With the aid of a creative young woman — a typist — who was clever at hand lettering and who could put the story together, he was able to prepare a very attractive portfolio describing the advantages of the new system of bookkeeping. She typed the pages neatly and pasted them in an ordinary scrapbook, which was used as a "silent salesman" with which the story of this new business was told so effectively that its owner soon had more accounts than he could handle.

There are thousands of people today in communities all over the country who could use the services of a merchandising specialist such as this woman, capable of preparing attractive materials for use in marketing personal services. The aggregate annual income from such a service might easily exceed that received by an employment agency, and the benefits of the service might be made far greater to the purchaser than any to be obtained from an employment agency.[4]

The IDEA here described was born of necessity, to meet an emergency which had to be covered, but it did not stop by merely serving one person. The woman who created the idea had a keen IMAGINATION. She saw in her newly born brainchild the making of a new profession, one that would render valuable service to thousands of people who needed practical guidance in marketing personal services.

Spurred to action by the instantaneous success of the first "Marketing Plan for Personal Services" she prepared, this energetic woman turned next to the solution of a similar problem for her son, who had just finished college, but had been totally unable to find a market for his services. The plan she originated for his use was the finest specimen of merchandising of personal services I have ever seen.

When the plan portfolio had been completed, it contained nearly 50 pages of beautifully typed, properly organized information, telling the story of her son's native ability, schooling, personal experiences, and a great variety of other information too extensive for description here. The portfolio also contained a complete description of the position her son desired, together with a marvelous word picture of the exact plan he would use in filling the position.

The preparation of the portfolio required several weeks' labor, during which time its creator sent her son to the public library almost daily to procure information needed to sell his services to best advantage. She sent him also to all the competitors of his prospective employer to gather from them vital information concerning their business methods, which was of great value in the formation of the plan he intended to use in filling the position he sought. When the plan was finished, it contained more than half a dozen excellent suggestions for the use and benefit of the prospective employer. (The suggestions were put into use by the company.)

One may be inclined to ask, "Why go to all this trouble to secure a job?" The answer is straight to the point, also dramatic, because it deals with a subject which assumes the proportion of a tragedy with millions of men and women whose sole source of income is personal services.

The answer is, "DOING A THING WELL NEVER IS TROUBLE! THE PLAN PREPARED BY THIS WOMAN FOR THE BENEFIT OF HER SON HELPED HIM GET THE JOB FOR WHICH HE APPLIED, AT THE FIRST INTERVIEW, AT A SALARY FIXED BY HIMSELF."

Moreover—and this, too, is important—THE POSITION DID NOT REQUIRE THE YOUNG MAN TO START AT THE BOTTOM.

HE BEGAN AS A JUNIOR EXECUTIVE, AT AN EXECUTIVE'S SALARY.

"Why go to all this trouble?" you ask. Well, for one thing, the PLANNED PRESENTATION of this young man's application for a position clipped off no less than ten years of time he would have required to get to where he began had he started at the bottom and worked his way up.

This idea of starting at the bottom and working one's way up may appear to be sound, but the major objection to it is this — too many of those who begin at the bottom never manage to lift their heads high enough to be seen by OPPORTUNITY, so they remain at the bottom. It should be remembered also that the outlook from the bottom is not so very bright or encouraging. It has a tendency to kill off ambition. We call it "getting into a rut," which means that we accept our fate because we form the HABIT of daily routine, a habit that finally becomes so strong we cease to try to throw it off. And that is another reason why it pays to start one or two steps above the bottom. By so doing, one forms the HABIT of looking around, of observing how others get ahead, of seeing OPPORTUNITY, and of embracing it without hesitation.

Dan Halpin[5] is a splendid example of what I mean. During his college days, he was manager of the famous National Championship Notre Dame football team when it was under the direction of Knute Rockne.

Perhaps he was inspired by the great football coach to aim high and NOT MISTAKE TEMPORARY DEFEAT FOR FAILURE, just as Andrew Carnegie, the great industrial leader, inspired his young business lieutenants to set high goals for themselves. At any rate, young Halpin finished college at a mighty unfavorable time, when the Depression had made jobs scarce, so, after a fling at investment banking and motion pictures, he took the first opening with a potential future he could find — selling hearing aids on a commission basis. ANYONE COULD START IN THAT SORT OF JOB, AND HALPIN KNEW IT, but it was enough to open the door of opportunity to him.

For almost two years he continued in a job not to his liking, and he would never have risen above that job if he had not done something about his dissatisfaction. He aimed first at the job of assistant sales manager of his company, and got the job. That one step upward placed him high enough above the crowd to enable him to see still greater opportunity.   Also, it placed him where OPPORTUNITY COULD SEE HIM.

He made such a fine record selling hearing aids that A. M. Andrews, chairman of the board of the Dictograph Products Company, a business competitor of the company for which Halpin worked, wanted to know something about "that man, Dan Halpin" who was taking big sales away from the long established Dictograph Company. He sent for Halpin. When the interview was over, Halpin was the new sales manager in charge of Dictograph's Acousticon Division. Then to test young Halpin's mettle, Mr. Andrews went away to Florida for three months, leaving him to sink or swim in his new job. He did not sink! Knute Rockne's spirit of "All the world loves a winner, and has no time for a loser" inspired him to put so much into his job that he was eventually elected vice president of the company and general manager of the Acousticon and Silent Radio Division, a job most executives would be proud to earn through ten years of loyal effort. Halpin turned the trick in little more than six months!

It is difficult to say whether Mr. Andrews or Mr. Halpin is more deserving of eulogy, for the reason that both showed evidence of having an abundance of that very rare quality known as IMAGINATION. Mr. Andrews deserves credit for seeing in young Halpin a go-getter of the highest order. Halpin deserves credit for REFUSING TO COMPROMISE WITH LIFE BY ACCEPTING AND KEEPING A JOB HE DID NOT WANT, and that is one of the major points I am trying to emphasize through this entire philosophy — that we rise to high positions or remain at the bottom BECAUSE OF CONDITIONS WE CAN CONTROL IF WE DESIRE TO CONTROL THEM.

I am also trying to emphasize another point, namely, that both success and failure are largely the results of HABIT! I have not the slightest doubt that Dan Halpin's close association with the greatest football coach America ever knew planted in his mind the same brand of DESIRE to excel which made the Notre Dame football team world famous. Truly, there is something to the idea that hero worship is helpful, provided one worships a WINNER. Halpin told me that Rockne[6] was one of the world's greatest leaders in all of history.

My belief in the theory that business associations are vital factors, both in failure and in success, was demonstrated when my son Blair was negotiating with Dan Halpin for a position. Mr. Halpin offered him a beginning salary of about one half what he could have gotten from a rival company. I brought parental pressure to bear, and induced him to accept the position with Mr. Halpin because I BELIEVE THAT CLOSE ASSOCIATION WITH ONE WHO REFUSES TO COMPROMISE WITH CIRCUMSTANCES HE DOES NOT LIKE IS AN ASSET THAT CAN NEVER BE MEASURED IN TERMS OF MONEY.

The bottom is a monotonous, dreary, unprofitable place for any person. That is why I have taken the time to describe how lowly beginnings may be circumvented by proper planning. That is why so much space has been devoted to the story about the woman who ended up creating a whole new business as a result of being inspired to do a fine job of PLANNING so that her son could get a favorable break.[7]

Perhaps some will find in the kind of IDEAS here briefly described the nucleus of the riches they DESIRE! Simple IDEAS have been the seedlings from which great fortunes have grown in America. Woolworth's Five and Ten Cent Store idea, for example, was so simple at the time as to be almost unworthy of consideration, but it piled up a fortune for its creator.[8]

There is no fixed price for sound IDEAS!

Back of all IDEAS is specialized knowledge. Unfortunately, for those who do not find riches in abundance, specialized knowledge is more abundant and more easily acquired than IDEAS. Capability means IMAGINATION, the one quality needed to combine specialized knowledge with IDEAS, in the form of ORGANIZED PLANS designed to yield riches.

If you have IMAGINATION, the stories that have been told in this chapter may stimulate you to come up with an idea sufficient to serve as the beginning of the riches you desire. Remember, the IDEA is the main thing. Specialized knowledge may be found just around the corner — any corner! But IMAGINATION is the catalyst that unites a good idea with the specialized knowledge required to translate it into SUCCESS.

Anybody can WISH for riches, and most people do, but only a few know that a definite plan, plus a BURNING DESIRE for wealth, are the only dependable means of accumulating wealth.

The only limitation is that which one sets up in one's own mind.

Chapter 5

IMAGINATION
The Workshop of the Mind
The Fifth Step to Riches

THE IMAGINATION is literally the workshop wherein are fashioned all plans created by humankind. The impulse, the DESIRE, is given shape, form, and ACTION through the aid of the imaginative faculty of the mind.

It has been said that anything can be created which a human being can imagine.

Of all the ages of civilization, the one in which we live is the most favorable for the development of the imagination because it is an age of rapid change. On every hand we may contact stimuli which develop the imagination.

Through the aid of the imaginative faculty, we have discovered, and harnessed, more of Nature's forces during the past 50 years than during the entire history of the human race previous to that time. We have conquered the air so completely that the birds are a poor match for us in flying. We have harnessed the electromagnetic spectrum and made it serve as a means of instantaneous communication with any part of the world. We have analyzed and weighed the sun at a distance of millions of miles and determined through the aid of IMAGINATION the elements of which it consists. We have discovered that our own brains are both a broadcasting and a receiving station for the "vibration of thought," although we have only barely begun to understand this phenomenon with the aim of making practical use of this discovery. We have increased the speed of travel until we may now breakfast in New York and lunch in San Francisco.

OUR ONLY LIMITATION, within reason, LIES IN OUR DEVELOPMENT AND USE OF OUR IMAGINATION. We have not yet reached the apex of development in the use of the "imaginative faculty." We have merely discovered that we *have* an imagination, and have commenced to use it only in a very elementary way.

Two Forms of Imagination

The imaginative faculty functions in two forms. One is known as Synthetic Imagination and the other as Creative Imagination.

SYNTHETIC IMAGINATION—Through this faculty, one can arrange old concepts, ideas, or plans into new combinations. This faculty *creates* nothing. It merely works with the material of experience, education, and observation with which it is fed. It is the faculty used most by the inventor—with the exception of the genius, who draws upon the Creative Imagination when unable to solve a problem through Synthetic Imagination.

CREATIVE IMAGINATION—Through the faculty of Creative Imagination, the finite human mind has direct communication with Infinite Intelligence. It is the faculty through which "hunches" and "inspirations" are received.[1] It is by this faculty that all basic or new ideas are handed over to us. It is through this faculty that "thought vibrations" or "influences" from the minds of others are received. It is through this faculty that one individual may "tune in" or communicate with the subconscious minds of others.

The Creative Imagination works automatically in the manner described in subsequent pages. This faculty functions ONLY when the conscious mind is functioning at an exceedingly high level of "intensity" or "energy," as for example, when the conscious mind is stimulated through the emotion of a *strong desire.*

The Creative Imagination becomes more alert, more receptive to influences from the sources mentioned, in proportion to its development through USE. This statement is significant! Ponder over it before passing on.

Keep in mind as you follow these principles that the entire story of how one may convert DESIRE into money cannot be told in one statement. The story will be complete only when one has MASTERED, ASSIMILATED, and BEGUN TO MAKE USE of *all* the success principles that are explained, and tied together, in this book.

The great leaders of business, industry, finance, and the great artists, musicians, poets, and writers became great because they developed the faculty of Creative Imagination.

Both the synthetic and creative faculties of imagination become more alert with use, just as any muscle or organ of the body develops through use.

Desire is only a thought, an impulse. It is nebulous and ephemeral. It is abstract, and of no value, until it has been transformed into its physical counterpart. While the Synthetic Imagination is the one which will be used most frequently in the process of transforming the impulse of DESIRE into money, you must keep in mind the fact that you may face circumstances and situations which demand the use of the Creative Imagination as well.

Your imaginative faculty may have become weak through inaction. It can be revived and made alert through USE. This faculty does not die, though it may become dormant through lack of use.

Center your attention, for the time being, on developing the Synthetic Imagination because this is the faculty which you will use more often in the process of converting desire into money.

Transforming the intangible impulse of DESIRE into the tangible reality of MONEY calls for the use of a plan or plans. These plans must be formed with the aid of the imagination, mainly Synthetic Imagination.

Read this entire book through, then come back to this chapter and begin at once to put your imagination to work on *building a plan or plans* to transform your DESIRE into money. Detailed instructions for building plans have been given in almost every chapter. Carry out the instructions best suited to your needs, and reduce your plan to writing if you have not already done so. The moment you complete this, you will have DEFINITELY given concrete form to the intangible DESIRE. Read the preceding sentence once more. Read it aloud, very slowly, and as you do so, remember that the moment you reduce the statement of your desire—and a plan for its realization—to writing, you have actually TAKEN THE FIRST of a series of steps which will enable you to convert the thought into its physical counterpart.

The earth on which you live, you yourself, and every other material thing are the result of evolutionary change—through which microscopic bits of matter have been organized and arranged in an orderly fashion.

Moreover—and this statement is of stupendous importance—this earth, every one of the billions of individual cells of your body, and every atom of matter *began as an intangible form of energy.*

DESIRE is thought impulse! Thought impulses are *forms of energy.* When you begin with the thought impulse of DESIRE TO ACCUMULATE MONEY or any other object of desire, you are drafting into your service the same stuff that Nature used in creating this earth and every material form in the universe, including the body and brain in which the thought impulses function.

As far as science has been able to determine, the entire universe consists of but two elements—matter and energy.

Through the combination of energy and matter has been created everything which we can perceive, from the largest star which floats in the heavens down to and including ourselves.

You are now engaged in the task of trying to profit by Nature's method. You are (sincerely and earnestly, we hope) trying to adapt yourself to Nature's laws by endeavoring to convert DESIRE into its physical or monetary equivalent. YOU CAN DO IT! IT HAS BEEN DONE BEFORE!

You can build a fortune through the aid of laws which are immutable. But first you must become familiar with these laws and learn to USE them. Through repetition, and by approaching the description of these principles from every conceivable angle, I hope to reveal to you the secret through which every great fortune has been accumulated. Strange and paradoxical as it may seem, the secret is NOT A SECRET. Nature herself advertises it in the earth on which we live, the stars, the planets suspended within our view, in the elements above and around us, in every blade of grass, and in every form of life within our vision.

Nature advertises this secret in the terms of biology, in the conversion of a tiny cell, so small that it may be lost on the point of a pin, into the HUMAN BEING now reading this line. The conversion of desire into its physical equivalent is certainly no more miraculous!

Do not become discouraged if you do not fully comprehend all that has been stated. Unless you have long been a student of the mind, it is not to be expected that you will assimilate all that is in this chapter upon a first reading.

But you will, in time, make good progress.

The principles that follow will open the way for understanding of imagination. Assimilate that which you understand as you read this philosophy for the first time, then when you reread and study it, you will discover that something has happened to clarify it and give you a broader understanding of the whole. Above all, DO NOT STOP nor hesitate in your study of these principles until you have read the book at least THREE times—for then you will not want to stop.

How to Make Practical Use of Imagination

Ideas are the beginning points of all fortunes. Ideas are products of the imagination. Let us examine a few well-known ideas which have yielded huge fortunes, with the hope that these illustrations will convey definite information concerning the method by which imagination may be used in accumulating riches.

The Enchanted Kettle

Fifty years ago, an old country doctor drove to town, hitched his horse, quietly slipped into a drugstore by the back door, and began dickering with the young drug clerk.

His mission was destined to yield great wealth to many people. It was destined to bring to the South the most far-flung benefit since the Civil War.

For more than an hour, behind the prescription counter, the old doctor and the clerk talked in low tones. Then the doctor left. He went out to the buggy and brought back a large, old-fashioned kettle, a big wooden paddle (used for stirring the contents of the kettle), and deposited them in the back of the store.

The clerk inspected the kettle, reached into his inside pocket, took out a roll of bills, and handed it over to the doctor. The roll contained exactly $500 — the clerk's entire savings!

The doctor handed over a small slip of paper on which was written a secret formula. The words on that small slip of paper were worth a king's ransom! *But not to the doctor!* Those magic words were needed to start the kettle to boiling, but neither the doctor nor the young clerk knew what fabulous fortunes were destined to flow from that kettle.

The old doctor was glad to sell the outfit for $500. The money would pay off his debts and give him freedom of mind. The clerk was taking a big chance by staking his entire life's savings on a mere scrap of paper and an old kettle! He never dreamed his investment would start a kettle to overflowing with gold that would surpass the miraculous performance of Aladdin's lamp.

What the clerk really purchased was an IDEA!

The old kettle, and the wooden paddle, and the secret message on a slip of paper were incidental. The strange performance of that kettle began to take place after the new owner mixed with the secret instructions an ingredient of which the doctor knew nothing.

Read this story carefully and give your imagination a test! See if you can discover what it was that the young man added to the secret message that caused the kettle to overflow with gold. Remember as you read that this is not a story from *Arabian Nights*. Here you have a story of facts, stranger than fiction, facts which began in the form of an IDEA.

Let us take a look at the vast fortunes of gold this idea has produced. It has paid, and still pays, huge fortunes to men and women all over the world who distribute the contents of the kettle to millions of people.

The Old Kettle is now one of the world's largest consumers of sugar, thus providing jobs of a permanent nature to thousands of men and women engaged in growing sugar cane, beets, other sugar producing crops, and in refining and marketing sugar.

The Old Kettle consumes millions and millions of bottles and cans each year, providing jobs to huge numbers of workers who manufacture those containers.

The Old Kettle gives employment to an army of clerks, stenographers, copywriters, and advertising experts throughout the nation. It has brought fame and fortune to scores of artists who have created magnificent pictures and ads describing the product.

The Old Kettle converted a small Southern city into the business capital of the South, where it now benefits, directly or indirectly, every business and practically every resident of the city.

The influence of this idea now benefits every civilized country in the world, pouring out a continuous stream of gold to all who touch it.

Gold from the kettle has built and maintains one of the most prominent universities of the South, where thousands of young people receive the training essential for success.

The Old Kettle has done other marvelous things. All during the Depression, when factories, banks and businesses were folding up and quitting by the thousands, the owner of this Enchanted Kettle went marching on, *giving continuous employment* to an army of men and women all over the world, and paying out extra portions of gold to those who long ago *had faith in the idea.*

If the product of that old brass kettle could talk, it would tell thrilling tales of romance in every language. Romances of love, romances of business, romances of professional men and women who are daily being stimulated by it.

I am sure of at least one such romance, for I was a part of it, and it all began not far from the very spot on which the drug clerk purchased the old kettle. It was here that I met my wife, and it was she who first told me of the Enchanted Kettle. It was the product of that kettle we were drinking when I asked her to accept me "for better or worse."[2]

Whoever you are, wherever you may live, whatever occupation you may be engaged in, just remember in the future, every time you see the words "Coca-Cola," that its vast empire of wealth and influence grew out of a single IDEA, and that the mysterious ingredient which the drug clerk—Asa Candler—mixed with the secret formula was.....IMAGINATION![3]

Stop and think of that for a moment.

Remember also that *The 13 Steps to Riches* described in this book were the media through which the influence of Coca-Cola has been extended to every city, town, village, and crossroads of the world, and that ANY IDEA you may create, which is as *sound* and *meritorious* as Coca-Cola, has the possibility of duplicating the stupendous record of this worldwide thirst-quencher.

Truly, thoughts are things, and their scope of operation is the world itself.

What I Would Do If I Had a Million Dollars

The following story proves the truth of the old saying, "Where there's a will, there's a way." It was told to me by that beloved educator and clergyman, the late Frank W. Gunsaulus, who began his preaching career in the stockyards region of South Chicago.

While Dr. Gunsaulus was going through college, he observed many defects in our educational system, defects which he believed he could correct if he were the head of a college. His deepest desire was to become the head of an educational institution in which young men and women would be taught to learn by doing.

He made up his mind to organize a new college in which he could carry out his ideas without being handicapped by orthodox methods of education.

He needed a million dollars to put the project across! Where was he to lay his hands on so large a sum of money? That was the question that absorbed most of this ambitious young preacher's thought.

But he couldn't seem to make any progress.

Every night he took that thought to bed with him. He got up with it in the morning. He took it with him everywhere he went.

He turned it over and over in his mind until it became a consuming *obsession* with him. A million dollars is a lot of money. He recognized that fact, but he also recognized the truth that *the only limitation is that which one sets up in one's own mind.*

Being a philosopher as well as a preacher, Dr. Gunsaulus recognized, as do all who succeed in life, that DEFINITENESS OF PURPOSE is the starting point from which one must begin. He recognized, too, that definiteness of purpose takes on animation, life, and power when backed by a BURNING DESIRE to translate that purpose into its material equivalent.

He knew all these great truths, yet he did not know where or how to lay his hands on a million dollars. The natural procedure would have been to give up and quit by saying, "Ah well, my idea is a good one, but I cannot do anything with it because I never can procure the necessary million dollars." That is exactly what the majority of people would have said, but it is not what Dr. Gunsaulus said. What he said and what he did are so important that I now introduce him and let him speak for himself.

"One Saturday afternoon I sat in my room thinking of ways and means of raising the money to carry out my plans. For nearly two years I had been thinking, but I *had done nothing but think!*

"The time had come for ACTION!

"I made up my mind, then and there, that I would get the necessary million dollars within a week. How? I was not concerned about that. The thing of importance was the *decision* to get the money within a specified time, and I want to tell you that the moment I reached a definite decision to get the money within a specified time, a strange feeling of assurance came over me such as I had never before experienced. Something inside me seemed to say, 'Why didn't you reach that decision a long time ago? The money was waiting for you all the time!'

"Things began to happen in a hurry. I called the newspapers and announced I would preach a sermon the following morning entitled, 'What I Would Do If I Had a Million Dollars.'

"I went to work on the sermon immediately, but I must tell you frankly the task was not difficult because I had been preparing that sermon for almost two years. The spirit back of it was a part of me!

"Long before midnight I had finished writing the sermon. I went to bed and slept with a feeling of confidence, for *I could see myself already in possession of the million dollars.*

"Next morning I arose early, went into the bathroom, read the sermon, then knelt on my knees and asked that my sermon might come to the attention of someone who would supply the needed money.

"While I was praying, I again had that feeling of assurance that the money would be forthcoming. In my excitement, I walked out without my sermon and did not discover the oversight until I was in my pulpit and about ready to begin delivering it.

"It was too late to go back for my notes, and what a blessing that I couldn't go back! Instead, my own subconscious mind yielded the material I needed. When I arose to begin my sermon, I closed my eyes, and spoke with all my heart and soul of my dreams. I not only talked to my audience, but I fancy I talked also to God. I told what I would do with a million dollars if that amount were placed in my hands. I described the plan I had in mind for organizing a great educational institution where young people would learn to do practical things and at the same time develop their minds.

"When I had finished and sat down, a man slowly arose from his seat, about three rows from the rear, and made his way toward the pulpit. I wondered what he was going to do. He came into the pulpit, extended his hand, and said, 'Reverend, I liked your sermon. I believe you can do everything you said you would if you had a million dollars. To prove that I believe in you and your sermon, if you will come to my office tomorrow morning, I will give you the million dollars. My name is Phillip D. Armour.'"[4]

Young Gunsaulus went to Mr. Armour's office and the million dollars was presented to him. With the money he founded the Armour Institute of Technology.

That is more money than the majority of preachers ever see in an entire lifetime, yet the thought impulse back of the money was created in the young preacher's mind in a fraction of a minute. The necessary million dollars came as a result of an idea. Back of the idea was a DESIRE which young Gunsaulus had been nursing in his mind for almost two years.

Observe this important fact—HE GOT THE MONEY WITHIN 36 HOURS AFTER HE REACHED A DEFINITE DECISION IN HIS OWN MIND TO GET IT—AND DECIDED UPON A DEFINITE PLAN FOR GETTING IT!

There was nothing new or unique about young Gunsaulus' vague thinking about a million dollars and weakly hoping for it. Others before him, and many since his time, have had similar thoughts. But there was something unique and different about the decision he reached on that memorable Saturday, when he put vagueness into the background and said definitely, "I WILL get that money within a week!"

God seems to throw Himself on the side of people who know exactly what they want, if they are determined to get JUST THAT!

Moreover, the principle through which Dr. Gunsaulus got his million dollars is still alive! It is available to you! This universal law is as workable today as it was when the young preacher made use of it so successfully. This book describes, step by step, the 13 elements of this great law and suggests how they may be put to use.[5]

Observe that Asa Candler and Dr. Frank Gunsaulus had one characteristic in common. Both knew the astounding truth that IDEAS CAN BE TRANSMUTED INTO CASH THROUGH THE POWER OF DEFINITE PURPOSE, PLUS DEFINITE PLANS.

If you are one of those who believe that hard work and honesty alone will bring riches, perish the thought! It is not true! Riches, when they come in huge quantities, are never the result of HARD work! Riches come, if they come at all, in response to definite demands, based upon the application of definite principles, and not by chance or luck.

Generally speaking, an idea is an impulse of thought that impels action by an appeal to the imagination. All master salespeople know that ideas can be sold where merchandise cannot. Ordinary salespeople do *not* know this—that is why they are ordinary.

A publisher of books which sell for a few dollars made a discovery that should be worth much to publishers generally. He learned that many people buy titles and not contents of books. By merely changing the name of one book that was not moving, his sales on that book jumped upward more than a million copies. The inside of the book was not changed in any way. He merely ripped off the cover bearing the title that did not sell, and put on a new cover with a title that had "box office" value.

That, as simple as it may seem, was an IDEA! It was IMAGINATION at work.

There is no standard price on ideas. Creators of ideas make their own price and, if they are smart, get it.

The movie industry created a whole flock of millionaires. Most of them were individuals who couldn't create ideas—BUT—they had the imagination to recognize ideas when they saw them.[6]

The story of practically every great fortune starts with the day when a creator of ideas and a seller of ideas get together and work in harmony. Carnegie surrounded himself with people who could do all that he could not do—people who created ideas and people who put ideas into operation—and by so doing made himself and the others fabulously rich.

Millions of people go through life hoping for favorable breaks. Perhaps a favorable break can get one an opportunity, but the safest plan is not to depend upon luck. It was a favorable "break" that gave me the biggest opportunity of my life—*but*—25 years of *determined effort* had to be devoted to that opportunity before it became an asset.

The break consisted of my good fortune in meeting and gaining the cooperation of Andrew Carnegie. On that occasion, Carnegie planted in my mind the idea of organizing the principles of achievement into a philosophy of success. Thousands of people have profited by the discoveries made in the 25 years of research, and numerous fortunes have been accumulated through the application of the philosophy. The beginning was simple. It was an IDEA which anyone might have developed.

The favorable break came through Andrew Carnegie, but what about the DETERMINATION, DEFINITENESS OF PURPOSE, the DESIRE TO ATTAIN THE GOAL, and the PERSISTENT EFFORT OF 25 YEARS? It was no ordinary DESIRE that survived disappointment, discouragement, temporary defeat, criticism, and the constant reminding of "waste of time." It was a BURNING DESIRE! An OBSESSION!

When the idea was first planted in my mind by Mr. Carnegie, it was coaxed, nursed, and enticed to *remain alive*. Gradually, the idea became a giant, under its own power, and it coaxed, nursed, and drove me. Ideas are like that. First you give life and action and guidance to ideas, then they take on power of their own and sweep aside all opposition.

Ideas are intangible forces, but they have more power than the physical brains that give birth to them. They have the power to live on, after the brain that creates them has returned to dust. For example, take the power of Christianity. That began with a simple idea. Its chief tenet was "Do unto others as you would have others do unto you." Christ has gone back to the source from whence He came, but His IDEA goes marching on. Some day, it may come fully into its own. Then it will have fulfilled Christ's deepest DESIRE. The IDEA has been developing only some two thousand years. Give it time!

Riches, when they come in huge quantities, are never the result of HARD work! Riches come, if they come at all, in response to definite demands, based upon the application of definite principles, and not by chance or luck.

§   §   §

SUCCESS REQUIRES NO APOLOGIES. FAILURE PERMITS NO ALIBIS.

Chapter 6

ORGANIZED PLANNING
The Crystallization of Desire Into Action
The Sixth Step to Riches

YOU HAVE LEARNED that everything worthwhile that an individual creates or acquires begins in the form of DESIRE—and that the first step of DESIRE'S journey from the *abstract* to the *concrete* is into the workshop of the IMAGINATION, where PLANS for DESIRE'S transition are created and organized.

In Chapter 1 you were instructed to take six definite, practical actions as your first move in translating the desire for money into its monetary equivalent. One of these steps is the formation of a DEFINITE, practical plan or plans through which this transformation may be made.

You will now be instructed on how to build plans which will be practical, namely:

(a) Ally yourself with a group of as many people as you may need to create and carry out your plan or plans for the accumulation of money. (To do this, you will make use of the Master Mind Principle, which is described in Chapter 9. Compliance with this instruction is *absolutely essential*. Do not neglect it.)

(b) Before forming your Master Mind Alliance, decide what advantages, and benefits, *you* may offer the individual members of your group in return for their cooperation.

No one will work indefinitely without some form of compensation. No intelligent person will either request or expect another to work without adequate compensation, although this may not always be in the form of money.

(c) Arrange to meet with the members of your Master Mind Group at least twice a week, and more often if possible, until you have jointly perfected the necessary plan or plans for the accumulation of money.

(d) Maintain PERFECT HARMONY between yourself and every member of your Master Mind Group. If you fail to carry out this instruction to the letter, you may expect to meet with failure. The Master Mind Principle *cannot* obtain where PERFECT HARMONY does not prevail.

Keep in mind these two facts:

First. You are engaged in an undertaking of major importance to you. To be sure of success, you must have plans which are faultless.

Second. You must have the advantage of the experience, education, native ability, and imagination of other minds. This is in harmony with the methods followed by every person who has accumulated a great fortune.

No individual has sufficient experience, education, native ability, and knowledge to ensure the accumulation of a great fortune without the cooperation of other people. Every plan you adopt in your endeavor to accumulate wealth should be the joint creation of yourself and every other member of your Master Mind Group. You may originate your own plans, either in whole or in part, but SEE THAT THOSE PLANS ARE CHECKED, AND APPROVED, BY THE MEMBERS OF YOUR MASTER MIND ALLIANCE.

If the first plan which you adopt does not work successfully, replace it with a new plan. If this new plan fails to work, replace it in turn with still another, and so on until you find a plan which DOES WORK. Right here is the point at which the majority of people meet with failure because of their lack of PERSISTENCE in creating new plans to take the place of those which fail.

The most intelligent individual cannot succeed in accumulating money—or in any other undertaking—without plans which are practical and workable. Just keep this fact in mind and remember, when your plans fail, that temporary defeat is not permanent failure. It may only mean that your plans have not been sound. Build other plans. Start over again.

Thomas A. Edison "failed" 10,000 times before he perfected the incandescent electric light bulb—that is, he met with *temporary defeat* 10,000 times before his efforts were crowned with success.

Temporary defeat should mean only one thing—the certain knowledge that there is something wrong with your plan. Millions of people go through life in misery and poverty because they lack a sound plan through which to accumulate a fortune.

Henry Ford accumulated a fortune not because of his superior mind, but because he adopted and followed a PLAN which proved to be sound. A thousand individuals could be pointed out, each with a better education than Ford's, yet each of whom lives in poverty because he or she does not possess the RIGHT plan for the accumulation of money.

Your achievement can be no greater than your PLANS are sound. That may seem to be an axiomatic statement, but it is true. And no one is ever whipped until that person QUITS—*in his or her own mind.*

This fact will be repeated many times because it is so easy to "take the count" at the first sign of defeat.

James J. Hill met with temporary defeat when he first endeavored to raise the necessary capital to build a railroad from the East to the West, but he, too, turned defeat into victory *through new plans.*

Henry Ford met with temporary defeat, not only at the beginning of his automobile career, but after he had gone far toward the top. He created new plans and went marching on to financial victory.

We see people who have accumulated great fortunes, but we often recognize only their triumph, overlooking the temporary defeats which they had to surmount before "arriving."

NO FOLLOWER OF THIS PHILOSOPHY CAN REASONABLY EXPECT TO ACCUMULATE A FORTUNE WITHOUT EXPER- IENCING TEMPORARY DEFEAT. When defeat comes, accept it as a signal that your plans are not sound, rebuild those plans, and set sail once more toward your coveted goal. If you give up before your goal has been reached, you are a quitter. A QUITTER NEVER WINS—AND A WINNER NEVER QUITS. Lift this sentence out, write it on a piece of paper in letters an inch high, and place it where you will see it every night before you go to sleep and every morning before you go to work.

When you begin to select members for your Master Mind Group, endeavor to select those who do not take defeat seriously.

Some people foolishly believe that only MONEY can make money. This is not true! DESIRE, transmuted into its monetary equivalent, through the principles laid down here, is the agency through which money is made. Money, of itself, is nothing but inert matter. It cannot move, think, or talk, but it can "hear" when a person who DESIRES it calls it to come!

Planning the Sale of Services

The remainder of this chapter is given over to a description of ways and means of marketing personal services. The information here conveyed will be of practical help to any person having any form of personal services to market, but it will be of priceless benefit to those who aspire to leadership in their chosen occupations.

Intelligent planning is essential for success in any undertaking designed to accumulate riches. The following pages provide detailed instructions to those who must begin the accumulation of riches by selling personal services.

It should be encouraging to know that practically all the great fortunes began in the form of compensation for personal services or from the sale of IDEAS. What else, except ideas and personal services, would one who owns little property have to give in return for riches?

Broadly speaking, there are two types of people in the world. One type is known as LEADERS and the other as FOLLOWERS.

Decide at the outset whether you intend to become a leader in your chosen calling or remain a follower. The difference in compensation is vast. The follower cannot reasonably expect the compensation to which a leader is entitled, although many followers make the mistake of expecting such pay.

It is no disgrace to be a follower. On the other hand, it is no credit to remain a follower. Most great leaders began in the capacity of followers. They became great leaders because they were INTELLIGENT FOLLOWERS. With few exceptions, the person who cannot follow a leader intelligently cannot become an efficient leader. The person who can follow a leader most efficiently is usually the one who develops into leadership most rapidly. An intelligent follower has many advantages, among them the OPPORTUNITY TO ACQUIRE KNOWLEDGE FROM HIS OR HER LEADER.

The 11 Major Factors of Leadership

The following are important attributes of leadership:

1. UNWAVERING COURAGE based upon knowledge of self and of one's occupation. No follower wishes to be dominated by a leader who lacks self-confidence and courage. No intelligent follower will be dominated by such a leader very long.

2. SELF-CONTROL. The person who lacks self-control can never control others. Self-control sets a mighty example for one's followers, which the more intelligent will emulate.

3. A KEEN SENSE OF JUSTICE. Without a sense of fairness and justice, no leader can command and retain the respect of his or her followers.

4. DEFINITENESS OF DECISION. Individuals who waver in their decisions show that they are not sure of themselves. They cannot lead others successfully.

5. DEFINITENESS OF PLANS. Successful leaders must plan their work and work their plan. Leaders who move by guesswork, without practical, definite plans, are

comparable to a ship without a rudder. Sooner or later they will land on the rocks.

6. THE HABIT OF DOING MORE THAN PAID FOR. One of the penalties of leadership is the necessity of willingness, upon the part of leaders, to do more than they require of their followers.

7. A PLEASING PERSONALITY. No slovenly, careless person can become a successful leader. Leadership calls for respect. Followers will not respect a leader who does not grade high on all of the factors of a "Pleasing Personality."

8. SYMPATHY AND UNDERSTANDING. Successful leaders must be in sympathy with their followers. Moreover, they must understand them and their problems.

9. MASTERY OF DETAIL. Successful leadership calls for mastery of details of the leader's position.

10. WILLINGNESS TO ASSUME FULL RESPONSIBILITY. Successful leaders must be willing to assume responsibility for the mistakes and the shortcomings of their followers. If they try to shift this responsibility, they will not remain the leader. If one of their followers makes a mistake and demonstrates incompetence, leaders must consider that it is *they themselves* who failed.

11. COOPERATION. Successful leaders must understand and apply the principle of cooperative effort and be able to induce their followers to do the same. Leadership calls for POWER and power calls for COOPERATION.

There are two forms of leadership. The first, by far the most effective, is LEADERSHIP BY CONSENT of, and with the sympathy of, the followers. The second is LEADERSHIP BY FORCE, without the consent and sympathy of the followers.

History is filled with evidence that Leadership by Force cannot endure. The downfall and disappearance of dictators and kings is significant. It means that people will not follow forced leadership indefinitely.

The world has just entered a new era of relationship between leaders and followers, which very clearly calls for new leaders and a new brand of leadership in business and industry. Those who belong to the old school of Leadership by Force must acquire an understanding of the new brand of leadership (cooperation) or be relegated to the rank and file of the followers. There is no other way out for them.

The relationship of employer and employee, or of leader and follower, in the future will be one of mutual cooperation, based upon an equitable division of the profits of business. In the future, the relationship of employer and employee will be more like a partnership than it has been in the past. Napoleon, Kaiser Wilhelm of Germany, the Czar of Russia, and the King of Spain were examples of leadership by force.[1] Their leadership passed. Without much difficulty, one might point to the prototypes of these ex-leaders among the business, financial, and labor leaders of America who have been dethroned or slated to go. *Leadership by Consent* (of the followers) is the only brand which can endure!

People may follow the forced leadership temporarily, but they will not do so willingly.

The new brand of LEADERSHIP will embrace the 11 Major Factors of Leadership described in this chapter, as well as some other factors. The individual who makes these the basis of his or her leadership will find abundant opportunity to lead in any walk of life. The difficult economic times we have faced have been prolonged in large part because the world lacked LEADERSHIP of the new brand. Now the demand for leaders who are competent to apply the new methods of leadership has greatly exceeded the supply. Some of the old type of leaders will reform and adapt themselves to the new brand of leadership, but generally speaking, the world will have to look for new timber for its leadership.

This necessity may be your OPPORTUNITY!

The 10 Major Causes of Failure in Leadership

We come now to the major faults of leaders who fail, because it is just as essential to know WHAT NOT TO DO as it is to know what to do.

1. INABILITY TO ORGANIZE DETAILS. Efficient leadership calls for ability to organize and to master details. Genuine leaders are never "too busy" to do anything which may be required of them in their capacity as leaders. Whenever people, whether they are leader or follower, admit that they are too busy to change their plans, or to give attention to any emergency, they admit their inefficiency. Successful leaders must be the master of all details connected with their position. That means, of course, that they must acquire the habit of delegating details to capable lieutenants.[2]

2. UNWILLINGNESS TO RENDER HUMBLE SERVICE. Truly great leaders are willing when the occasion demands to perform any sort of labor which they would ask another to perform. "The greatest among ye shall be the servant of all" is a truth which all able leaders observe and respect.

3. EXPECTATION OF PAY FOR WHAT THEY KNOW, INSTEAD OF WHAT THEY *DO* WITH THAT WHICH THEY KNOW. The world does not pay people for that which they know. It pays them for what they DO or induce others to do.

4. FEAR OF COMPETITION FROM FOLLOWERS. Leaders who fear that one of their followers may take their position are practically sure to realize that fear sooner or later. Able leaders train understudies to whom they may delegate, at will, any of the details of their position. Only in this way can leaders multiply themselves and prepare themselves to be at many places and give attention to many things at one time. It is an eternal truth that people receive more pay for their ABILITY TO GET OTHERS TO

PERFORM than they could possibly earn by their own efforts. Efficient leaders may, through their knowledge of their job and the magnetism of their personality, greatly increase the efficiency of others and induce them to render more service and better service than they could render without the leader's aid.

5. LACK OF IMAGINATION. Without imagination, leaders are incapable of meeting emergencies and of creating plans by which to guide their followers efficiently.

6. SELFISHNESS. Leaders who claim all the honor for the work of their followers are sure to be met by resentment. Great leaders CLAIM NONE OF THE HONORS. They are contented to see the honors, when there are any, go to their followers because they know that most people will work harder for commendation and recognition than they will for money alone.[3]

7. INTEMPERANCE. Followers do not respect an intemperate leader. Moreover, intemperance in any of its various forms destroys the endurance and the vitality of all who indulge in it.

8. DISLOYALTY. Perhaps this should have come at the head of the list. Leaders who are not loyal to their trust and to their associates, those above and those below, cannot long maintain their leadership. Disloyalty marks one as being less than the dust of the earth, and brings down on one's head the contempt he or she deserves. Lack of loyalty is one of the major causes of failure in every walk of life.

9. OVEREMPHASIS ON THE AUTHORITY OF LEADER-SHIP. Efficient leaders lead by encouraging and not by trying to instill fear in the hearts of their followers. Leaders who try to impress their followers with their "authority" come within the category of Leadership by Force. If leaders are REAL LEADERS, they will have no need to advertise that fact except by their conduct — their

sympathy, understanding, fairness, and a demonstration that they know their job.

10. OVEREMPHASIS ON TITLE. Competent leaders require no title to give them the respect of their followers. The individual who makes too much over his or her title generally has little else to emphasize. The doors to the office of real leaders are open to all who wish to enter, and their working quarters are free from formality or ostentation.

These are among the more common of the causes of failure in leadership. Any one of these faults is sufficient to induce failure. Study the list carefully if you aspire to leadership, and make sure that you are free of these faults.

Some Fertile Fields in Which New Leadership Will Be Required

Before leaving this chapter, your attention is called to a few of the fertile fields in which there has been a decline of leadership and in which the new type of leader may find an abundance of OPPORTUNITY.

First. In the field of politics there is a most insistent demand for new leaders—a demand which indicates nothing less than an emergency. The majority of politicians have seemingly become high-grade, legalized racketeers. They have increased taxes and debauched the machinery of industry and business until the people can no longer stand the burden.

Second. The banking business is undergoing a reform. The leaders in this field have almost entirely lost the confidence of the public. Already the bankers have sensed the need of reform, and they have begun it.

Third. Industry calls for new leaders. The old type of leaders thought and moved in terms of dividends, instead of thinking and moving in terms of human equations! Future leaders in industry, to endure, must regard themselves as quasi-public officials whose duty it is to manage their trust in such a way that it will work hardship on no individual or group of individuals. Exploitation of working people is a thing of the past. Let the man or woman who aspires to leadership in the field of business, industry, and labor remember this.

Fourth. Religious leaders of the future must give more attention to the temporal needs of their followers in the solution of their present economic and personal problems, and less attention to the dead past and the yet unborn future.

Fifth. In the professions of law, medicine, and education, a new brand of leadership, and to some extent new leaders, will become a necessity. This is especially true in the field of education. The leader in that field must in the future find ways and means of teaching people HOW TO APPLY the knowledge they receive in school. The educator must deal more with PRACTICE and less with THEORY.

Sixth. New leaders will be required in the field of journalism. Newspapers of the future, to be operated successfully, must be divorced from "special privilege" and relieved from the subsidy of advertising. They must cease to be organs of propaganda for the interests which patronize their advertising columns. The type of newspaper which publishes scandal and lewd pictures will eventually go the way of all forces which debauch the human mind.[4]

These are but a few of the fields in which opportunities for new leaders and a new brand of leadership are now available. The world is undergoing a rapid change. This means that the media through which the changes in human habits are promoted must be adapted to the changes. The media here described are the ones which more than any others determine the trend of civilization.

The information to be described next about when and how to apply for a position is the net result of many years of experience during which thousands of men and women were helped to market their services effectively. It can, therefore, be relied upon as sound and practical.

Media through Which Services May Be Marketed

Experience has proved that the following media offer the most direct and effective methods of bringing the buyer and seller of personal services together.

1. EMPLOYMENT AGENCIES. Care must be taken to select only reputable agencies, the management of which can show adequate records of achievement of satisfactory results. There are comparatively few such agencies.

2. ADVERTISING in newspapers, trade journals, and magazines. Classified advertising may usually be relied upon to produce satisfactory results in the case of those who apply for clerical or ordinary salaried positions. Display advertising is more desirable in the case of those who seek executive connections. The copy should be prepared by an expert, who understands how to inject sufficient selling qualities to produce replies.

3. PERSONAL LETTERS OF APPLICATION, directed to particular firms or individuals most apt to need such services as are being offered. Letters should be *neatly typed*, ALWAYS, and signed by hand with a bold signature. With the letter should be sent a complete brief or outline of the applicant's qualifications. Both the letter of application and the resume of experience or qualifications should be prepared by an expert — or be of the same quality and appearance as one prepared by an expert. (See instructions as to information to be supplied).

4. APPLICATION THROUGH PERSONAL ACQUAINT-ANCES. When possible, the applicant should endeavor to approach prospective employers through some mutual acquaintance. This method of approach is particularly advantageous in the case of those who seek executive connections and do not wish to appear to be "peddling" themselves.[5]

5. APPLICATION IN PERSON. In some instances, it may be more effective if the applicant offers personally, his or her services to prospective employers, in which event a complete written statement of qualifications for the position should be presented because prospective employers often wish to discuss with associates one's record.

Eight Musts for an Effective Resume

A resume should be prepared as carefully as a lawyer would prepare the brief of a case to be tried in court. Unless the applicant is experienced in the preparation of resumes, an expert should be consulted and hired for this purpose. Successful merchants employ men and women who understand the art and the psychology of advertising to present the merits of their merchandise. One who has personal services for sale should do the same. The following eight items of information should appear in the resume:

1. *Education.* State briefly, but specifically, what education you have had and in what subjects you specialized, giving the reasons for that specialization.

2. *Experience.* If you have had experience in connection with positions similar to the one you seek, describe it fully, and state names and addresses of former employers. Be sure to bring out clearly any *special* experience you may have had which would equip you to fill the position you seek.

3. *References.* Practically every business firm desires to know all about the previous records, antecedents, etc., of prospective employees who seek positions of responsibility. Attach to your resume photostatic copies of letters from:

   a. former employers
   b. teachers under whom you studied
   c. prominent people whose judgment may be relied upon

4. *Photograph.* Attach to your resume a recent, unmounted photograph of yourself (or, if your resume is being printed professionally, have the photograph suitably reproduced).

5. *Apply for a specific position.* Avoid applying for a position without describing EXACTLY what particular position you seek. Never apply for "just a position." That indicates you lack specialized qualifications.

6. *State your qualifications* for the particular position for which you apply. Give full details as to the reason you believe you are qualified for the particular position you seek. This is THE MOST IMPORTANT DETAIL OF YOUR APPLICATION. It will determine more than anything else what consideration you receive.

7. *Offer to go to work on probation.* In the majority of instances, if you are determined to have the position for which you apply, it will be most effective if you offer to work for a week, or a month, or for a sufficient length of time to enable your prospective employer to judge your value WITHOUT PAY. This may appear to be a radical suggestion, but experience has proved that it seldom fails to win at least a trial. If you are SURE OF YOUR QUALIFICATIONS, a trial is all you need. Incidentally, such an offer indicates that you have confidence in your ability to fill the position you seek. It is most convincing. If your offer is accepted, and you make good, more than likely you will be paid for your probation period. Make clear the fact that your offer is based upon:
   a. your confidence in your ability to fill the position
   b. your confidence in your prospective employer's decision to employ you after trial
   c. your DETERMINATION to have the position you seek

8. *Knowledge of your prospective employer's business.* Before applying for a position, do sufficient research in connection with the business to familiarize yourself thoroughly

with that business, and indicate in your resume the knowledge you have acquired in this field. This will be impressive, as it will indicate that you have imagination and a real interest in the position you seek.

Remember that it is not the lawyer who knows the most law, but the one who prepares the best case who wins. If your "case" is properly prepared and presented, your victory will have been more than half won at the outset.

Do not be afraid of making your resume too long. Employers are just as much interested in purchasing the services of well-qualified applicants as you are in securing employment. In fact, the success of most successful employers is due mainly to their ability to select well-qualified lieutenants. They want all the information available.

Remember another thing: Neatness and care in the preparation of your resume will indicate that you are a painstaking person. I have helped to prepare resumes for clients which were so striking and out of the ordinary that they resulted in the employment of the applicant without a personal interview.

When your resume has been completed, have it neatly bound and printed by an experienced printer. Its cover should appear similar to the following:

RESUME OF
Robert K. Smith
APPLYING FOR THE POSITION OF
Assistant Manager at
THE BLANK COMPANY, INC.

This personal touch is sure to command attention. Have your resume neatly typed or printed on the finest paper you can obtain and then suitably bound or placed in an appropriate presentation folder. The cover should, of course, be changed and the proper firm name and job title inserted if it is to be shown to more than one company. Your photograph should be pasted or printed on one of the pages of your resume. Follow these instructions to the letter, improving upon them wherever your imagination suggests.

Successful salespeople groom themselves with care. They understand that first impressions are lasting. Your resume is your sales representative. Give it a good suit of clothes so it will stand out in bold contrast to anything your prospective employer ever saw in the way of an application for a position. If the position you seek is worth having, it is worth going after with care. Moreover, if you sell yourself to employers in a manner that impresses them with your individuality, you may very well receive more money for your services from the very start than you would if you applied for employment in the usual way.

If you seek employment through an employment agency, make sure they use copies of your resume — or produce and provide one that meets all the above criteria — in marketing your services. This will help to gain preference for you both with the agency and prospective employers.

How to Get the Exact Position You Desire

Everyone enjoys doing the kind of work for which they are best suited. An artist loves to work with paints, a craftsman with his or her hands, a writer loves to write. Those with less definite talents have their preferences for certain fields of business or industry. If America does anything well, it offers a full range of occupations, from tilling the soil and manufacturing, to marketing, commerce, and the professions.

Here are seven actions to take to guarantee yourself the exact position you wish:

First. Decide — and DEFINE briefly in writing — EXACTLY what kind of job you desire. If the job does not already exist, perhaps you can create it.

Second. Choose the specific company, or the specific individual, for whom you wish to work.

Third. Study your prospective employer as to policies, personnel, and chances of advancement.

Fourth. By analysis of yourself, your talents and capabilities, figure WHAT YOU CAN OFFER and plan ways and means of giving advantages, services, developments, and ideas that *you believe* you can successfully deliver.

Fifth. Forget about "a job." Forget whether or not there is an opening. Forget the usual routine of "have you got a job for me?" Concentrate on what *you can give*.

Sixth. Once you have your plan in mind, arrange with an experienced writer to put it on paper, in neat form and in full detail.

Seventh. Present it to the *proper person with authority* and he or she will do the rest. Every company is looking for people who can give something of value, whether it be ideas, services, or "connections." Every company has room for the individual who has a definite plan of action which is to the advantage of that company.

This line of procedure may take a few days or weeks of extra time, but the difference in income, in advancement, and in gaining recognition will save years of hard work at small pay. It has many advantages, the main one being that it will often save from one to five years of time in reaching a chosen goal.

Every person who starts, or "gets in," halfway up the ladder does so by deliberate and careful planning (excepting, of course, the Boss' kid.)

THE NEW WAY TO MARKET SERVICES

"Jobs" Are Now "Partnerships"

Men and women who market their services to best advantage in the future must recognize the stupendous change which has taken place in connection with the relationship between employer and employee.

In the future, the "Golden Rule," not the "Rule of Gold," will be the dominating factor in the marketing of merchandise, as well as personal services.[6] The future relationship between employers and their employees will be more in the nature of a partnership consisting of:

a. the employer
b. the employee
c. the public they serve

This new way of marketing personal services is called "new" for many reasons. First, both the employer and the employee of the future will be considered as "fellow employees" whose business it will be to SERVE THE PUBLIC EFFICIENTLY. In times past, employers and employees have bartered among themselves, driving the best bargains they could with one another, not considering that in the final analysis they were in reality BARGAINING AT THE EXPENSE OF THE THIRD PARTY—THE PUBLIC THEY SERVED.[7] The real employer of the future will be the public. This should be kept uppermost in mind by every person seeking to market personal services effectively.[8]

HOW TIMES HAVE CHANGED! That is just the point I am trying to emphasize. TIMES HAVE CHANGED! Moreover, the change is reflected in all occupations and all walks of life as well. The "public be damned" policy is now passé. It has been supplanted by the "we-are-obligingly-at-your-service, sir" policy.[9]

"Courtesy" and "service" are the watchwords of merchandising today, and they apply to the person who is marketing personal services even more directly than to the employer whom he or she serves because, in the final analysis, both the employer and the employee are EMPLOYED BY THE PUBLIC THEY SERVE. If they fail to serve well, they pay by the loss of their privilege of serving.[10]

During the Depression, I spent several months in the anthracite coal region of Pennsylvania, studying conditions which all but destroyed the coal industry. Among several very significant discoveries was the fact that greed on the part of operators and their employees was the chief cause of the loss of business for the operators and loss of jobs for the miners.

Through the pressure of a group of overzealous labor leaders representing the employees, and the greed for profits on the part of the operators, the anthracite business suddenly dwindled. The coal operators and their employees drove sharp bargains with one another, adding the cost of the bargaining to the price of the coal until finally they discovered they had BUILT UP A WONDERFUL BUSINESS FOR THE MANUFACTURERS OF OIL BURNING OUTFITS AND THE PRODUCERS OF CRUDE OIL.

"The wages of sin is death!" Many have read this in the Bible, but few have discovered its meaning. Now, and for several years, America and the world have been listening to a sermon which might well be called "WHATSOEVER A MAN SOWETH, THAT SHALL HE ALSO REAP."

Nothing as widespread as the depressed economic times we have lived through could possibly be "just a coincidence." Behind it all there was a CAUSE. Nothing ever happens without a CAUSE. In the main, the cause here is traceable directly to the economic habit of trying to REAP without SOWING.

This should not be mistaken to mean that these tough economic times represent a crop which we are being FORCED to reap without having SOWN. The trouble is that we sowed the wrong sort of seed. All farmers know they cannot sow the seed of thistles and reap a harvest of grain. For a very long period, the people of America and some other lands began to sow the seed of service which was inadequate in both quality and quantity. Nearly everyone was engaged in the pastime of trying to GET WITHOUT GIVING.

This whole issue is brought to the attention of those who have personal services to market, to show that we are where we are and what we are because of our own conduct! If there is a principle of cause and effect which controls business, finance, and transportation, this same principle controls individuals and determines their economic status.

What Is Your QQS Rating?

The causes of success in marketing services EFFECTIVELY and permanently have been clearly described. Unless those causes are studied, analyzed, understood, and APPLIED, no one can market personal services effectively and permanently. Every individual must "sell" his or her services. The QUALITY and the QUANTITY of service rendered, and the SPIRIT in which it is rendered, determine to a large extent the price and the duration of employment. To market personal services effectively (which means a permanent market, at a satisfactory price, under pleasant conditions), one must adopt and follow the "QQS Formula" — QUALITY, plus QUANTITY, plus the proper SPIRIT of cooperation equals perfect salesmanship of service. Remember the QQS Formula, but do more — APPLY IT AS A HABIT!

Let us analyze the formula to make sure we understand exactly what it means.

1. **QUALITY** of service shall be construed to mean the performance of every detail in connection with your position in the most efficient manner possible, with the object of greater efficiency always in mind.

2. **QUANTITY** of service shall be understood to mean the HABIT of rendering all the service of which you are capable, at all times, with the purpose of increasing the amount of service rendered as greater skill is developed through practice and experience. Emphasis is again placed on the word HABIT.

3. **SPIRIT** of service shall be construed to mean the HABIT of agreeable, harmonious conduct which will induce cooperation from associates and fellow employees. Adequacy of QUALITY and QUANTITY of service is not sufficient to maintain a permanent market for your services. The conduct, or the SPIRIT in which you deliver service, is a strong determining factor in connection with both the price you receive and the duration of your employment. Andrew Carnegie stressed this point more than others in connection with his description of the factors which lead to success in the marketing of personal services. He emphasized again and again the necessity for HARMONIOUS CONDUCT. He stressed

the fact that he would not retain any person, no matter how great a QUANTITY or how efficient the QUALITY of that person's work, unless the individual worked in a spirit of HARMONY. Mr. Carnegie insisted upon people being AGREEABLE. To prove that he placed a high value upon this quality, he permitted many individuals who conformed to his standards to become very wealthy. Those who did not conform had to make room for others.

The importance of a pleasing personality has been stressed because it is a factor which enables one to render service in the proper SPIRIT. If one has a personality which PLEASES and renders service in a spirit of HARMONY, these assets often make up for deficiencies in both the QUALITY and the QUANTITY of service one renders. Nothing, however, can be SUCCESSFULLY SUBSTITUTED FOR PLEASING CONDUCT.

The Capital Value of Your Services

The person whose income is derived entirely from the sale of personal services is no less a merchant than the person who sells goods or products, and it might well be added that such a person is subject to EXACTLY THE SAME RULES of conduct as the merchant who sells merchandise.

This has been emphasized because the majority of people who live by the sale of personal services make the mistake of considering themselves free from the rules of conduct and the responsibilities which are attached to those who are engaged in marketing goods and products.

The new way of marketing services has practically forced both employer and employee into partnership alliances, through which both take into consideration the rights of the third party, THE PUBLIC THEY SERVE.

The day of the "go-getter" has passed. The go-getter has been supplanted by the "go-giver." High-pressure methods in business finally blew the lid off. There will never be the need to put the lid back on because in the future business will be conducted by methods that will require no pressure.

The actual capital value of your brains may be determined by the amount of income you can produce (by marketing your services). A fair estimate of the capital value of your services may be made by multiplying your annual income by $16^{2/3}$ (or 16.667), as it is reasonable to estimate that your annual income represents approximately six percent of your capital value. (Money is worth no more than brains. It is often worth much less.)

Competent brains, if effectively marketed, represent a much more desirable form of capital than that which is required to conduct a business dealing in goods and products because brains are a form of capital which cannot be permanently depreciated through economic depressions and cannot be stolen or spent. Moreover, the money which is essential for the conduct of business is as worthless as a sand dune until it has been mixed with efficient brains.

THE 30 MAJOR CAUSES OF FAILURE

How Many of These Are Holding You Back?

Life's greatest tragedy consists of men and women who earnestly try and fail! The tragedy lies in the overwhelmingly large majority of people who fail as compared to the few who succeed.

I have had the privilege of analyzing several thousand men and women, 98 percent of whom were classed as failures. There is something radically wrong with a civilization, and a system of education, which permit 98 percent of the people to go through life as failures. But I did not write this book for the purpose of moralizing on the rights and wrongs of the world. That would require a book a hundred times the size of this one.

My research and analysis proved that there are 30 major reasons for failure and 13 major principles (*The 13 Steps to Riches*) through which people accumulate fortunes. In this chapter, a description of the 30 major causes of failure will be given. As you go over the list, check yourself by it point by point for the purpose of discovering how many of these causes of failure stand between you and success.

1. UNFAVORABLE HEREDITARY BACKGROUND. There is but little, if anything, which can be done for people who are born with a deficiency in brain power. *The Think and Grow Rich Philosophy* offers but one method of bridging this weakness—through the aid of the Master Mind. Observe with profit, however, that this is the ONLY one of the 30 causes of failure which may not be easily corrected by any individual.

2. LACK OF A WELL-DEFINED PURPOSE IN LIFE. There is no hope of success for the person who does not have a central purpose, or definite goal, at which to aim. At least 98 out of every 100 of those people whom I have analyzed had no such aim. Perhaps this was the MAJOR CAUSE OF THEIR FAILURE.

3. LACK OF AMBITION TO AIM ABOVE MEDIOCRITY. We offer no hope for the person who is so indifferent as not to want to get ahead in life, and who is not willing to pay the price.

4. INSUFFICIENT EDUCATION. This is a handicap which may be overcome with comparative ease. Experience has proven that the best-educated people are often those who are known as "self-made," or self-educated. It takes more than a college degree to make one a person of education. Any person who is educated is one who has learned to get whatever he or she wants in life without violating the rights of others. Education consists not so much of knowledge, but of knowledge effectively and persistently APPLIED. People are paid not merely for what they know, but more particularly for WHAT THEY DO WITH THAT WHICH THEY KNOW.

5. LACK OF SELF-DISCIPLINE. Discipline comes through self-control. This means that one must control all negative qualities. Before you can control conditions, you must first control yourself. Self-mastery is the hardest job you will ever tackle. If you do not conquer self, you will be conquered by self. You may see at one and the same

time both your best friend and your greatest enemy by stepping in front of a mirror.

6. ILL HEALTH. No person may enjoy outstanding success without good health. Many of the causes of ill health are subject to mastery and control. These in the main are:

   a. overeating of foods that are not nutritious and conducive to good health

   b. wrong habits of thought; giving expression to negatives

   c. wrong use of and overindulgence in sex

   d. inadequate physical exercise

   e. an inadequate supply of fresh air, resulting from improper breathing

7. UNFAVORABLE ENVIRONMENTAL INFLUENCES DURING CHILDHOOD. "As the twig is bent, so shall the tree grow." Most people who have criminal tendencies acquire them as the result of bad environment and improper associates during childhood.

8. PROCRASTINATION. This is one of the most common causes of failure. "Old Man Procrastination" stands within the shadow of every human being, awaiting his opportunity to spoil one's chances of success. Most people go through life as failures because they habitually wait for the "time to be right" to start doing something worthwhile. Do not wait. The time will never be "just right." Start where you stand and work with whatever tools you may have at your command, and better tools will be found as you go along.

9. LACK OF PERSISTENCE. Most of us are good starters, but poor finishers of everything we begin. Moreover, people are prone to give up at the first signs of defeat. There is no substitute for PERSISTENCE. The person who makes PERSISTENCE a personal watchword discovers that "Old Man Failure" finally becomes tired and makes his departure. Failure cannot cope with PERSISTENCE.

10. NEGATIVE PERSONALITY. There is no hope of success for the person who repels people through a negative personality. Success comes through the application of POWER, and power is attained through the cooperative efforts of other people. A negative personality will not induce cooperation.

11. LACK OF CONTROLLED SEXUAL URGE. Because of the way human beings are "wired," biologically and genetically, sex energy is the most powerful of all the stimuli which move people into ACTION. Because it is the most powerful of the emotions, it must be controlled -- through a process of transmutation—and converted into other channels. (More about this in Chapter 10.)

12. UNCONTROLLED DESIRE FOR "SOMETHING FOR NOTHING." The gambling instinct drives   millions of people to failure. Evidence of this may be found in a study of the Wall Street crash of 1929 during which millions of people tried to make money by gambling on stock margins.

13. LACK OF A WELL-DEFINED POWER OF DECISION. People who succeed reach decisions promptly and change them, if at all, very slowly. People who fail, reach decisions, if at all, very slowly and change them quickly and frequently. Indecision and procrastination are twin brothers. Where one is found the other may usually be found also. Kill off this pair before they completely hog-tie you to the treadmill of FAILURE.

14. ONE OR MORE OF THE SIX BASIC FEARS. These fears are analyzed for you in a later chapter. They must be mastered before you can market your services effectively.

15. WRONG SELECTION OF A MATE IN MARRIAGE. This a most common cause of failure. The relationship of marriage brings people intimately into contact. Unless this relationship is harmonious, failure is likely to follow. Moreover, it will be a form of failure that is

marked by misery and unhappiness, destroying all signs of AMBITION.

16. OVER-CAUTION. The person who takes no chances generally has to take whatever is left when others are through choosing. Over-caution is as bad as under-caution. Both are extremes to be guarded against. Life itself is filled with the element of chance.

17. WRONG SELECTION OF ASSOCIATES IN BUSINESS. This is one of the most common causes of failure in business. In marketing personal services, one should use great care to select an employer who will be an inspiration and who is intelligent and successful. We emulate those with whom we associate most closely. Pick an employer who is worth emulating.

18. SUPERSTITION AND PREJUDICE. Superstition is a form of fear. It is also a sign of ignorance. People who succeed keep open minds and are afraid of nothing.

19. WRONG SELECTION OF A VOCATION. No one can succeed in a line of endeavor which he or she does not like. The most essential step in the marketing of personal services is that of selecting an occupation into which you can throw yourself wholeheartedly.

20. LACK OF CONCENTRATION OF EFFORT. The jack-of-all-trades is seldom good at any. Concentrate all of your efforts on one DEFINITE CHIEF AIM.

21. THE HABIT OF INDISCRIMINATE SPENDING. Spendthrifts cannot succeed mainly because they stand eternally in FEAR OF POVERTY. Form the habit today of systematic saving by putting aside a definite percentage of your monthly income (15% to 20% is ideal, if difficult; 5% is an absolute minimum). Money in the bank gives one a very safe foundation of COURAGE when bargaining for the sale of personal services. Without money, one must take what one is offered and be glad to get it.

22. LACK OF ENTHUSIASM. Without enthusiasm one cannot be convincing. Moreover, enthusiasm is contagious,

and the person who has it, under control, is generally welcome in any group of people.

23. INTOLERANCE. The person with a closed mind on any subject seldom gets ahead. Intolerance means that one has stopped acquiring knowledge. The most damaging forms of intolerance are those connected with religious, racial, and political differences of opinion.

24. INTEMPERANCE. The most damaging forms of intemperance are connected with eating, strong drink, drugs, and sexual activities. Overindulgence in any of these is fatal to success.

25. INABILITY TO COOPERATE WITH OTHERS. More people lose their positions and their big opportunities in life because of this fault than for all other reasons combined. It is a fault which no well-informed business person or leader will tolerate.

26. POSSESSION OF POWER THAT WAS NOT ACQUIRED THROUGH SELF EFFORT (for example, sons and daughters of wealthy families and others who inherit money which they did not earn). Power in the hands of one who did not acquire it gradually is often fatal to success. QUICK RICHES are more dangerous than poverty.

27. INTENTIONAL DISHONESTY. There is no substitute for honesty. One may be temporarily dishonest, by force of circumstances over which one has no control, without permanent damage. But there is NO HOPE for those who are dishonest by choice. Sooner or later, their deeds will catch up with them, and they will pay by loss of reputation and perhaps even loss of liberty.

28. EGOTISM AND VANITY. These qualities serve as red lights which warn others to keep away. THEY ARE FATAL TO SUCCESS.

29. GUESSING INSTEAD OF THINKING. Most people are too indifferent or lazy to acquire FACTS with which to THINK ACCURATELY. They prefer to act on "opinions" created by guesswork or snap-judgments.

30. LACK OF CAPITAL. This is a common cause of failure among those who start out in business for the first time without sufficient reserve of capital to absorb the shock of their mistakes, and to carry them over until they have established a REPUTATION.

31. (Here, name any particular cause of failure from which you have suffered that has not been included in the foregoing list.)

In the list of "30 (or 31) Major Causes of Failure" is found a description of the tragedy of life, which obtains for practically every person who tries and fails. It will be helpful if you can induce someone who knows you well to go over this list with you and help you analyze yourself for the 30 causes of failure. It may be beneficial if you try this alone. Most people cannot see themselves as others see them. You may be one who cannot.

The oldest of admonitions is "Know thyself!" If you market merchandise successfully, you must know the merchandise. The same is true in marketing personal services. You should know all of your weaknesses in order that you may either bridge them or eliminate them entirely. You should know your strengths in order that you may call attention to them when selling your services. You can know yourself only through accurate analysis.

The folly of ignorance in connection with self was displayed by a young man who applied to the manager of a well-known business for a position. He made a very good impression until the manager asked him what salary he expected. He replied that he had no fixed sum in mind (lack of a definite aim). The manager then said, "We will pay you all you are worth after we try you out for a week."

"I will not accept it," the applicant replied, "because I AM GETTING MORE THAN THAT WHERE I AM NOW EMPLOYED."

Before you even start to negotiate for a readjustment of your salary in your present position or seek employment elsewhere, BE SURE THAT YOU ARE WORTH MORE THAN YOU NOW RECEIVE.

It is one thing to WANT money—everyone wants more—but it is something entirely different to be WORTH MORE! Many people mistake their WANTS for their JUST DUES. Your financial requirements or wants have nothing whatever to do with your WORTH. Your value is established entirely by your ability to render useful service or your capacity to induce others to render such service.

TAKE INVENTORY OF YOURSELF

28 Questions You Should Answer

Annual self-analysis is an essential in the effective marketing of personal services, as is annual inventory in merchandising. Moreover, the yearly analysis should disclose a DECREASE IN FAULTS and an increase in VIRTUES. One goes ahead, stands still, or goes backward in life. One's object should be, of course, to go ahead. Annual self-analysis will disclose whether advancement has been made, and if so, how much. It will also disclose any backward steps one may have made. The effective marketing of personal services requires one to move forward even if the progress is slow.

Your annual self-analysis should be made at the end of each year so that you can include in your New Year's Resolutions any improvements which the analysis indicates should be made. Take this inventory by asking yourself the following questions and by checking your answers with the aid of someone who will not permit you to deceive yourself as to their accuracy.

Self-Analysis Questionnaire for Personal Inventory

1. Have I attained the goal which I established as my objective for this year? (You should work with a definite yearly objective to be attained as a part of your major life objective).
2. Have I delivered service of the best possible QUALITY of which I was capable, or could I have improved any part of this service?

3. Have I delivered service in the greatest possible QUANTITY of which I was capable?

4. Has the spirit of my conduct been harmonious and cooperative at all times?

5. Have I permitted the habit of PROCRASTINATION to decrease my efficiency, and if so, to what extent?

6. Have I improved my PERSONALITY, and if so, in what ways?

7. Have I been PERSISTENT in following my plans through to completion?

8. Have I reached DECISIONS PROMPTLY AND DEFINITELY on all occasions?

9. Have I permitted any one or more of the Six Basic Fears to decrease my efficiency?

10. Have I been either over-cautious or under-cautious?

11. Has my relationship with my associates in work been pleasant or unpleasant? If it has been unpleasant, has the fault been partly or wholly mine?

12. Have I dissipated any of my energy through lack of CONCENTRATION of effort?

13. Have I been open-minded and tolerant in connection with all subjects?

14. In what way have I improved my ability to render service?

15. Have I been intemperate in any of my habits?

16. Have I expressed either openly or secretly any form of EGOTISM?

17. Has my conduct toward my associates been such that it has induced them to RESPECT me?

18. Have my opinions and DECISIONS been based upon guesswork or accuracy of analysis and THOUGHT?

19. Have I followed the habit of budgeting my time, my expenses, and my income, and have I been conservative in these budgets?

20. How much time have I devoted to UNPROFITABLE effort which I might have used to better advantage?

21. How may I REBUDGET my time, and change my habits so I will be more efficient during the coming year?
22. Have I been guilty of any conduct which was not approved by my conscience?
23. In what ways have I rendered MORE SERVICE AND BETTER SERVICE than I was paid to render?
24. Have I been unfair to anyone, and if so, in what way?
25. If I had been the purchaser of my own services for the year, would I be satisfied with my purchase?
26. Am I in the right vocation, and if not, why not?
27. Has the purchaser of my services been satisfied with the service I have rendered, and if not, why not?
28. What is my present rating on the fundamental principles of success? (Make this rating fairly and frankly and have it checked by someone who is courageous enough to do it accurately.)

Having read and assimilated the information conveyed through this chapter, you are now ready to create a practical plan for marketing your personal services. In this chapter is found an adequate description of every principle essential in planning the sale of personal services, including the major attributes of leadership, the most common causes of failure in leadership, a description of the fields of opportunity for leadership, the main causes of failure in all walks of life, and the important questions which should be used in self-analysis.

This extensive and detailed presentation of accurate information has been included because it will be needed by all who must begin the accumulation of riches by marketing personal services. Those who have lost their jobs, property, and fortunes, and those who are just beginning to earn money, have nothing but personal services to offer in return for riches; therefore, it is essential that they have available the practical information needed to market services to best advantage.

The information contained in this chapter will be of great value to all who aspire to attain leadership in any calling. It will be particularly helpful to those aiming to market their services as business or industrial executives.

Complete assimilation and understanding of the information here conveyed will be helpful in marketing one's own services, and it will also help one to become more analytical and capable of judging people. The information will be priceless to personnel directors and all supervisors and executives charged with the selection of employees and the maintenance of efficient organizations. If you doubt this statement, test its soundness by answering in writing the 28 self-analysis questions. That might be both interesting and profitable, even if you do not doubt the soundness of the statement.

Where and How One May Find Opportunities
to Accumulate Riches

Now that we have analyzed six of *The 13 Steps to Riches*, we naturally ask, "Where may one find favorable opportunities to apply these principles?" Very well, let us take inventory and see what the United States of America offers the person seeking riches, great or small.

To begin with, let us remember that we live in a country where every law-abiding citizen enjoys freedom of thought and freedom of deed unequaled anywhere in the world. Most of us have never taken inventory of the advantages of this freedom. We have never compared our unlimited freedom with the curtailed freedom in other countries.

Here we have freedom of thought and expression, freedom in the choice and enjoyment of education, freedom of religion, freedom in politics, freedom in the choice of a business, profession or occupation, freedom to accumulate and own without molestation ALL THE PROPERTY WE CAN ACCUMULATE, freedom to choose our place of residence, freedom in marriage, freedom through equal opportunity to all races, freedom of travel from one state to another, freedom in our choice of foods, and freedom to AIM FOR ANY STATION IN LIFE FOR WHICH WE HAVE PREPARED OURSELVES—even for the Presidency of the United States.

We have other forms of freedom, but this list will give a bird's-eye-view of the most important which constitute OPPORTUNITY of the highest order. This advantage of freedom is all the more conspicuous because the United States is the only country that guarantees to every citizen, whether native born or naturalized, so broad and varied a list of freedoms.

Next, let us recount some of the blessings which our widespread freedom has placed within our hands. Take the average American family, for example (the family of average income), and sum up the benefits available to every member of the family in this land of OPPORTUNITY and plenty!

a. FOOD. Next to freedom of thought and deed comes FOOD, CLOTHING, and SHELTER, the three basic necessities of life.

Because of our universal freedom, the average American family has available at its very door the choicest selection of food to be found anywhere in the world, and at prices within its financial range.

A family of four, living in a small to medium-size American city, far removed from the source of production of foods, took careful inventory of the cost of a simple breakfast, with this astonishing result:

Items of food: Cost at the breakfast table:*

orange juice (from Florida)................................. .56
cereal (wheat from Kansas farm)........................ .44
tea (from China)... .20
bananas (from South America)............................ .28
toasted bread (again, wheat from Kansas farm).... .19

---

* Using today's prices.

fresh eggs (from regional farm)................……….... .18
sugar (from Utah or Texas)....................…………. .01
margarine (from Illinois)......................…………….... .16
milk (from local dairy)........................……………..... .74

Grand total.....$2.76

It is not very difficult to obtain FOOD in a country where four people can have breakfast consisting of all they want or need for 69 cents apiece! Observe that this simple breakfast was gathered, by some strange form of magic (?), from China, South America, Utah, Kansas, and Illinois and delivered on the breakfast table, ready for consumption, in the very heart of an average American city, at a cost well within the means of the most humble laborer.

The cost included all federal, state and city taxes![11]

b. SHELTER. This family lives in a comfortable apartment, heated by natural gas, lighted with electricity, with gas for cooking, all for $800 a month. In a smaller city, the same apartment could be had for as low as $685 a month.

The toast they had for breakfast in the food estimate was toasted in an electric toaster which cost but $15. The apartment is cleaned with a vacuum cleaner that is run by electricity. Hot and cold water is available at all times in the kitchen and the bathroom. The food is kept cool in a refrigerator that is run by electricity. The wife curls her hair, washes the clothes and dries them with easily operated electrical equipment, on power obtained by sticking a plug into the wall. The husband shaves with an electric razor, and they receive entertainment from all over the world, 24 hours a day if they want it, without charge, by merely turning the dial of their television or radio. There are other conveniences in this apartment, but the foregoing list will give a fair idea of some of the concrete evidences of the freedom that we in America enjoy.[12]

c. CLOTHING. Anywhere in the United States, the woman of average clothing requirements can dress very comfortably and neatly for less than $1,500 a year, and the average man can dress for the same, or less.

Only the three basic necessities of food, clothing, and shelter have been mentioned. The average American citizen has other privileges and advantages available in return for modest effort, not exceeding eight hours per day of labor. Among these is the privilege of automobile transportation, with which one can go and come at will, at relatively small cost.

Average Americans have security of property rights not found in any other country in the world. They can place their surplus money in a bank with the assurance that their government will protect it and make good to them if the bank fails. If American citizens want to travel from one state to another, they need no passport, no one's permission. They may go when they please and return at will. Moreover, they may travel by private automobile, airplane, bus, train, or ship as their pocketbook permits.[13]

The Miracle That Has Provided
These Blessings

We often hear politicians proclaiming the freedoms of America when they solicit votes, but seldom do they take the time or devote sufficient effort to the analysis of the source or nature of this freedom. Having no axe to grind, no grudge to express, no ulterior motives to be carried out, I have the privilege of going into a frank analysis of that mysterious, abstract, greatly misunderstood "SOMETHING" which gives to every citizen of America more blessings, more opportunities to accumulate wealth, and more freedom of every nature than may be found in any other country.

I have the right to analyze the source and nature of this UNSEEN POWER because I know and have known for more than a quarter of a century many of the persons who organized that power, and many who are now responsible for its maintenance.

The name of this mysterious benefactor of humankind is CAPITAL!

CAPITAL consists not alone of money, but more particularly of highly organized, intelligent groups of individuals who plan ways and means of using money efficiently for the good of the public and profitably to themselves.

These groups consist of scientists, educators, chemists, inventors, business analysts, advertising executives, transportation experts, accountants, lawyers, doctors, and both men and women who have highly specialized knowledge in all fields of industry and business. They pioneer, experiment, and blaze trails in new fields of endeavor. They support colleges, hospitals, public schools, build good roads, publish newspapers, operate television and radio stations, pay most of the cost of government, and take care of the multitudinous detail essential to human progress. Stated briefly, the capitalists are *the brains of civilization* because they supply the entire fabric of which all education, enlightenment and human progress consists.

Money, without brains, always is dangerous. Properly used, it is the most important essential of civilization. The simple breakfast described earlier could not have been delivered to that family of four at 69 cents each or at any other price if organized capital had not provided the machinery, the ships, the railroads, the trucks, and the huge armies of trained workers to operate them.

Some slight idea of the importance of ORGANIZED CAPITAL may be had by trying to imagine yourself burdened with the responsibility of collecting, without the aid of capital, and delivering to that family the simple breakfast described.

To supply the tea you would have to make a trip to China or India, both a very long way from America. Unless you are an excellent swimmer, you would become rather tired before making the round trip. Then, too, another problem would confront you.

What would you use for money, even if you had the physical endurance to swim the ocean?

To supply the sugar, you would have to take another long journey to the sugar beet section of Utah or to the fields of Louisiana or Texas. But even then, you might come back without the sugar because organized effort and money are necessary to produce sugar, to say nothing of what is required to refine, transport, and deliver it to the breakfast table anywhere in the United States.

The eggs you could deliver easily enough from small farms located in the countryside not far from the city, but you would have a very long walk to Florida and back before you could serve the four glasses of orange juice. You would have another long walk to Kansas or one of the other wheat growing states when you went after the four slices of wheat bread.

The breakfast cereal would have to be omitted from the menu because they would not be available except through the labor of a trained organization of workers and suitable machinery, ALL OF WHICH CALL FOR CAPITAL.

While resting, you could take off for another little swim down to South America, where you would pick up a couple of bananas, and on your return you could take a short walk to the nearest farm having a dairy and pick up some milk (and perhaps some butter because you would have to do without the margarine, which, like the box of cereal, would require CAPITAL for its manufacture). Then your family would be ready to sit down and enjoy breakfast, and you could collect your six dimes and seven pennies for your labor!

Seems absurd, doesn't it? Well, the procedure described would be the only possible way these simple items of food could be delivered to the breakfast table of the family in that heartland city — IF we had no capitalistic system.

The sum of money required for the building and maintenance of the railroads, ships, and trucking lines used in the delivery of that simple breakfast is so huge that it staggers one's imagination. It runs into billions of dollars, not to mention the armies of trained employees required to operate the ships, truck lines, and trains.

But, transportation is only a part of the requirements of modern civilization in capitalistic America. Before there can be anything to haul, something must be grown from the ground or manufactured and prepared for market. This calls for more billions of dollars for equipment, machinery, boxing, marketing, and for the wages of millions of men and women.

Ships, railroads, airlines, and trucking networks do not spring up from the earth and function automatically. They come in response to the call of civilization, through the labor and ingenuity and organizing ability of people who have IMAGINATION, FAITH, ENTHUSIASM, DECISION, PERSISTENCE! These individuals are known as capitalists. They are motivated by the desire to build, construct, achieve, render useful service, earn profits and accumulate riches. And because they RENDER SERVICE WITHOUT WHICH THERE WOULD BE NO CIVILIZATION, they put themselves in the way of great riches.

Just to keep the record simple and understandable, I will add that these capitalists are the self-same people of whom most of us have heard soapbox orators speak. They are the same people to whom radicals, racketeers, dishonest politicians and grafting labor leaders have referred to as the "predatory interests," or "Wall Street," or "big business."

I am not attempting to present an argument for or against any group or any system of economics. I am not attempting to condemn collective bargaining when I refer to "grafting labor leaders," nor do I aim to give a clean bill of health to all individuals known as capitalists or entrepreneurs.

The purpose of this book—a purpose to which I have faithfully devoted over a quarter of a century—is to present to all who want the knowledge, the most dependable philosophy through which individuals may accumulate riches in whatever amounts they desire.

I have here analyzed the economic advantages of the capitalistic system for the two-fold purpose of showing:

1. that all who seek riches must recognize and adapt themselves to the system that controls all approaches to fortunes, large or small

2. to present the side of the picture opposite that being shown by politicians and demagogues who deliberately becloud the issues they bring up by referring to organized capital or free enterprise as if it were something poisonous.

This is a free enterprise, capitalistic country. It was developed through the use of capital, and we who claim the right to partake of the blessings of freedom and opportunity, we who seek to accumulate riches here, may as well know that neither riches nor opportunity would be available to us if ORGANIZED CAPITAL had not provided these benefits.

For decades, it has been a somewhat popular and growing pastime for radicals, self-seeking politicians, racketeers, crooked labor leaders, and on occasion religious leaders, to take potshots at "WALL STREET" and "BIG BUSINESS."[14]

The practice became so general that we witnessed for a time during the Depression the unbelievable sight of high government officials lining up with cheap politicians and labor leaders for the openly avowed purpose of throttling the system which has made Industrial America the richest country on earth. The lineup was so general and so well organized that it prolonged the worst depression America had ever known. It cost millions of people their jobs because those jobs were inseparably a part of the industrial and capitalistic system which form the very backbone of the nation.

During this unusual alliance of government officials and self-seeking individuals who were endeavoring to profit by declaring "open season" on the American system of industry, a certain type of labor leader joined forces with the politicians and offered to deliver voters in return for legislation designed to permit people to TAKE RICHES AWAY FROM INDUSTRY BY ORGANIZED FORCE OF NUMBERS, INSTEAD OF THE BETTER METHOD OF GIVING A FAIR DAY'S WORK FOR A FAIR DAY'S PAY.

Millions of men and women throughout the nation are still engaged in this popular pastime of trying to GET without GIVING.

Some of them are lined up with labor unions, where they demand SHORTER HOURS AND MORE PAY! Others do not take the trouble to work at all. THEY DEMAND GOVERNMENT RELIEF AND ARE GETTING IT.[15]

If you are one of those who believe that riches can be accumulated by the mere act of individuals who organize themselves into groups and demand MORE PAY for LESS SERVICE, if you are one of those who DEMAND government relief without being willing to return any service for it, if you are one of those who believe in trading their votes to politicians in return for the passing of laws which permit the raiding of the public treasury, then you may rest securely on your belief, with certain knowledge that no one will disturb you, because THIS IS A FREE COUNTRY WHERE EVERYONE MAY THINK AS HE OR SHE PLEASES, where nearly everybody can live with but little effort, where many may live well without doing any work whatsoever.

However, you should know the full truth concerning this FREEDOM of which so many people boast and so few understand. As great as it is, as far as it reaches, as many privileges as it provides, IT DOES NOT, AND CANNOT, BRING RICHES WITHOUT EFFORT.

There is but one dependable method of accumulating and legally holding riches, and that is *by rendering useful service*. No system has ever been created by which people can legally acquire riches through mere force of numbers or without giving in return an equivalent value of one form or another.

There is a principle known as the LAW OF ECONOMICS! This is more than a theory. It is a law no one can beat. Mark well the name of the principle and remember it because it is far more powerful than all the politicians and political machines. It is above and beyond the control of all the special interest groups and labor unions. It cannot be swayed nor influenced nor bribed by racketeers or self-appointed leaders in any calling. Moreover, IT HAS AN ALL-SEEING EYE AND A PERFECT SYSTEM OF BOOKKEEPING in which it keeps an accurate account of the transactions of every human being engaged in the business of trying to get without giving.

Sooner or later its auditors come around, look over the records of individuals both great and small, and demand an accounting.

"Wall Street," "Big Business," "Capital Predatory Interests" or whatever name you choose to give the system which has given us AMERICAN FREEDOM represents a group of people who understand, respect, and adapt themselves to this powerful LAW OF ECONOMICS! Their financial continuation depends upon their respecting the law.

Most people living in America like this country, its capitalistic system and all. I must confess I know of no better country where one may find greater opportunities to accumulate riches. Judging by their acts and deeds, there are some in this country who do not like it. That of course is their privilege: If they do not like this country, its capitalistic system, and its boundless opportunities, *THEY HAVE THE PRIVILEGE OF CLEARING OUT!* Always there are other countries where one may try one's hand at enjoying freedom and accumulating riches, providing one is not too particular.[16]

America provides all the freedom and all the opportunity to accumulate riches that any honest person may require. When one goes hunting for game, one selects hunting grounds where game is plentiful. When seeking riches, the same rule would naturally obtain.

If it is riches you seek, do not overlook the possibilities of a country whose citizens are so rich that they spend more than $29 billion[17] a year for hair, nail and skin care. Think twice, you who seek riches, before trying to destroy the Capitalistic System of a country whose citizens spend more than $25 billion a year for newspapers, $31 billion on books, almost $14 billion on sound recordings, and almost $54 billion on motion pictures, all of which express the FREEDOM of expression!

By all means give plenty of consideration to a country whose people spend annually more than $115 billion on fast food and $13.3 billion to pay bar and tavern tabs.

Do not be in too big a hurry to get away from a country whose people willingly, even eagerly, hand over $34 billion annually to buy toys, $38 billion to take care of their lawns and gardens, and $74 billion to purchase sporting goods. And, by all means, STICK by a country whose inhabitants spend more than $91 billion a year for furniture and home furnishings, $167 billion on clothing and accessories, $22 billion for laundry and dry cleaning, $87 billion in appliance and electronics stores, and almost $14 billion to bury their dead.

Remember also that this is but the beginning of the available sources for the accumulation of wealth. Only a few of the luxuries and non-essentials have been mentioned. But remember that the business of producing, transporting, and marketing these few items of merchandise gives regular employment to MANY MILLIONS OF MEN AND WOMEN who receive for their service BILLIONS OF DOLLARS MONTHLY and spend it freely for both the luxuries and the necessities of life.

Especially remember that back of all this exchange of merchandise and personal services may be found an abundance of OPPORTUNITY to accumulate riches. Here our AMERICAN FREEDOM comes to one's aid. There is nothing to stop you, or anyone, from engaging in any portion of the effort necessary to carry on these businesses. If one has superior talent, training, and experience, one may accumulate riches in large amounts. Those not so fortunate may accumulate smaller amounts. Anyone may earn a living in return for a very nominal amount of labor.

So — there you are!

OPPORTUNITY has spread its wares before you. Step up to the front, select what you want, create your plan, put the plan into action, and follow through with PERSISTENCE. "Capitalistic" America will do the rest. You can depend upon this much — CAPITALISTIC AMERICA ENSURES EVERY PERSON THE OPPORTUNITY TO RENDER USEFUL SERVICE AND TO COLLECT RICHES IN PROPORTION TO THE VALUE OF THE SERVICE RENDERED.

The "system" denies no one this right, but it does not, and cannot, promise SOMETHING FOR NOTHING because the system itself is irrevocably controlled by the LAW OF ECONOMICS, which neither recognizes nor tolerates for long, GETTING WITHOUT GIVING.

The LAW OF ECONOMICS was passed by Nature! There is no Supreme Court to which violators of this law may appeal. The law hands out both penalties for its violation and appropriate rewards for its observance, without interference or the possibility of interference by any human being. The law cannot be repealed. It is as fixed as the stars in the heavens and subject to, and a part of, the same system that controls the stars.

May one refuse to adapt one's self to the LAW OF ECONOMICS?

Certainly! This is a free country, where all people are born with equal rights, including the privilege of ignoring the LAW OF ECONOMICS. What happens then? Well, nothing happens until large numbers of people join forces for the avowed purpose of ignoring the law and taking what they want by force. *THEN COMES THE DICTATOR, WITH WELL-ORGANIZED FIRING SQUADS AND MACHINE GUNS!*

We have never reached that stage in America! But we now know all we want to know about how the system works.[18] Perhaps we shall be fortunate enough not to demand personal knowledge of so gruesome a reality. Doubtless we shall prefer to continue with our FREEDOM OF SPEECH, FREEDOM OF DEED, and FREEDOM TO RENDER USEFUL SERVICE IN RETURN FOR RICHES.

The practice by government officials of extending to men and women the privilege of raiding the public treasury in return for votes sometimes results in election, but as night follows day, the final payoff will always come when every penny wrongfully used must be repaid with compound interest upon compound interest. If those who "make the grab" are not forced to repay, the burden falls on their children, and their children's children, "even unto the third and fourth generations." There is no way to avoid the debt.[19]

People can, and sometimes do, form themselves into groups for the purpose of "crowding" wages up and working hours down. There is a point beyond which they cannot go. It is the point at which the LAW OF ECONOMICS steps in, and the sheriff gets both the employer and the employees.[20]

For six years, from 1929 to 1935, the people of America, both rich and poor, barely missed seeing "Old Man Economics" hand over to the sheriff all the businesses, industries, and banks. It was not a pretty sight! It did not increase our respect for mob psychology through which people cast reason to the winds and start trying to GET without GIVING.

We who went through those six discouraging years — when FEAR WAS IN THE SADDLE AND FAITH WAS ON THE GROUND — cannot forget how ruthlessly the LAW OF ECONOMICS exacted its toll from both rich and poor, weak and strong, old and young. We shall not wish to go through another such experience.

These observations are not founded upon short-time experience. They are the result of 25 years of careful analysis of the methods of the most successful individuals America has known. These resourceful, hard-working, smart-thinking people — and people like them today and people like them who have gone before — represent the real genius of the American system of free enterprise and the American way of life. Their attributes helped the nation survive the Great Depression and flourish. One of those attributes is DEFINITENESS OF DECISION, the mastery of which represents *The Seventh Step to Riches.* And it is on that step that we will now focus our attention.

God seems to throw Himself on the side of the individual who knows exactly what he wants, if he is determined to get
JUST THAT!

Chapter 7

DECISION
The Mastery of Procrastination
The Seventh Step to Riches

CAREFUL ANALYSIS of thousands of men and women who had experienced failure revealed that LACK OF DECISION was near the head of the list of the 30 Major Causes of Failure (Chapter 6). This is no mere statement of a theory — *it is a fact.*

PROCRASTINATION, the opposite of DECISION, is a common enemy which practically every individual must conquer.

You will have an opportunity to test your capacity to reach *quick* and *definite* DECISIONS when you finish reading this book and are ready to begin putting into ACTION the principles which it describes.

Analysis of several hundred people who had accumulated fortunes well beyond the million-dollar mark disclosed the fact that *every one of them* had the habit of REACHING DECISIONS PROMPTLY and of changing these decisions slowly, if and when they were changed. People who fail to accumulate money, *without exception*, have the habit of reaching decisions, IF AT ALL, very *slowly* and of *changing these decisions quickly and often.*

One of Henry Ford's most outstanding qualities was his habit of reaching decisions quickly and definitely, and changing them slowly. This quality was so pronounced in Mr. Ford that it gave him the reputation of being obstinate. It was this quality which prompted Mr. Ford to continue to manufacture his famous Model T (the world's ugliest car), when all of his advisors and many of the purchasers of the car were urging him to change it.

Perhaps Mr. Ford delayed too long in making the change, but the other side of the story is that Mr. Ford's firmness of decision yielded a huge fortune before the change in model became necessary. There is but little doubt that Mr. Ford's habit of definiteness of decision assumed the proportion of obstinacy, but this quality is preferable to slowness in reaching decisions and quickness in changing them.

The majority of people who fail to accumulate money sufficient for their needs are, in general, easily influenced by the opinions of others. They permit the newspapers and the "gossiping" neighbors to do their thinking for them. Opinions are the cheapest commodities on earth. Everyone has a flock of opinions ready to be wished upon anyone who will accept them. If you are influenced by others' opinions when you reach DECISIONS, you will not succeed in any undertaking, much less in that of transmuting YOUR OWN DESIRE into money.

If you are too easily influenced by the opinions of others, you will have no DESIRE of your own.

Keep your own counsel when you begin to put into practice the principles described in this book *by reaching your own decisions and following them.* Take no one into your confidence EXCEPT the members of your Master Mind Group, and be very sure in your selection of this group that you choose ONLY those who will be in COMPLETE SYMPATHY AND HARMONY WITH YOUR PURPOSE.

Close friends and relatives, while not meaning to do so, often handicap one through opinions and sometimes through ridicule, which is meant to be humorous. Thousands of men and women carry inferiority complexes with them all through life because some well-meaning, but ignorant person destroyed their confidence through opinions or ridicule.

You have a brain and a mind of your own. USE THEM and reach your own decisions. If you need facts or information from other people to enable you to reach decisions, as you probably will in many instances, acquire these facts or secure the information you need quietly, without disclosing your purpose.

It is characteristic of people who have but a smattering or a veneer of knowledge to try to give the impression that they have much knowledge. Such people generally do TOO MUCH talking and TOO LITTLE listening. Keep your eyes and ears wide open—and your mouth CLOSED—if you wish to acquire the habit of prompt DECISION. Those who talk too much do little else. If you talk more than you listen, you not only deprive yourself of many opportunities to accumulate useful knowledge, but you also disclose your PLANS and PURPOSES to people who will take great delight in defeating you because they envy you.

Remember also that every time you open your mouth in the presence of a person who has an abundance of knowledge, you display to that person your exact stock of knowledge or your LACK of it! Genuine wisdom is usually conspicuous through *modesty and silence*.

Keep in mind the fact that every person with whom you associate is, like yourself, seeking the opportunity to accumulate money. If you talk about your plans too freely, you may be surprised when you learn that some other person has beaten you to your goal by PUTTING INTO ACTION AHEAD OF YOU the plans of which you talked unwisely.

Let one of your first decisions be to KEEP A CLOSED MOUTH AND OPEN EARS AND EYES.

As a reminder to yourself to follow this advice, it will be helpful if you copy the following epigram in large letters and place it where you will see it daily:

"TELL THE WORLD WHAT YOU INTEND TO DO, BUT FIRST SHOW IT."

This is the equivalent of saying that "deeds, and not words, are what count most."

Freedom or Death on a Decision

The value of decisions depends upon the courage required to render them. The great decisions, which have served as the foundation of civilization, were reached by assuming great risks, which often meant the possibility of death.

Lincoln's decision to issue his famous "Proclamation of Emancipation," which gave freedom to the slaves of America, was rendered with full understanding that his act would turn thousands of friends and political supporters against him. He knew, too, that the carrying out of that proclamation would mean death to thousands of men on the battlefield. In the end, it cost Lincoln his life. That required courage.

Socrates' decision to drink the cup of poison, rather than compromise in his personal belief, was a decision of courage. It turned time ahead a thousand years and gave to people then unborn the right to freedom of thought and of speech.

The decision of Gen. Robert E. Lee, when he came to the parting of the way with the Union and took up the cause of the South, was a decision of courage, for he well knew that it might cost him his own life and that it would surely cost the lives of others.

But the greatest decision of all time, as far as any American citizen is concerned, was reached in Philadelphia on July 4, 1776, when 56 individuals signed their names to a document which they well knew would bring freedom to all Americans or *leave every one of the 56 hanging from a gallows!*

You have heard of this famous document, but you may not have drawn from it the great lesson in personal achievement it so plainly taught.

We all remember the date of this momentous decision, but few of us realize what courage that decision required. We remember our history as it was taught; we remember dates and the names of those who fought; we remember Valley Forge and Yorktown; we remember George Washington and Lord Cornwallis. But we know little of the real forces back of these names, dates, and places. We know still less of that intangible POWER which ensured us freedom *long before Washington's armies reached Yorktown.*

We read the history of the American Revolution and falsely imagine that George Washington was the Father of our Country, that it was he who won our freedom, while the truth is that Washington was only an accessory after the fact because victory for his armies had been ensured long before Lord Cornwallis surrendered. This is not intended to rob Washington of any of the glory he so richly merited. The purpose is rather to give greater attention to the astounding POWER that was the real cause of his victory.

It is nothing short of a tragedy that the writers of history have missed entirely even the slightest reference to the irresistible POWER which gave birth and freedom to the nation destined to set up new standards of independence for all the peoples of the earth. I say it is a tragedy because it is the self-same POWER which must be used by every individual who surmounts the difficulties of life and forces life to pay the price asked.

Let us briefly review the events which gave birth to this POWER. The story begins with an incident in Boston on March 5, 1770. British soldiers were patrolling the streets, by their presence openly threatening the citizens. The colonists resented armed soldiers marching in their midst. They began to express their resentment openly, hurling stones as well as epithets at the marching soldiers until the commanding officer gave orders, "Fix bayonets — Charge!"

The battle was on. It resulted in the death and injury of many. The incident aroused such resentment that the Provincial Assembly (made up of prominent colonists) called a meeting for the purpose of taking definite action. Two of the members of that Assembly were John Hancock and Samuel Adams — LONG LIVE THEIR NAMES! They spoke up courageously and declared that a move must be made to eject all British soldiers from Boston.

Remember this — a DECISION, in the minds of two individuals, might properly be called the beginning of the freedom which we of the United States now enjoy. Remember, too, that the DECISION of these two men called for FAITH and COURAGE because it was dangerous.

Before the Assembly adjourned, Samuel Adams was appointed to call on the Governor of the Province, Thomas Hutchinson, and demand the withdrawal of the British troops.

The request was granted, the troops were removed from Boston, but the incident was not closed. It had caused a situation destined to change the entire trend of civilization. Strange, is it not, how the great changes, such as the American Revolution and the First World War, often have their beginnings in circumstances which seem unimportant. It is interesting also to observe that these important changes usually begin in the form of a DEFINITE DECISION in the minds of a relatively small number of people. Few of us know the history of our country well enough to realize that John Hancock, Samuel Adams, and Richard Henry Lee (of the Province of Virginia) were the real Fathers of our Country.

Richard Henry Lee became an important factor in this story by reason of the fact that he and Samuel Adams communicated frequently (by correspondence), sharing freely their fears and their hopes concerning the welfare of the people of their provinces. From this practice, Adams conceived the idea that a mutual exchange of letters among the 13 colonies might help to bring about the coordination of effort so badly needed in connection with the solution of their problems. In March 1772, two years after the clash with the soldiers in Boston, Adams presented this idea to the Assembly in the form of a motion that a Correspondence Committee be established among the colonies, with definitely appointed correspondents in each colony, "for the purpose of friendly cooperation for the betterment of the Colonies of British America."

Mark well this incident! It was the beginning of the organization of the far-flung POWER destined to give freedom to you and to me. The Master Mind had already been organized. It consisted of Adams, Lee, and Hancock. (It is as the gospel writer says in Matthew 18:19, "I tell you further, that if two of you agree upon the earth concerning anything for which you ask, it will come to you from My Father, who is in Heaven.")

The Committee of Correspondence was organized. Observe that this move provided the way for increasing the power of the Master Mind by adding to it people from all the Colonies. Take notice that this procedure constituted the first ORGANIZED PLANNING of the disgruntled colonists.

In union there is strength! The citizens of the colonies had been waging disorganized warfare against the British soldiers through incidents similar to the Boston riot, but nothing of benefit had been accomplished. Their individual grievances had not been consolidated under one Master Mind. No group of individuals had put their hearts, minds, souls, and bodies together in one definite DECISION to settle their difficulty with the British once and for all—until Adams, Hancock, and Lee got together.

Meanwhile, the British were not idle. They, too, were doing some PLANNING and "Master-Minding" on their own account, with the advantage of having back of them money and organized soldiery.

The Crown appointed Brig. General Thomas Gage to supplant Hutchinson as Governor of Massachusetts. One of the new Governor's first acts was to send a messenger to call on Samuel Adams for the purpose of endeavoring to stop his opposition—FEAR.

We can best understand the spirit of what happened by quoting the conversation between a Col. Fenton (the messenger sent by Gage) and Adams.

Col. Fenton: "I have been authorized by Governor Gage to assure you, Mr. Adams, that the Governor has been empowered to confer upon you such benefits as would be satisfactory, upon the condition that you engage to cease in your opposition to the measures of the government. It is the Governor's advice to you, Sir, not to incur the further displeasure of his majesty. Your conduct has been such as makes you liable to penalties of an Act of Henry VIII, by which persons can be sent to England for trial for treason, or misprison* of treason, at the discretion of a governor of a province. But, BY CHANGING YOUR POLITICAL COURSE, you will not only receive great personal advantages but you will make your peace with the King."

---

* "Misprison" is any violation of an official duty, or any failure by an individual who is not actively involved in committing a crime, to prevent its commission or report it to the authorities.

Samuel Adams had the choice of two DECISIONS. He could cease his opposition and receive personal bribes, or he could CONTINUE AND RUN THE RISK OF BEING HANGED!

Clearly, the time had come when Adams was *forced to reach instantly* a DECISION which could have cost his life. The majority of people would have found it difficult to reach such a decision. The majority would have sent back an evasive reply, but not Adams! He insisted upon Col. Fenton's word of honor that the Colonel would deliver to the Governor the answer exactly as Adams would give it to him.

Adams' answer was this: "Then you may tell Governor Gage that I trust I have long since made my peace with the King of Kings. No personal consideration shall induce me to abandon the righteous cause of my Country. And TELL GOVERNOR GAGE IT IS THE ADVICE OF SAMUEL ADAMS TO HIM, no longer to insult the feelings of an exasperated people."

Comment as to the character of this man seems unnecessary. It must be obvious to all who read this astounding message that its sender possessed loyalty of the highest order. *This is important.*[1]

When Governor Gage received Adams' caustic reply, he flew into a rage and issued a proclamation which read, "I do, hereby, in his majesty's name, offer and promise his most gracious pardon to all persons who shall forthwith lay down their arms, and return to the duties of peaceable subjects, excepting only from the benefit of such pardon, SAMUEL ADAMS AND JOHN HANCOCK, whose offenses are of too flagitious a nature to admit of any other consideration but that of condign punishment."

As one might put it more commonly, Adams and Hancock were "on the spot!" The threat of the irate governor forced the two men to reach another DECISION, equally dangerous. They hurriedly called a secret meeting of their staunchest followers. (Here the Master Mind began to take on momentum.) After the meeting had been called to order, Adams locked the door, placed the key in his pocket, and informed all present that it was imperative that a Congress of the Colonists be organized and that NO ONE SHOULD LEAVE

THE ROOM UNTIL THE DECISION FOR SUCH A CONGRESS HAD BEEN REACHED.

Great excitement followed. Some weighed the possible consequences of such radicalism (Old Man Fear). Some expressed grave doubt as to the wisdom of so *definite a decision* in defiance of the Crown. Locked in that room were TWO MEN immune to fear, blind to the possibility of failure. Hancock and Adams. Through the influence of their minds, the others were induced to agree that through the Correspondence Committee arrangements should be made for a meeting of the First Continental Congress, to be held in Philadelphia on September 5, 1774.

Remember this date. It is more important than July 4, 1776. If there had been no DECISION to hold a Continental Congress, there could have been no signing of the Declaration of Independence.

Before the first meeting of the new Congress, another leader in a different section of the country was deep in the throes of publishing a "Summary View of the Rights of British America." He was Thomas Jefferson of the Province of Virginia, whose relationship to Lord Dunmore (representative of the Crown in Virginia) was as strained as that of Hancock and Adams with their Governor.

Shortly after his famous "Summary of Rights" was published, Jefferson was informed that he was subject to prosecution for high treason against his majesty's government. Inspired by the threat, one of Jefferson's colleagues, Patrick Henry, boldly spoke his mind, concluding his remarks with a sentence which shall remain forever a classic, "*If this be treason, then make the most of it.*"

It was such men as these who without power, without authority, without military strength, and without money sat in solemn consideration of the destiny of the colonies, beginning at the opening of the First Continental Congress and continuing at intervals for two years—until June 7, 1776, when Richard Henry Lee arose, addressed the chair, and to the startled Assembly made this motion:

"Gentlemen, I make the motion that these United Colonies are, and of right ought to be free and independent states, that they be absolved from all allegiance to the British Crown, and that all political connection between them and the state of Great Britain is, and ought to be, totally dissolved."

Lee's astounding motion was discussed fervently and at such length that he began to lose patience. Finally, after days of argument, he again took the floor and declared in a clear, firm voice, "Mr. President, we have discussed this issue for days. It is the only course for us to follow. Why then, Sir, do we longer delay? Why still deliberate? Let this happy day give birth to an American Republic. Let her arise, not to devastate and to conquer, but to reestablish the reign of peace and of law. The eyes of Europe are fixed upon us. She demands of us a living example of freedom that may exhibit a contrast, in the felicity of the citizen, to the ever-increasing tyranny."

Before his motion was finally voted upon, Lee was called back to Virginia because of serious family illness, but before leaving, he placed his cause in the hands of his friend Thomas Jefferson, who promised to fight until favorable action was taken. Shortly thereafter the President of the Congress (Hancock) appointed Jefferson as chairman of a committee to draw up a Declaration of Independence.

Long and hard the Committee labored on a document which would mean, when accepted by the Congress, that EVERYONE WHO SIGNED IT WOULD BE SIGNING HIS OWN DEATH WARRANT should the colonies lose in the fight with Great Britain that was sure to follow.

The document was drawn, and on June 28 the original draft was read before the Congress. For several days it was discussed, altered, and made ready. On July 4, 1776, Thomas Jefferson stood before the Assembly and fearlessly read the most momentous DECISION ever placed upon paper.

"When in the course of human events it is necessary for one people to dissolve the political bands which have connected them with another, and to assume, among the powers of the earth, the separate and equal station to which the laws of Nature, and of Nature's God entitle them, a decent respect to the opinions of mankind requires that they should declare the causes which impel them to the separation...."

When Jefferson finished, the document was voted upon, accepted, and signed by the 56 representatives, every one staking his own life upon his DECISION to write his name. By that DECISION came into existence a nation destined to bring to people forever the privilege and right of making DECISIONS.

By decisions made in a similar spirit of FAITH, and only by such decisions, can people solve their personal problems and win for themselves high estates of material and spiritual wealth. Let us not forget this!

Analyze the events which led to the Declaration of Independence and be convinced that this nation, which now holds a position of commanding respect and power among all nations of the world, was born of a DECISION created by a Master Mind consisting of 56 persons. Note well the fact that it was their DECISION which ensured the success of Washington's armies because the *spirit* of that decision was in the heart of every soldier who fought with him. It served as a spiritual power which recognizes no such thing as FAILURE.

Note also (with great personal benefit) that the POWER which gave this nation its freedom is the self-same power that must be used by every individual who becomes self-determining. This POWER is made up of the 13 principles described in this book. It will not be difficult to detect in the story of the Declaration of Independence at least six of these principles: DESIRE, DECISION, FAITH, PERSISTENCE, THE MASTER MIND, and ORGANIZED PLANNING.

Throughout this philosophy will be found the suggestion that thought, backed by strong DESIRE, has a tendency to transmute itself into its physical equivalent. Before passing on, I wish to leave with you the suggestion that one may find in this story, and in the story of the organization of the United States Steel Corporation (Chapter 2), a perfect description of the method by which thought makes this astounding transformation.

In your search for the secret of the method, do not look for a miracle because you will not find it. You will find only the eternal laws of Nature. These laws are available to every person who has the

FAITH and the COURAGE to use them. They may be used to bring freedom to a nation, or to accumulate riches, or to accomplish any other worthwhile goal. There is no charge save the time necessary to understand and appropriate them.

Those who reach DECISIONS promptly and definitely know what they want and generally get it. The leaders in every walk of life DECIDE quickly and firmly. That is the major reason why they are leaders. The world has the habit of making room for those individuals whose words and actions show that they know where they are going.

INDECISION is a habit which usually begins in youth. The habit takes on permanency as the youth goes through grade school, high school, and even through college without DEFINITENESS OF PURPOSE. The major weakness of all educational systems is that they neither teach nor encourage the habit of DEFINITE DECISION.

It would be beneficial if no college would permit the enrollment of any student unless and until the student declared his or her major purpose in matriculating. It would be of still greater benefit if every student in grade school were compelled to accept training in the HABIT OF DECISION and forced to pass a satisfactory examination on this subject before being permitted to advance in the grades.

The habit of INDECISION acquired because of the deficiencies of our school system goes with students into the occupations they choose—IF, in fact, they *choose* their occupations at all. Generally, young people just out of school seek any job that can be found. They take the first position they find because they have fallen into the habit of INDECISION. Ninety-eight out of every one hundred people working for wages today are in the positions they hold because they lacked the DEFINITENESS OF DECISION to PLAN A DEFINITE POSITION and the knowledge of how to choose an employer.

DEFINITENESS OF DECISION always requires courage, sometimes very great courage. The 56 men who signed the Declaration of Independence staked their lives on the DECISION to affix their signatures to that document. Individuals who reach a DEFINITE DECISION to procure a *particular* job, and make life pay the price they ask, do not stake their lives on that decision. They stake their ECONOMIC FREEDOM. Financial independence, riches, and desirable business and professional positions are not within reach of the person who neglects or refuses to EXPECT, PLAN, and DEMAND these things. The person who desires riches—in the same spirit that Samuel Adams desired freedom for the Colonies—is sure to accumulate wealth.

In Chapter 6 on Organized Planning, you were given complete instructions for marketing every type of personal service. You were also given detailed information on how to choose the employer you prefer and the particular job you desire. These instructions will be of no value to you UNLESS YOU DEFINITELY DECIDE to organize them into a plan of action—and unless you pursue that plan with PERSISTENCE, which is *The Eighth Step to Riches*.

Riches do not respond to wishes. They respond only to definite plans, backed by definite desires, through constant PERSISTENCE.

§ § §

EVERY FAILURE BRINGS WITH IT THE SEED OF AN EQUIVALENT SUCCESS.

Chapter 8

PERSISTENCE

The Sustained Effort Necessary to Induce Faith
The Eighth Step to Riches

PERSISTENCE is an essential factor in the procedure of transmuting DESIRE into its monetary equivalent. The basis of persistence is the POWER OF WILL.

Willpower and desire, when properly combined, make an irresistible pair. People who accumulate great fortunes are generally thought of as cold-blooded and sometimes ruthless. Often they are misunderstood. What they have is willpower, which they mix with PERSISTENCE and place back of their desires to ensure the attainment of their objectives.

Henry Ford was generally misunderstood to be ruthless and cold-blooded. This misconception grew out of Ford's habit of following through in all of his plans with PERSISTENCE.

The majority of people are ready to throw their aims and purposes overboard and give up at the first sign of opposition or misfortune. A few carry on DESPITE all opposition until they attain their goal. These few are the Fords, Carnegies, Rockefellers, Edisons, and other outstanding achievers of the world.

There may be no heroic connotation to the word "persistence," but the quality is to a person's character what carbon is to steel.

The building of a fortune generally involves the application of the entire 13 principles of *The Think and Grow Rich Philosophy*. These principles must be understood, and they must be applied with PERSISTENCE by all who would accumulate money.

If you are following this book with the intention of applying the knowledge it conveys, your first test as to your PERSISTENCE will come when you begin to take the six actions described in Chapter 1. Unless you are one of the two out of every hundred persons who already have a DEFINITE GOAL at which you are aiming and a DEFINITE PLAN for its attainment, you *may* read those instructions, then pass on with your daily routine, and never comply with those instructions.

I ask you to evaluate yourself on this point because lack of persistence is one of the major causes of failure. Moreover, experience with thousands of people has proved that lack of persistence is a weakness common to the majority of them. It is a weakness which may be overcome by effort. The ease with which lack of persistence may be conquered will depend *entirely* upon the INTENSITY OF ONE'S DESIRE.

The starting point of all achievement is DESIRE. Keep this constantly in mind. Weak desires bring weak results, just as a small amount of fire makes a small amount of heat. If you find yourself lacking in persistence, this weakness may be remedied by building a stronger fire under your desires.

Continue to read through to the end of this chapter, then go back to Chapter 1 and start *immediately* to carry out the instructions given in connection with the six action steps. The eagerness with which you follow these instructions will indicate clearly how much, or how little, you really DESIRE to accumulate money. If you find that you are indifferent, you may be sure that you have not yet acquired the "money consciousness" which you must possess before you can be sure of accumulating a fortune.

Fortunes gravitate to individuals whose minds have been prepared to "attract" them, just as surely as water gravitates to the ocean. In this book may be found all the stimuli necessary to "attune" any normal mind to the "thought vibrations" which will attract the object of one's desires.

If you find you are weak in PERSISTENCE, center your attention upon the instructions contained in the chapter on POWER OF THE MASTER MIND (Chapter 9). Surround yourself with a MASTER MIND GROUP, and through the cooperative efforts of the members of this group you can develop persistence. You will find additional instructions for the development of persistence in the chapters on autosuggestion and the subconscious mind (Chapter 3 and Chapter 11). Follow the instructions outlined in these chapters until your "habit nature" hands over *a clear picture* of the object of your DESIRE to your subconscious mind, which works continuously while you are awake and while you are asleep. From that point on you will not be handicapped by lack of persistence.

Spasmodic or occasional effort to apply the rules will be of no value to you. To get RESULTS, you must apply all of the rules until their application becomes a fixed habit with you. In no other way can you develop the necessary money-consciousness.

POVERTY is attracted to the one whose mind is favorable to it, as money is attracted to the one whose mind has been deliberately prepared to attract it, and through the same laws. POVERTY CONSCIOUSNESS WILL VOLUNTARILY SEIZE THE MIND WHICH IS NOT OCCUPIED WITH MONEY CONSCIOUSNESS. A poverty consciousness develops without *conscious* application of habits favorable to it. The money consciousness must be created to order, unless one is born with such a consciousness.

Catch the full significance of the statements in the preceding paragraph, and you will understand the importance of PERSIS-TENCE in the accumulation of a fortune. Without PERSISTENCE, you will be defeated even before you start. With PERSISTENCE you will win.

If you have ever experienced a nightmare, you will realize the value of persistence. You are lying in bed half awake, with a feeling that you are about to smother. You are unable to turn over or move a muscle. You realize that you MUST BEGIN to regain control over your muscles. Through persistent effort of willpower, you finally manage to move the fingers of one hand. By continuing to move your fingers, you extend your control to the muscles of one arm until you can lift it. Then you gain control of the other arm in the same manner. You finally gain control over the muscles of one leg and then extend it to the other leg. THEN WITH ONE SUPREME EFFORT OF WILL you regain complete control over your muscular system and snap out of your nightmare. The trick has been turned step by step.

You may find it necessary to snap out of your mental inertia through a similar procedure, moving slowly at first, then increasing your speed until you gain complete control over your will. Be PERSISTENT no matter how slowly you may at first have to move. WITH PERSISTENCE WILL COME SUCCESS.[1]

If you select your Master Mind Group with care, you will have in it at least one person who will aid you in the development of PERSISTENCE. Some individuals who have accumulated great fortunes did so because of NECESSITY. They developed the habit of PERSISTENCE because they were so closely driven by circumstances that they *had to become persistent.*

THERE IS NO SUBSTITUTE FOR PERSISTENCE! It cannot be supplanted by any other quality! Remember this and it will hearten you in the beginning, when the going may seem difficult and slow.

Those who have cultivated the HABIT of persistence seem to enjoy insurance against failure. No matter how many times they are defeated, they finally arrive at the top of the ladder. Sometimes it appears that they have a hidden Guide whose duty is to test them through all sorts of discouraging experiences. Those who pick themselves up after defeat and keep on trying, arrive — and the world cries, "Bravo! I knew you could do it! " The hidden Guide lets no one enjoy great achievement without passing the PERSISTENCE TEST. Those who can't take it simply do not make the grade.

Those who *can* take it are bountifully rewarded for their PERSISTENCE. They receive as their compensation whatever goal they are pursuing. That is not all! They receive something infinitely more important than material compensation — the knowledge that EVERY FAILURE BRINGS WITH IT THE SEED OF AN EQUIVALENT ADVANTAGE.

There are exceptions to this rule. A few people know from experience the soundness of persistence. They are the ones who have not accepted defeat as being anything more than temporary. They are the ones whose DESIRES are so PERSISTENTLY APPLIED that defeat is finally changed into victory. We who stand on the sidelines of life see the overwhelmingly large number who go down in defeat, never to rise again. We see the few who take the punishment of defeat *as an urge to greater effort.* These, fortunately, never learn to accept life's "reverse gear." But what we DO NOT SEE, what most of us never suspect of existing, is the silent but irresistible POWER which comes to the rescue of those who fight on in the face of discouragement. If we speak of this power at all, we call it PERSISTENCE and let it go at that. One thing we all know — if one does not possess PERSISTENCE, one does not achieve noteworthy success in any calling.

As these lines are being written, I look up from my work and see before me less than a block away the great mysterious Broadway of New York, the "Graveyard of Dead Hopes" and the "Front Porch of Opportunity." From all over the world, people have come to Broadway seeking fame, fortune, power, love, or whatever it is that human beings call success. Once in a great while someone steps out from the long procession of seekers, and the world hears that another person has mastered Broadway. But Broadway is not easily nor quickly conquered. She acknowledges talent, recognizes genius, and pays off in money only *after* one has refused to QUIT.

The secret of how to conquer Broadway is always inseparably attached to one word — PERSISTENCE! The secret is told in the struggle of Fannie Hurst, whose PERSISTENCE conquered the Great White Way. She came to New York in 1915 to convert writing into riches. The conversion did not come quickly, BUT IT CAME. For four years Miss Hurst learned about "The Sidewalks of New York" from firsthand experience. She spent her days laboring and her nights HOPING. When hope grew dim, she did not say, "All right Broadway, you win!" She said, "Very well, Broadway, you may whip some, but not me. I'm going to force you to give up."[2]

One publisher (*The Saturday Evening Post*) sent her 36 rejection slips before she broke the ice and got a story across. The average writer, like the "average" in other walks of life, would have given up the job when the first rejection slip came. She pounded the pavements for four years to the tune of the publisher's "NO" because she was determined to win.

Then came the payoff. The spell had been broken, the unseen Guide had tested Fannie Hurst, and she could take it. From that time on, publishers beat a path to her door. Money came so fast she hardly had time to count it. Then the motion picture crowd discovered her, and money came not in small change, but in floods. The movie rights to her novel *Great Laughter* brought $100,000, said at the time to be the highest price ever paid for a story before publication. Her royalties from the sale of the book increased her fortune further.

Briefly, you now have a description of what PERSISTENCE is capable of achieving. Fannie Hurst is no exception. Wherever men and women accumulate great riches, you may be sure they first acquired PERSISTENCE. Broadway will give any beggar a cup of coffee and a sandwich, but it demands PERSISTENCE of those who go after the big stakes.

Kate Smith would have said "Amen" in reading this. For years she sang, without money and without price, in front of any microphone she could reach. Broadway said to her, "Come and get it, if you can take it." She did take it until one happy day Broadway got tired and said, "Aw, what's the use? You don't know when you're whipped, so name your price, and go to work in earnest." Miss Smith named her price! It was plenty—up in figures so high that one week of her salary was far more than most people made in a whole year.[3]

Verily it pays to be PERSISTENT!

And here is an encouraging statement which carries with it a suggestion of great significance: THOUSANDS OF SINGERS WHOSE VOCAL SKILLS EXCEED THOSE OF KATE SMITH ARE WALKING UP AND DOWN BROADWAY TODAY LOOKING FOR A "BREAK"—WITHOUT SUCCESS. Countless others have come and gone. Many of them sang well enough, but they failed to make the grade because they lacked the courage to keep on keeping on until Broadway became tired of turning them away.

Persistence is a state of mind, therefore, it can be cultivated. Like all states of mind, persistence is based upon definite causes, among them what I call:

The Eight Factors of Persistence

1. DEFINITENESS OF PURPOSE. Knowing what one wants is the first and, perhaps, the most important step toward the development of persistence. A strong motive forces one to surmount many difficulties.
2. DESIRE. It is comparatively easy to acquire and to maintain persistence in pursuing the object of intense desire.
3. SELF-RELIANCE. Belief in one's ability to carry out a plan encourages one to follow the plan through with persistence. (Self-reliance can be developed through the principle described in Chapter 3 on Autosuggestion.)
4. DEFINITENESS OF PLANS. Organized plans, even though they may be weak and entirely impractical, encourage persistence.
5. ACCURATE KNOWLEDGE. Knowing that one's plans are sound, based upon experience or observation, encourages persistence. Guessing, instead of knowing, destroys persistence.
6. COOPERATION. Sympathy, understanding, and harmonious cooperation with others tend to develop persistence.
7. WILL POWER. The habit of concentrating one's thoughts upon the building of plans for the attainment of a definite purpose leads to persistence.
8. HABIT. Persistence is the direct result of habit. The mind absorbs and becomes a part of the daily experiences upon which it feeds. Fear, the worst of all enemies, can be effectively cured by forced repetition of acts of

courage. Everyone who has seen active service in war knows this.

Before leaving the subject of PERSISTENCE, take inventory of yourself and determine in what particular, if any, you are lacking in this essential quality. Measure yourself courageously, point by point, and see how many of the Eight Factors of Persistence you lack. The analysis may lead to discoveries that will give you a new grip on yourself.

The 16 Symptoms of Lack of Persistence

Here you will find the real enemies which stand between you and noteworthy achievement. Here you will find not only the 16 symptoms that indicate weakness of PERSISTENCE, but also the deeply seated subconscious causes of this weakness. Study the list carefully and face yourself squarely IF YOU REALLY WISH TO KNOW WHO YOU ARE AND WHAT YOU ARE CAPABLE OF DOING. These are the 16 weaknesses which must be mastered by all who accumulate riches.

1. Failure to recognize and to clearly define exactly what one wants.
2. Procrastination, with or without cause. (Usually backed up with a formidable array of alibis and excuses.)
3. Lack of interest in acquiring specialized knowledge.
4. Indecision, the habit of passing the buck on all occasions instead of facing issues squarely. (Also backed by alibis.)
5. The habit of relying upon alibis instead of creating definite plans for the solution of problems.
6. Self-satisfaction. There is but little remedy for this affliction and no hope for those who suffer from it.
7. Indifference, usually reflected in one's readiness to compromise on all occasions, rather than meet opposition and fight it.
8. The habit of blaming others for one's mistakes, and accepting unfavorable circumstances as being unavoidable.

9. WEAKNESS OF DESIRE, resulting from neglect in the choice of MOTIVES that impel action.

10. Willingness, even eagerness, to quit at the first sign of defeat. (Based upon one or more of the Six Basic Fears.)

11. Lack of ORGANIZED PLANS, placed in writing where they may be analyzed.

12. The habit of neglecting to move on ideas or to grasp opportunity when it presents itself.

13. WISHING instead of WILLING.

14. The habit of compromising with POVERTY instead of aiming at riches. General absence of ambition to *be*, to *do*, and to *own*.

15. Searching for all the shortcuts to riches, trying to GET without GIVING a fair equivalent, usually reflected in the habit of gambling or endeavoring to drive "sharp" bargains.

16. FEAR OF CRITICISM, which leads to failure to create plans and put them into action because of what other people will think, do, or say. This enemy belongs at the head of the list because it generally exists in one's subconscious mind, where its presence is not recognized. (See the Six Basic Fears on page 240.)

Let us examine some of the symptoms of No. 16, the fear of criticism. The majority of people permit relatives, friends, and the public at large to so influence them that they cannot live their own lives because they fear criticism.

Huge numbers of people make mistakes in marriage, stand by the bargain, and go through life miserable and unhappy because they fear criticism which may follow if they correct the mistake. (Anyone who has submitted to this form of fear knows the irreparable damage it does by destroying ambition, self-reliance, and the desire to achieve.) Millions of people neglect to acquire belated educations, after having left school, because they fear criticism.

Countless numbers of men and women, both young and old, permit relatives to wreck their lives in the name of DUTY because they fear criticism. (Duty does not require *anyone* to submit to the destruction of one's personal ambitions and the right to live one's own life in one's own way).

People refuse to take chances in business because they fear the criticism which may follow if they fail. *The fear of criticism in such cases is stronger than the DESIRE for success.*

Too many people refuse to set high goals for themselves, or even neglect selecting a career, because they fear the criticism of relatives and friends who may say, "Don't aim so high, people will think you are crazy."

When Andrew Carnegie suggested that I devote 20 years to the organization of a philosophy of individual achievement, my first impulse of thought was fear of what people might say. The suggestion set up a goal for me, far out of proportion to any I had ever conceived. As quick as a flash, my mind began to create alibis and excuses, all of them traceable to the inherent FEAR OF CRITICISM. Something inside me said, "You can't do it—the job is too big and requires too much time—what will your relatives think of you?—how will you earn a living?—no one has ever organized a philosophy of success, what right have you to believe you can do it?—who are you, anyway, to aim so high?—remember your humble birth—what do you know about philosophy?—people will think you are crazy—(and they did)—why hasn't some other person done this before now?"

These and many other questions flashed into my mind and demanded attention. It seemed as if the whole world had suddenly turned its attention to me with the purpose of ridiculing me into giving up all desire to carry out Mr. Carnegie's suggestion.

I had a fine opportunity then and there to kill off ambition before it gained control of me. Later in life, after having analyzed thousands of people, I discovered that MOST IDEAS ARE STILLBORN AND NEED THE BREATH OF LIFE INJECTED INTO THEM THROUGH DEFINITE PLANS OF IMMEDIATE ACTION. The time to nurse an idea is at the time of its birth. Every minute it lives gives it a better chance of surviving. The FEAR OF CRITICISM is at the bottom of the destruction of most ideas which never reach the PLANNING and ACTION stage.

Many people believe that material success is the result of favorable breaks. There is some element of truth in the belief, but people who depend entirely upon luck are nearly always disappointed because they overlook another important factor which must be present before one can be sure of success. It is the knowledge with which favorable breaks can be made to order.

During the Depression, W. C. Fields, the comedian, lost all his money and found himself without income, without a job, and with his means of earning a living (vaudeville) made obsolete. Moreover, he was past 60, the age when many people consider themselves old. He was so eager to stage a comeback that he offered to work without pay in a new field (movies). In addition to his other troubles, he fell and injured his neck. To many that would have been the place to give up and QUIT. But Fields was PERSISTENT. He knew that if he carried on he would get the breaks sooner or later, and he did get them, but not by chance.[4]

Marie Dressler found herself down and out, with her money gone and with no job, when she was about 60. She, too, went after the breaks and got them. Her PERSISTENCE brought an astounding triumph late in life, long beyond the age when most men and women are done with ambition to achieve.[5]

Eddie Cantor lost his money in the 1929 stock market crash, but he still had his PERSISTENCE and his courage. With these, plus two prominent eyes, he exploited himself back into an income of $10,000 a week![6] Verily, if one has PERSISTENCE, one can get along very well without many other qualities.

The only break anyone can afford to rely upon is a self-made one. These come through the application of PERSISTENCE. The starting point is DEFINITENESS OF PURPOSE.[7]

Examine the first 100 people you meet, ask them what they want most in life, and 98 of them will not be able to tell you. If you press them for an answer, some will say SECURITY; many will say MONEY; a few will say HAPPINESS; others will say FAME AND POWER; and still others will say SOCIAL RECOGNITION,

EASE IN LIVING, ABILITY TO SING, DANCE, or WRITE—but none of them will be able to define these terms or give the slightest indication of a PLAN by which they hope to attain these vaguely expressed wishes. Riches do not respond to wishes. They respond only to definite plans, backed by definite desires, through constant PERSISTENCE.

How To Develop Persistence

There are four simple steps which lead to the habit of PERSISTENCE. They call for no great amount of intelligence, no particular amount of education, and but little time or effort. The necessary steps are:

1. A DEFINITE PURPOSE BACKED BY BURNING DES-IRE FOR ITS FULFILLMENT.
2. A DEFINITE PLAN, EXPRESSED IN CONTINUOUS ACTION.
3. A MIND CLOSED TIGHTLY AGAINST ALL NEGATIVE AND DISCOURAGING INFLUENCES, including nega-tive suggestions of relatives, friends and acquaintances.
4. A FRIENDLY ALLIANCE WITH ONE OR MORE PER-SONS WHO WILL ENCOURAGE ONE TO FOLLOW THROUGH WITH BOTH PLAN AND PURPOSE.

These four steps are essential for success in all walks of life. The entire purpose of the 13 principles of *The Think and Grow Rich Philosophy* is to enable one to take these four steps as a matter of *habit*.

These are the steps by which one may control one's economic destiny.

They are the steps that lead to freedom and independence of thought.

They are the steps that lead to riches, in small or great quantities.

They lead the way to power, fame, and worldly recognition.

They are the four steps which guarantee favorable breaks.

They are the steps that convert dreams into physical realities.

They lead also to the mastery of FEAR, DISCOURAGEMENT, and INDIFFERENCE.

There is a magnificent reward for all who learn to take these four steps. It is the privilege of writing one's own ticket and of making life yield whatever price is asked.

I have no way of knowing the facts, but I venture to conjecture that Mrs. Wallis Simpson's great love for a man was not accidental, nor the result of favorable breaks alone. There was a burning desire and careful searching at every step of the way. Her first duty was to love.[8] What is the greatest thing on earth? Jesus called it love — not manmade rules, criticism, bitterness, slander, or "political marriages" — but love.

Wallace Simpson knew what she wanted not after she met the Prince of Wales, but long before that. Twice when she had failed to find it, she had the courage to continue her search. "To thine own self be true, and it must follow, as the night the day, thou canst not then be false to any man."

Her rise from obscurity was of the slow, progressive, PERSISTENT order, but it was SURE! She triumphed over unbelievably long odds. And no matter who you are or what you may think of Wallis Simpson or the king who gave up his crown for her love, she was an astounding example of applied PERSISTENCE, an instructor on the rules of self-determination from whom the entire world might profitably take lessons.

And what of King Edward? What lesson may we learn from his part in one of the 20th century's greatest personal dramas? Did he pay too high a price for the affections of the woman he loved?[9]

No one but he could have answered that question. The rest of us can only conjecture. This much we know — the king came into the world without his own consent. He was born to great riches, without requesting them. He was persistently sought in marriage. Politicians and statesmen throughout Europe tossed dowagers and princesses at his feet. Because he was the first born of his parents, he inherited a crown which he did not seek and perhaps did not desire. For more than 40 years he was not a free agent, could not live his life in his own way, had but little privacy, and finally assumed duties inflicted upon him when he ascended the throne.

Some will say, "With all these blessings, King Edward should have found peace of mind, contentment, and joy of living." The truth is that back of all the privileges of a crown, all the money, the fame, and the power inherited by King Edward, there was an emptiness which could be filled only by love.

His greatest DESIRE was for love. Long before he met Wallis Simpson, he doubtless felt this great universal emotion tugging at the strings of his heart, beating upon the door of his soul and crying out for expression.[10]

King Edward's DECISION to give up the British crown for the privilege of going the remainder of the way through life with the woman of his choice was a decision that required courage. The decision also had a price, but who has the right to say the price was too great?[11]

As a suggestion to anyone who would find fault with the Duke of Windsor because his DESIRE for LOVE led him to openly declare that love and give up his throne for it, let it be remembered that his "open declaration" was not essential. He could have followed the custom of "clandestine liaison," or secret affair, which had prevailed in Europe for centuries, without giving up either his throne or the woman of his choice — and there would have been NO COMPLAINT FROM EITHER CHURCH OR THE PUBLIC. But this unusual man was built of sterner stuff. His love was deep and sincere. It represented the one thing which above ALL ELSE he truly DESIRED, therefore, he took what he wanted and paid the price demanded.[12]

Most of the world today would applaud the Duke of Windsor and Wallis Simpson because of their PERSISTENCE in searching until they found life's greatest reward. ALL OF US CAN PROFIT by following their example in our own search for that which we demand of life.[13]

What mystical power gives to people of PERSISTENCE the capacity to master difficulties? Does the quality of PERSISTENCE set up in one's mind some form of spiritual, mental, or chemical activity which gives one access to supernatural forces? Does Infinite Intelligence throw itself on the side of the person who still fights on after the battle has been lost, with the whole world on the opposing side?

These and many other similar questions have arisen in my mind as I have observed individuals such as Henry Ford, who started from scratch and built an industrial empire of huge proportions with little else in the way of a beginning but PERSISTENCE, or Thomas A. Edison, who with less than three months of schooling became the world's leading inventor and converted PERSISTENCE into the phonograph, the movie projector, and the incandescent light, to say nothing of a hundred other useful inventions.

I had the happy privilege of analyzing and studying at close range both Mr. Edison and Mr. Ford year by year over a long period of years, so I speak from firsthand knowledge when I say that I found no quality save PERSISTENCE in either of them that would even remotely suggest the major source of their stupendous achievements.

As one makes an impartial study of the prophets, philosophers, miracle workers, and religious leaders of the past, one is drawn to the inevitable conclusion that PERSISTENCE, concentration of effort, and DEFINITENESS OF PURPOSE were the major sources of their achievements.

Consider, for example, the strange and fascinating story of Mohammed. Analyze his life, compare him with individuals of achievement in this modern age of industry and finance, and observe how they all have one outstanding trait in common— PERSISTENCE!

If you are keenly interested in studying the strange power which gives potency to PERSISTENCE, read a biography of Mohammed, especially the one by Essad Bey. This brief review of that book, by Thomas Sugrue in the *New York Herald-Tribune*, will provide a preview of the rare treat in store for those who take the time to read the entire story of one of the most astounding examples of the power of PERSISTENCE known to civilization.

The Last Great Prophet
Reviewed by Thomas Sugrue

Mohammed was a prophet, but he never performed a miracle. He was not a mystic; he had no formal schooling; he did not begin his mission until he was forty. When he announced that he was the Messenger of God, bringing word of the true religion, he was ridiculed and labeled a lunatic. Children tripped him and women threw filth upon him. He was banished from his native city, Mecca, and his followers were stripped of their worldly goods and sent into the desert after him. When he had been preaching ten years, he had nothing to show for it but banishment, poverty and ridicule. Yet before another ten years had passed, he was dictator of all Arabia, ruler of Mecca, and the head of a new world religion which was to sweep to the Danube and the Pyrenees before exhausting the impetus he gave it. That impetus was three-fold: the power of words, the efficacy of prayer, and man's kinship with God.

His career never made sense. Mohammed was born to impoverished members of a leading family of Mecca. Because Mecca, the crossroads of the world, home of the magic stone called the Caaba, great city of trade and the center of trade routes, was unsanitary, its children were sent to be raised in the desert by Bedouins. Mohammed was thus nurtured, drawing strength and health from the milk of nomad, vicarious mothers. He tended sheep and soon hired out to a rich widow as leader of her caravans. He traveled to all parts of the Eastern World, talked with many men of diverse beliefs and observed the decline of Christianity into warring sects. When he was twenty-eight, Khadija, the widow, looked upon him with favor and married him. Her father would have objected to such a marriage, so she got him drunk and held him up while he gave the paternal blessing. For the next twelve years Mohammed lived as a rich and respected and very shrewd trader. Then he took to wandering in the desert, and one day he returned with the first verse of the *Koran* and told Khadija that the archangel Gabriel had appeared to him and said that he was to be the Messenger of God.

The Koran, the revealed word of God, was the closest thing to a miracle in Mohammed's life. He had not been a poet; he had no gift of words. Yet the verses of the Koran, as he received them and recited them to the faithful, were better than any verses which the professional poets of the tribes could produce. This, to the Arabs, was a miracle. To them the gift of words was the greatest gift, the poet was all-powerful. In addition the Koran said that all men were equal before God, that the world should be a democratic state — Islam. It was this political *heresy*, plus Mohammed's desire to destroy all the 360 idols in the courtyard of the Caaba, which brought about his banishment. The idols brought the desert tribes to Mecca, and that meant trade. So the businessmen of Mecca, the capitalists, of which he had been one, set upon Mohammed. Then he retreated to the desert and demanded sovereignty over the world.

The rise of Islam began. Out of the desert came a flame which would not be extinguished — a democratic army fighting as a unit and prepared to die without wincing. Mohammed had invited the Jews and Christians to join him, for he was not building a new religion. He was calling all who believed in one God to join in a single faith. If the Jews and Christians had accepted his invitation, Islam would have conquered the world. They didn't. They would not even accept Mohammed's innovation of humane warfare. When the armies of the prophet entered Jerusalem, not a single person was killed because of his faith. When the crusaders entered the city, centuries later, not a Moslem man, woman, or child was spared. But the Christians did accept one Moslem idea — the place of learning, the university.

Religious visionaries such as Mohammed; business leaders such as Thomas Edison, Henry Ford, and Andrew Carnegie; political leaders such as Samuel Adams; entertainers such as Fannie Hurst, Kate Smith, and W. C. Fields; cosmopolites such as Wallis Simpson and the Duke of Windsor—no matter what their walk of life, individuals such as these in all eras of human history have demonstrated the tremendous power of *The Eighth Step to Riches*—PERSISTENCE, sustained effort in the face of all odds and all adversity.

PERSISTENCE creates FAITH. And FAITH is the only known antidote for failure, it is the starting point of all accumulation of riches, and it is the *only* agency through which one can tap the force of Infinite Intelligence.

GREAT POWER CAN BE ACCUMULATED THROUGH NO OTHER PRINCIPLE THAN THAT OF THE MASTER MIND!

Chapter 9

POWER OF THE MASTER MIND

The Ninth Step to Riches
The Driving Force

PERSISTENCE creates FAITH.

From FAITH comes POWER.

And POWER is essential for success in the accumulation of money.

PLANS alone are inert and useless, without sufficient POWER to translate them into ACTION. This chapter will describe the method by which an individual may attain and apply POWER.

POWER may be defined as "organized and intelligently directed KNOWLEDGE." Power, as the term is here used, refers to ORGANIZED effort, sufficient to enable an individual to transmute DESIRE into its monetary equivalent. ORGANIZED effort is produced through the coordination of effort of two or more people who work toward a DEFINITE end, in a spirit of harmony.

POWER IS REQUIRED FOR THE ACCUMULATION OF MONEY! POWER IS NECESSARY FOR THE RETENTION OF MONEY AFTER IT HAS BEEN ACCUMULATED!

Let us ascertain how power may be acquired. If power is "organized knowledge," let us examine:

The Three Major Sources of Knowledge

1. INFINITE INTELLIGENCE. This source of knowledge may be contacted, with the aid of Creative Imagination, through the procedure described in Chapter 5.
2. ACCUMULATED EXPERIENCE. The accumulated experience of civilization (or that portion of it which has been organized and recorded) may be found in any well-equipped public library. An important part of this accumulated experience is taught in public schools and colleges, where it has been classified and organized.
3. EXPERIMENT AND RESEARCH. In the field of science and in practically every other walk of life, people are gathering, classifying, and organizing new facts daily. This is the source to which one must turn when knowledge is not available through "accumulated experience." Here, too, the Creative Imagination must often be used.

Knowledge may be acquired from any of the foregoing sources. It may be converted into POWER by organizing it into definite PLANS and by expressing those plans in terms of ACTION.

Examination of the Three Major Sources of Knowledge will readily disclose the difficulty you would have if you depended upon your own efforts alone in assembling knowledge and expressing it through definite plans in terms of ACTION. If your plans are comprehensive and if they require vast sums of information, you must generally induce others to cooperate with you before you can inject into them the necessary element of POWER.

Gaining Power through the Master Mind

The Master Mind may be defined as: "Coordination of knowledge and effort, in a spirit of harmony between two or more people, for the attainment of a definite purpose."[1]

No individual can have great power without availing himself or herself of the Master Mind Principle. In Chapter 1 instructions were given for the creation of PLANS for the purpose of translating DESIRE into its monetary equivalent. If you carry out these instructions with PERSISTENCE and intelligence, and use discrimination in the selection of your Master Mind Group, your objective will have been halfway reached even before you begin to recognize it.

So you may better understand the intangible potentialities of power available to you through a properly chosen Master Mind Group, I will here explain the two characteristics of the Master Mind Principle, one of which is economic in nature and the other psychic. The economic feature is obvious. Economic advantages may be created by any person who surrounds himself or herself with the advice, counsel, and personal cooperation of a group of people who are willing to lend wholehearted aid, in a spirit of PERFECT HARMONY. This form of cooperative alliance has been the basis of nearly every great fortune. Your understanding of this great truth may definitely determine your financial status.

The psychic phase of the Master Mind Principle is much more abstract, much more difficult to comprehend, because it has reference to the spiritual forces with which the human race, as a whole, is not well acquainted. You may catch a significant suggestion from this statement: "No two minds ever come together without, thereby, creating a third, invisible, intangible force which may be likened a third mind."

Keep in mind the fact that there are only two known substances in the whole universe—energy and matter. It is a well-known fact that matter may be broken down into units of molecules, atoms, protons, neutrons, and electrons. There are units of matter which may be isolated, separated, and analyzed.

Likewise, there are units of energy.

The human mind is a form of "energy," a part of it being spiritual in nature. When the minds of two people are coordinated in a SPIRIT OF HARMONY, the spiritual units of energy of each mind form an "affinity," which constitutes the psychic phase of the Master Mind.

The Master Mind Principle—or rather, the "economic" feature of it—was first called to my attention by Andrew Carnegie back during the earliest years of my research. Discovery of this part of the principle was responsible for the choice of my life's work.

Mr. Carnegie's Master Mind Group consisted of a staff of approximately 50 individuals with whom he surrounded himself for the DEFINITE PURPOSE of manufacturing and marketing steel. He attributed his entire fortune to the POWER he accumulated through this Master Mind.

Analyze the record of anyone who has accumulated a great fortune and many who have accumulated modest fortunes and you will find that they have either consciously or unconsciously employed the Master Mind Principle.

GREAT POWER CAN BE ACCUMULATED THROUGH NO OTHER PRINCIPLE!

ENERGY is Nature's universal set of building blocks, out of which she constructs every material thing in the universe, including human beings and every form of animal and vegetable life. Through a process which only Nature completely understands, she translates energy into matter.

Nature's building blocks are available to humanity in the energy involved in THINKING! The human brain may be compared to an electric battery. It absorbs energy from what may be called "The Mysterious Unifying Force of the Universe," which permeates every atom of matter—including the atoms that compose the human brain—and fills the entire universe.[2]

It is a well-known fact that a group of electric batteries will provide more energy than a single battery. It is also a well-known fact that an individual battery will provide energy in proportion to the number and capacity of the cells it contains.

The brain functions in a similar fashion. This accounts for the fact that some brains are more efficient than others, and leads to this significant statement: *A group of brains coordinated (or connected) in a spirit of harmony will provide more thought-energy than a single brain, just as a group of electric batteries will provide more energy than a single battery.*

Through this metaphor it becomes immediately obvious that the Master Mind Principle holds the secret of the POWER wielded by people who surround themselves with the minds of other capable individuals.

There follows now another statement which will lead still nearer to an understanding of the *psychic* phase of the Master Mind Principle: When a group of individual brains are coordinated and function in harmony, the increased energy created through that alliance becomes available to every individual brain in the group.

Henry Ford began his business career under the handicap of poverty, illiteracy, and ignorance. Within the inconceivably short period of ten years Mr. Ford mastered these three handicaps, and within 25 years he made himself one of the richest people in America. Connect with those facts the additional knowledge that Mr. Ford's most rapid strides became noticeable from the time he became a personal friend of Thomas A. Edison, and you will begin to understand what the influence of one mind upon another can accomplish. Go a step further and consider the fact that Mr. Ford's most outstanding achievements began from the time that he formed the acquaintances of Harvey Firestone, John Burroughs, and Luther Burbank (each an individual of great intellectual capacity), and you will have further evidence that POWER may be produced through a friendly alliance of minds.[3]

There is little, if any, doubt that Henry Ford was one of the best informed leaders of the business and industrial world of his time. The question of his wealth needs no discussion. Analyze Mr. Ford's intimate personal friends, some of whom have already been mentioned, and you will be prepared to understand the following statement: "Individuals take on the nature and the habits and the POWER OF THOUGHT of those with whom they associate in a spirit of sympathy and harmony."

Henry Ford whipped poverty, illiteracy, and ignorance by allying himself with great minds, whose "vibrations of thought" he absorbed into his own mind. Through his association with Edison, Burbank, Burroughs, and Firestone, Mr. Ford added to his own brain power the sum and substance of the intelligence, experience, knowledge, and spiritual forces of these four individuals. Moreover, he appropriated and made use of the Master Mind Principle through the methods of procedure described in this book.

This principle is available to you!

I have already mentioned Mahatma Gandhi. Perhaps the majority of people who know anything about Gandhi look upon him as merely an eccentric little man who went around without formal wearing apparel making trouble for the British Government.

In reality, Gandhi was not eccentric, but HE WAS THE MOST POWERFUL MAN ALIVE DURING HIS TIME (judging by the number of followers he had and their faith in him). Moreover, he is arguably one of the most powerful individuals who have ever lived. His power was passive, but it was real.

Let us study the method by which he attained his stupendous POWER. It may be explained in a few words. He attained POWER through inducing more than 200 million people to cooperate, with mind and body, in a spirit of HARMONY, for a DEFINITE PURPOSE.

In brief, Gandhi accomplished a MIRACLE, for it is a miracle when 200 million people can be induced — not forced — to cooperate in a spirit of HARMONY for a limitless time. If you doubt that this is a miracle, try to induce ANY TWO PERSONS to cooperate in a spirit of harmony for any length of time.

Every individual who manages a business knows what a difficult matter it is to get employees to work together in a spirit even remotely resembling HARMONY.

The list of the chief sources from which POWER may be attained is headed, as has been shown, by INFINITE INTELLIGENCE. When two or more people coordinate in a spirit of HARMONY and work toward a definite objective, they place themselves in a position through that alliance to absorb power directly from the great universal storehouse of Infinite Intelligence. This is the greatest of all sources of POWER. It is the source to which the genius turns. It is the source to which every great leader turns, whether consciously or not.

The other two major sources from which the knowledge necessary for the accumulation of POWER may be obtained — "accumulated experience" and "experiment and research" — are no more reliable than the five human senses. The senses are not always reliable. However, Infinite Intelligence DOES NOT ERR.

In subsequent chapters, the methods by which Infinite Intelligence may be most readily contacted will be adequately described.

This book is not a course on religion. No fundamental principle described in this book should be interpreted as being intended to interfere either directly or indirectly with any person's religious habits. This book is confined, primarily, to instructing the reader how to transmute the DEFINITE PURPOSE OF DESIRE FOR MONEY into its monetary equivalent.

Read, *THINK*, and meditate as you read. Soon the entire subject will unfold, and you will see it *in perspective*. For now, you are seeing the *detail* of the individual chapters.

Money is shy and elusive. It must be wooed and won by methods not unlike those used by the determined lover in pursuit of the beloved. And, coincidental as it is, the POWER used in the wooing of money is not greatly different from that used in wooing a person. That power, when successfully used in the pursuit of money, must be mixed with FAITH. It must be mixed with DESIRE. It must be mixed with PERSISTENCE. It must be applied through a plan, and that plan must be set into ACTION.

When money comes in quantities known as "the big money," it flows to the one who accumulates it as easily as water flows downhill. There exists in life a great unseen *STREAM OF POWER* which may be compared to a river — except that one side flows in one direction, carrying all who get into that side of the stream onward and upward to WEALTH, while the other side flows in the opposite direction, carrying all who are unfortunate enough to get into it (and not able to extricate themselves from it), downstream to misery and POVERTY.

Every person who has accumulated a great fortune has recognized the existence of this stream of life. It consists of one's THINKING PROCESS. The positive emotions of thought form the side of the stream which carries one to fortune. The negative emotions form the side which carries one down to poverty.

Understanding that you yourself can control where you will be in this stream of life is of stupendous importance to the person who is following this book with the object of accumulating a fortune, for such understanding leads to the recognition that ANYBODY can WISH for riches, and most people do, but only a few know that a definite plan, plus a BURNING DESIRE for wealth, are the only dependable means of accumulating wealth.

If you find yourself in the side of the *stream of life* which leads to poverty, understand that you have within you the power to propel yourself over to the other side of the stream. Your oar is the philosophy and the principles set forth in this book. They can serve you ONLY through application and use. Merely reading and passing judgment on these principles, either one way or another, will in no way benefit you. You must take your oar in hand and ACT.[4]

Some people undergo the experience of alternating between the positive and negative sides of the stream, being at times on the positive side and at times on the negative side. Recent economic hard times have swept millions of people from the positive to the negative side of the stream. These millions are struggling, some of them in desperation and fear, to get back to the positive side of the stream. This book was written especially for those millions.

Poverty and riches often change places. Rapidly changing economic conditions have taught the world this truth, although many people may not long remember the lesson. Poverty may, and generally does, voluntarily take the place of riches. When riches take the place of poverty, the change is usually brought about through well-conceived and carefully executed PLANS. Poverty needs no plan. It needs no one to aid it because it is bold and ruthless. Riches are shy and timid. They have to be attracted. But they will rarely be attracted, and retained, until one learns, first, to tap the POWER OF THE MASTER MIND, and then proceed to understand *The Tenth Step to Riches,* which involves the "Mystery of Sex Transmutation."

Chapter 10

THE MYSTERY OF SEX TRANSMUTATION
The Tenth Step to Riches

THE MEANING of the word "transmute" is, in simple language, "the changing, or transferring of one element, or form of energy, into another."

The emotion of sex brings into being a state of mind.

Because of ignorance on the subject, this state of mind is generally associated only with the *physical* side of human nature. And because of the improper influences to which most people have been subjected in acquiring their knowledge about sex, this emphasis on the purely physical aspects of sex has created strong, and often destructive, biases in most people's minds.

The emotion of sex has back of it the possibility of three constructive potentialities. They are:

1. the perpetuation of the human race
2. the maintenance of sound physical and emotional health
3. the transformation of mediocrity into genius through transmutation

"Sex transmutation," which is involved in the third constructive potentiality, is simple and easily explained. It means the switching of one's mind, or "dominating mental focus," from thoughts (and consequent actions) of a merely physical expression to thoughts (and consequent actions) of another nature. It does *not* mean in any sense "celibacy" or "repression of natural instincts." It *does* mean approaching sex and engaging in sexual conduct from a completely positive, completely constructive, balanced and appropriate state of awareness.

Sexual desire is the most powerful of human desires. Its exercise in proper relation and proportion to all other aspects of life is positive and healthy. People who are driven by this desire — in a positive, constructive sense — can "channel" it to develop keenness of imagination, courage, willpower, persistence, and creative ability that are all but unknown at other times. So strong and impelling is the desire for sexual contact that some people freely run the risk of life and reputation to indulge it. When "harnessed" and "redirected" constructively, this motivating force maintains all of its attributes of keenness of imagination, courage, and so forth, which may be used as powerful creative forces in literature, art, or in any other profession, calling, or undertaking — including, of course, the accumulation of riches.[1]

The transmutation of sex energy calls for the exercise of willpower, to be sure, but the reward is worth the effort. The desire for sexual expression is inborn and natural. The desire cannot and should not be submerged or eliminated. But it should not be allowed to dominate or dictate one's behavior. It should be given an extra outlet through forms of expression which enrich the body, mind, and spirit. If not given this form of outlet, through the process of transmutation, it will seek outlets through purely physical channels.

A river may be dammed, and its water controlled for a time, but eventually it will force an outlet. The same is true of the emotion of sex. It may be submerged and controlled for a time, but its very nature causes it ever to be seeking a means of expression. If it is not transmuted into some creative effort, it will find a less positive, less productive outlet. Fortunate, indeed, are those individuals who have discovered how to give their sexual emotion an outlet through some form of creative effort, for they have, by that discovery, lifted themselves to the level of "genius performance."

Research has disclosed these two significant facts:

1. The individuals of greatest achievement tend to be those who have highly developed sexual natures and who have learned the art of sex transmutation.
2. Generally speaking, those who have accumulated great fortunes and achieved outstanding recognition in literature, art, industry, architecture, and the professions, were motivated by the influence of romantic love for another person.

The research in which these astounding discoveries were made went back through the pages of biography and history for more than 2,000 years. Wherever there was evidence available in connection with the lives of men and women of great achievement, it indicated most convincingly that they possessed highly developed sexual natures.

The emotion of sex is an irresistible force against which there can be no such opposition as an immovable body. When driven by this emotion, individuals become gifted with a super power for action. Understand this truth and you will catch the significance of the statement that sex transmutation can lift one to genius-level performance.

The emotion of sex contains the secret of creative ability.

Destroy the sex glands, whether in a human being or a beast, and you have removed a major source of action. For proof of this, observe what happens to any animal after it has been neutered. A bull or a bulldog becomes thoroughly docile after it has been altered sexually. Sex alteration takes out of any male animal all the FIGHT that was in him. Sex alteration of the female has the same quieting effect.[2]

The 10 Mind Stimuli

The human mind responds to stimuli, through which it may be "keyed up" to high rates of vibration known as enthusiasm, Creative Imagination, intense desire, and so forth. The ten stimuli to which the mind responds most freely are:

1. the desire for sexual expression
2. love
3. a burning desire for fame, power, or financial gain—
   MONEY
4. music
5. close friendship between either those of the same sex or
   those of the opposite sex
6. a Master Mind Alliance based upon the harmony of
   two or more people who ally themselves for spiritual or
   temporal advancement
7. mutual suffering, such as that experienced by people who
   are persecuted
8. autosuggestion
9. fear
10. narcotics and alcohol

The desire for sexual expression comes at the head of the list of stimuli which most effectively step up the vibrations of the mind and, thus, "start the wheels" of physical action. Eight of these stimuli are natural and constructive. Two are destructive. The list is here presented for the purpose of enabling you to make a comparative study of the major sources of mind stimulation. From this study it will be readily seen that the emotion of sex is, by great odds, the most intense and powerful of all mind stimuli.

This comparison is necessary as a foundation for proof of the statement that transmutation of sex energy may lift one to genius-level performance. Let us find out what constitutes a genius.

Some wiseacre once said that a genius is someone who "wears long hair, eats odd food, lives alone, and serves as a target for comedians." A better definition of a genius is "an individual who has discovered how to increase mental intensity and concentration to the point where he or she can freely communicate with sources of knowledge *not available through ordinary levels of thought.*"

The person who thinks will want to ask some questions concerning this definition. The first question will be, "How can one communicate with sources of knowledge which are not available through the ORDINARY 'intensity' and 'concentration' of thought?"

The next question will be, "Are there known sources of knowledge which are generally available only to geniuses, and if so, WHAT ARE THESE SOURCES and exactly how can they be reached?"

I shall offer proof of the soundness of some of the more important statements made in this book—or at least I shall offer evidence through which you may secure your own proof through experimentation. In doing so, I shall answer both of these questions.

Genius Is Developed Through the Sixth Sense

The reality of a sixth sense in human beings has been well established. This sixth sense is "Creative Imagination." The faculty of Creative Imagination is one which the majority of people never use during an entire lifetime, and if used at all, it usually happens by mere accident. A relatively small number of people use WITH DELIBERATION, PURPOSE, AND FORETHOUGHT the faculty of Creative Imagination. Those who use this faculty voluntarily and with understanding of its functions are, by definition, geniuses.

The faculty of Creative Imagination is the direct link between the finite human mind and Infinite Intelligence. All so-called revelations referred to in the realm of religion, and all discoveries of basic or new principles in the field of invention, take place through the faculty of Creative Imagination.

When ideas or concepts flash into one's mind through what is popularly called a hunch, they come from one or more of the following four sources:

1. Infinite Intelligence
2. one's subconscious mind, wherein is stored every sense impression and thought impulse which ever reached the brain through any of the five regular senses
3. the mind of some other person who has just "released" the thought, or "picture" of the idea or concept, through conscious thought
4. the other person's subconscious storehouse

The first, third, and fourth sources above are tapped through some mysterious process or processes, perhaps extra-sensory in nature and manifestation, which we cannot yet explain and which we do not even dimly comprehend. What we *do* comprehend is that these sources are tapped, every day around the globe, and that there are no other KNOWN sources from which "inspired" ideas or hunches may be received.

The Creative Imagination functions best when the mind is operating — or functioning, concentrating, "vibrating" (as a result of some form of mind stimulation) — at a level of intensity and awareness that is significantly higher than that of ordinary, normal thought.

When brain action has been stimulated through one or more of the ten mind stimulants, it has the effect of lifting a person far above the horizon of ordinary thought and permitting that individual to envision distance, scope, quality, and character of THOUGHTS that are not available on lower planes, such as the one where a person is engaged in the solution of the everyday problems of business and professional routine.

When lifted to this "higher level of thought" through any form of mind stimulation, an individual occupies, relatively speaking, the same position as one who has ascended in an airplane to a height from which may be seen objects beyond the horizon line that limits one's vision while on the ground. Moreover, while on this higher level of thought, the individual is not hampered or bound by any of the stimuli which circumscribe and limit one's vision while wrestling with the problems of gaining the three basic necessities of food, clothing, and shelter. The individual is in a world of thought in which ORDINARY, workaday thoughts have been as effectively removed as are the hills and valleys and other limitations of physical vision when that person rises in the airplane.

While on this exalted plane of THOUGHT, the creative faculty of the mind is given freedom for action. The way has been cleared for the Sixth Sense to function. It becomes receptive to ideas which could not reach the individual under any other circumstances.

The Sixth Sense is the defining faculty which marks the difference between a genius and an ordinary individual.

The more this creative faculty is used, the more it becomes alert and receptive to thought vibrations originating outside the individual's subconscious mind—and the more the individual will come to rely upon it and make demands upon it for thought impulses (hunches, inspirations, or insights). This faculty can be cultivated and developed only through use.

That which is known as one's "conscience" operates entirely through the faculty of the Sixth Sense.

The great artists, writers, musicians, and poets become great because they acquire the habit of relying upon the "still small voice" which speaks from within through the faculty of Creative Imagination. It is a fact well known to people who have keen imaginations that their best ideas come through so-called hunches.

There is a great orator who does not reach his performance peak until he closes his eyes and begins to rely entirely upon the faculty of Creative Imagination. When asked why he closed his eyes just before the climaxes of his oratory, he replied, "I do it because then I speak *through ideas which come to me from within.*"

One of America's most successful and best-known financiers followed the habit of closing his eyes for two or three minutes before making a decision. When asked why he did this, he replied, "With my eyes closed, I am able to draw upon *a source of superior intelligence.*"[3]

Dr. Elmer R. Gates of Chevy Chase, Maryland, created more than 200 useful patents, many of them basic, through the process of cultivating and using the creative faculty. His method is both significant and interesting to anyone interested in achieving "genius status," a category to which Dr. Gates unquestionably belonged. Dr. Gates was one of the truly great, though generally less publicized scientists of the world.

In his laboratory he had what he called his "personal communication room." It was practically soundproof and so arranged that all light could be shut out. It was equipped with a small table on which he kept a pad of writing paper. When Dr.

Gates desired to draw upon the forces available to him through his Creative Imagination, he would go into this room, seat himself at the table, lower the lights, and CONCENTRATE upon the KNOWN factors of the invention on which he was working, remaining in that position until ideas began to flash into his mind in connection with the UNKNOWN factors of the invention.

On one occasion, ideas came so fast that he wrote continuously for almost three hours. When the thoughts stopped flowing and he examined his notes, he found they contained a description of principles which had no parallel among known scientific data. Moreover, the answer to his problem was intelligently presented in those notes. In this manner Dr. Gates completed more than 200 patents which had been begun, but not completed, by other inventors who were less resourceful than Dr. Gates. Evidence of the truth of this statement lies in the United States Patent Office.

Dr. Gates earned his living by "sitting for ideas" for individuals and corporations. While they may not have realized it, some of the largest corporations in America paid him substantial fees, by the hour, for sitting for ideas.[4]

The normal faculty of reason is often faulty because it is largely guided by one's accumulated experience. But not all knowledge which one accumulates through experience is accurate. Ideas received through the creative faculty are much more reliable because they come from sources more reliable than any which are available to the reasoning faculty of the mind.

The major difference between the genius and the ordinary "crank" inventor can be found in the fact that the genius works through the faculty of Creative Imagination, while the crank knows nothing of this faculty. The scientific inventor (such as Mr. Edison or Dr. Gates) makes use of both the synthetic and the creative faculties of imagination.

For example, the scientific inventor operating in the genius mode begins an invention by organizing and combining known ideas, or principles accumulated through experience, through the synthetic faculty (the reasoning faculty). If this accumulated knowledge turns out to be insufficient for the completion of the invention, the scientific inventor then draws upon the other sources of knowledge that are made available through the *creative faculty*. The exact method by which this is accomplished varies with the individual, but this is the sum and substance of the procedure that genius inventors use:

1. THEY "STIMULATE" THEIR MINDS SO THAT THEIR BRAIN FUNCTIONS ON A HIGHER-THAN-AVERAGE PLANE AND AT A HIGHER-THAN-AVERAGE LEVEL OF INTENSITY, using one or more of the ten mind stimulants or some other stimulant of their choice.

2. THEY CONCENTRATE upon the known factors (the finished part) of their invention and create in their mind a perfect picture of unknown factors (the unfinished part) of their invention. They hold this picture in mind until it has been taken over by their subconscious mind, then they relax by clearing their mind of ALL thought and waiting for their answer to flash into their mind.

Sometimes the results are both definite and immediate. At other times the results are negative, depending upon the state of development of their Sixth Sense, or creative faculty.

Mr. Edison tried out more than 10,000 different combinations of ideas through the synthetic faculty of his imagination before he tuned in through the creative faculty and got the answer which perfected the incandescent light. His experience was similar when he invented the phonograph.

There is plenty of reliable evidence that the faculty of Creative Imagination exists. This evidence is available through accurate analysis of people who have become leaders in their respective callings without having had extensive educations. Lincoln is a notable example of a great leader who achieved greatness through the discovery and use of his faculty of Creative Imagination. He discovered and began to use this faculty as the result of the stimulation of love which he experienced after he met Anne Rutledge, a statement of the highest significance in connection with the study of the source of genius.

The pages of history are filled with the records of great leaders whose achievements may be traced directly to the influence of their beloved, the person who aroused the creative faculties of their minds through the stimulation of sex desire. Napoleon Bonaparte was one of these. When inspired by his first wife, Josephine, he was irresistible and invincible. When his "better judgment" or reasoning faculty prompted him to put Josephine aside, he began to decline. His defeat and St. Helena were not far distant.

If good taste would permit, I might easily mention scores of individuals well known to the American people who climbed to great heights of achievement under the stimulating influence of their spouses, only to drop back to destruction AFTER money and power went to their heads and they cast aside their original loves for someone new. Napoleon was not the only person to discover that sex influence, *from the right source*, is more powerful than any substitute of expediency, which may be created by mere reason.

The human mind responds to stimulation!

Among the greatest and most powerful of these stimuli is the sexual urge. When harnessed and transmuted, this driving force is capable of lifting individuals into that higher sphere of thought which enables them to master the sources of worry and petty annoyance which beset their pathway on the lower planes.

Unfortunately, only the geniuses have made this discovery. Others have accepted the experience of sexual urge without discovering one of its major potentialities — a fact which accounts for the great number of "others" as compared to the limited number of geniuses.

For the purpose of refreshing the memory, in connection with the facts available from the biographies of certain individuals, we here present the names of a few outstanding achievers, each of whom was known to have had a highly sexual nature. The genius which was theirs undoubtedly found its source of power in transmuted sex energy:

GEORGE WASHINGTON
NAPOLEON BONAPARTE

WILLIAM SHAKESPEARE
ABRAHAM LINCOLN
RALPH WALDO EMERSON
ROBERT BURNS
THOMAS JEFFERSON
ELBERT HUBBARD[5]
ELBERT H. GARY[6]
OSCAR WILDE
WOODROW WILSON
JOHN H. PATTERSON[7]
ANDREW JACKSON
ENRICO CARUSO[8]

Your own knowledge of biography will enable you to add to this list. Find, if you can, a single individual in all the history of civilization who achieved outstanding success in any calling who was not driven by a well-developed sexual nature.

If you do not wish to rely upon biographies of persons who are no longer alive, take inventory of those whom you know to be individuals of great achievement today and see if you can find one among them who does not have high sexual energy.

It may be a controversial contention, but sexual energy is the creative energy of virtually all geniuses. *There never has been and never will be a great leader, builder, or artist lacking in this driving force of sex.*

Surely no one will misunderstand these statements to mean that ALL who are highly sexed are geniuses! Individuals attain the status of genius ONLY when, and IF, they stimulate their mind so that it draws upon the forces available through the creative faculty of the imagination. Chief among the stimuli which can produce this stepping up of mental functions is sex energy. The mere *possession* of this energy itself is not sufficient to produce a genius. The energy must be *transmuted* from desire for merely physical contact, into some *other* form of desire and action before it will lift one to the status of a genius.

Far from becoming geniuses because of great sex desires, the majority of people lower themselves, through misunderstanding and misuse of this great force, to the status of the lower animals.

Why Most People Seldom Succeed Before 40

I discovered from the analysis of more than 25,000 people that individuals who succeed in an outstanding way seldom do so before the age of 40, and more often they do not strike their real pace until they are well beyond 50. This fact was so astounding that it prompted me to go into the study of its cause most carefully, carrying the investigation over a period of more than 12 years.

This study disclosed the fact that one major reason why the majority of people who succeed do not begin to do so before the age of 40 to 50 is their tendency to DISSIPATE their energies through overindulgence in the *physical* expression of the emotion of sex. Most people never learn that the sexual urge has other possibilities which far transcend in importance that of mere physical expression. The majority of those who do make this discovery, do so *after having wasted many years* at a period when sexual energy is at its height, prior to the age of 45 to 50. This usually is followed by noteworthy achievement.

The lives of many people up to and sometimes well past the age of 40 reflect a continued dissipation of energies, which could have been more profitably turned into better channels. Their finer and more powerful emotions are sown wildly to the four winds. Out of this habit grew the term, "sowing one's wild oats."

The desire for sexual expression is by far the strongest and most impelling of all the human emotions, and for this very reason this desire — when harnessed and transmuted into action other than that of physical expression — may lift one into the "genius mode."[9]

History is not lacking in examples of individuals who sometimes attained the status of genius with the aid of artificial mind stimulants in the form of alcohol and narcotics. Edgar Allen Poe wrote "The Raven" while under the influence of liquor, "dreaming dreams that mortal never dared to dream before." James Whitcomb Riley[10] did some amazing writing while under the influence of alcohol.

Perhaps it was thus he saw "the ordered intermingling of the real and the dream, the mill above the river, and the mist above the stream." Robert Burns wrote under the influence of intoxicants the immortal words, "For Auld Lang Syne, my dear, we'll take a cup of kindness yet, for Auld Lang Syne."

But let it be remembered that many such individuals have destroyed themselves in the end.[11] Nature has prepared her own potions — for example, deep love, sexual drive, and the power of autosuggestion — with which people may *safely* stimulate their minds so they function on a higher plane that enables them to tune in to fine and rare thoughts which come from — no one knows where! No satisfactory substitute for Nature's natural stimulants has ever been found.

The world is ruled and the destiny of civilization is established by the human emotions. People are influenced in their actions not by reason so much as by feelings. The creative faculty of the mind is set into action entirely by emotions *and not by cold reason*. The most powerful of all human emotions is that of sex. There are other mind stimulants, some of which have been listed, but no one of them, nor all of them combined, can equal the driving power of sex.

A mind stimulant is any influence which will either temporarily or permanently increase significantly the freedom, intensity, and concentration of thought. The 10 Mind Stimuli described earlier are those most commonly used. Through these sources, or combinations of them, one may commune with Infinite Intelligence or enter, at will, the storehouse of the subconscious mind — either one's own, or that of another person, a procedure *which is all there is of genius*.

A teacher, who has trained and directed the efforts of more than 30,000 people involved in sales, made the astounding discovery that individuals with high sex drives generally make the most efficient salespeople. The explanation is that the factor of personality known as personal magnetism is nothing more nor less than sex energy. Individuals with high sex drives always have a plentiful supply of personal magnetism. Through cultivation and understanding, this vital force may be drawn upon and used to great advantage in relationships with other people. This powerful energy may be communicated to others through the following:

1. *The handshake.* The touch of the hand indicates instantly the presence of magnetism or the lack of it.
2. *The tone of voice.* Magnetism, or sex energy, is the factor with which the voice may be colored or made musical and charming.
3. *Posture and carriage of the body.* People with high sexual energy move briskly and with grace and ease.
4. *The vibrations of thought.* Highly sexual people, perhaps unconsciously, mix the emotion of sex with their thoughts, or may do so at will, and in that way may influence those around them.
5. *Body adornment.* People with high sex drives are usually very careful about their personal appearance. They usually select clothing of a style becoming to their personality, physique, complexion, etc.

When employing salespeople, the more capable sales manager looks for the quality of personal magnetism as the *first requirement* of a sales representative. Men and women who lack sex energy will never become enthusiastic nor inspire others with enthusiasm, and enthusiasm is one of the most important requisites in salesmanship, no matter what one is selling. The public speaker, orator, preacher, lawyer, or salesperson who is lacking in sex energy is generally a flop when it comes to being able to influence others. Couple with this the fact that most people can be influenced only through an appeal to their emotions, and you will understand the importance of sexual energy as a part of the salesperson's native ability. Top salespeople attain the status of mastery in selling because they either consciously or unconsciously *transmute* the energy of sex into SALES ENTHUSIASM! In this statement may be found a very practical suggestion as to the actual meaning of sex transmutation.

Salespeople who know how to take their mind off the subject of sex itself and direct that energy into sales effort—with as much enthusiasm and determination as they would apply it to its original purpose—have already acquired the art of sex transmutation whether they know it or not. The majority of salespeople who transmute their sex energy do so without being in the least aware of what they are doing or how they are doing it.

Transmutation of sex energy calls for more willpower than the average person cares to use for this purpose. Those who find it difficult to summon willpower sufficient for transmutation may gradually acquire this ability. Though this requires willpower, the reward for the practice is more than worth the effort.

The entire subject of sex is one about which the majority of people appear to be unpardonably ignorant. The sexual urge has been grossly misunderstood, slandered, and burlesqued by the ignorant and the evil minded for so long that the very word "sex" has taken on lascivious and often sordid connotations. Men and women who are known to be blessed—yes, BLESSED—with high sex drives are frequently looked upon with suspicion and even contempt. Instead of being considered normal, healthy, and blessed, they are often considered abnormal, flawed, and even base.

Millions of people, even in this age of enlightenment, have inferiority complexes which they developed because of this false belief that a high sex drive is a curse. Yet statements about the virtue of sexual energy should *not* be construed as a justification for the libertine. The emotion of sex is a virtue ONLY when used intelligently and with discrimination. It may be misused, and often is, to such an extent that it debases, instead of enriches, both body and mind. The better use of this power is the purpose of the explanations in this chapter.

It seemed quite significant when I discovered that practically every great leader whom I had the privilege of analyzing was a person whose achievements were largely inspired by someone that individual loved deeply. In many instances, the beloved was a modest, self-denying spouse of whom the public had heard little or nothing, although in a few instances the source of inspiration turned out to be a lover. Perhaps such cases may not be entirely unknown to you.

Intemperance in sex habits is just as detrimental as intemperance in habits of drinking and eating. In the age we live in, sexual intemperance is common. This orgy of indulgence may help account for the relative shortage of great leaders today. No individual can avail himself or herself of the forces of Creative Imagination while dissipating them. Human beings are the only creatures on earth which violate Nature's purpose in this connection. Every other animal indulges its sexual nature in moderation and with purpose which harmonizes with the laws of nature. Every other animal responds to the call of sex only "in season." Human beings are inclined to declare "open season."

Every intelligent person knows that stimulation in excess through alcoholic drink and narcotics is a form of intemperance which destroys the vital organs of the body, including the brain. Not every person knows, however, that over indulgence in sexual expression may become a habit as destructive and as detrimental to creative effort as narcotics or liquor.

A sex-obsessed individual is not essentially different from a drug addict! Both have lost control over their faculties of reason and willpower. Sexual overindulgence may not only destroy reason and willpower, but it may also lead to either temporary or permanent mental dysfunction. Many cases of hypochondria (imaginary illness) grow out of habits developed in ignorance of the true function of sex.

From these brief references to the subject, it may be readily seen that ignorance on the subject of sex transmutation forces stupendous penalties upon the ignorant, on the one hand, and withholds from them equally tremendous benefits, on the other.

Widespread ignorance on the subject of sex is due to the fact that the subject has been surrounded with mystery and beclouded by dark silence. The conspiracy of mystery and silence has had the same effect upon the minds of young people that the psychology of prohibition had. The result has been increased curiosity and desire to acquire more knowledge on this forbidden subject. And to the great shame of all lawmakers and most physicians — who by training are best qualified to educate youth on that subject —

appropriate information has all too often not been made readily available.

Seldom does an individual enter upon highly creative effort in any field of endeavor before the age of 40. The average person reaches the period of greatest capacity to create between 40 and 60. These statements are based upon careful observation and analysis of thousands of men and women. They should be encouraging to those who fail to arrive before the age of 40, and to those who become frightened at the approach of old age. The years between 40 and 50 are, as a rule, the most fruitful. Individuals should approach this age not with fear and trembling, but with hope and eager anticipation.

If you want evidence that most people do not begin to do their best work before the age of 40, study the records of the most successful individuals known to the American people, and you will find it. Henry Ford had not hit his pace of achievement until he had passed the age of 40. Andrew Carnegie was well past 40 before he began to reap the reward of his efforts. James J. Hill was still running a telegraph key at the age of 40. His stupendous achievements took place after that age.[12] Biographies of American industrialists and financiers are filled with evidence that the period from age 40 to 60 is the most productive age for almost everyone.

Between the ages of 30 and 40, people begin to learn (if they ever learn), the art of sex transmutation. This discovery is generally accidental, and, more often than otherwise, individuals who make it are totally unconscious of their discovery. They may observe that their powers of achievement have increased around the age of 35 to 40, but in most cases they are not familiar with the cause of this change — the fact that Nature begins to harmonize the emotions of love and sex in the individual between the ages of 30 and 40 so that they may draw upon these great forces and apply them jointly as stimuli to action.

Sex alone is a mighty urge to action, but its forces are like a cyclone — they are often uncontrollable. When the emotion of love begins to mix itself with the emotion of sex, the result is calmness of purpose, poise, accuracy of judgment, and balance. What person who has attained the age of 40 is so unfortunate as to be unable to analyze these statements and to corroborate them by his or her own experience?

When driven by the desire to please a member of the opposite sex, based solely upon the emotion of sex, individuals may be and usually are capable of great achievement, but their actions may be disorganized, distorted, and totally destructive. When driven by their desire to please someone they love, based upon the motive of sex alone, an individual may steal, cheat — even, in an extreme case, commit murder. But when the emotion of LOVE is mixed with the emotion of sex, these same individuals will guide their actions with sanity, balance, and reason.

Criminologists have discovered that some of the most hardened criminals can be reformed through the influence of a strong love. There is no record of a criminal's having been reformed solely through the influence of sex. These facts are well known, but their cause is not. Reformation comes, if at all, through the heart, or the emotional side, not through the head, or the reasoning side. Reformation means, "a change of heart." It does not mean a "change of head." A person may, because of reason, make certain changes in his or her personal conduct to avoid the consequences of undesirable effects, but GENUINE REFORMATION comes only through a change of heart — through a DESIRE to change.

Love, romance, and sex are all emotions capable of driving individuals to heights of super-achievement. Love is the emotion which serves as a safety valve and ensures balance, poise, and constructive effort. When combined, these three emotions may lift one to the "altitude" of a genius. There are geniuses, however, who know but little of the emotion of love. Most of them may be found engaged in some form of action which is destructive or at least not based upon justice and fairness toward others. If good taste would permit, a dozen geniuses could be named in the field of industry and finance who ride ruthlessly over the rights of their fellow human beings. They seem totally lacking in conscience. The reader can easily supply his own list of such individuals.

The emotions are states of mind. Nature has provided human beings with a chemistry of the mind which operates in a manner similar to the principles of chemistry of matter. It is a well-known fact that through the aid of the science of chemistry, a chemist can create a deadly poison by mixing certain elements, none of which are in themselves harmful.[13] The emotions may likewise be combined so as to create a deadly poison. The emotions of sex and jealousy, when mixed, may turn a person into an insane beast.

The presence of any one or more of the destructive emotions in the human mind, through the chemistry of the mind, creates a poison which may destroy one's sense of justice and fairness. In extreme cases, the presence of any combination of these emotions in the mind may destroy one's reason.

The road to genius consists of the development, control, and proper use of sex, love, and romance. The process involves *encouraging* the presence of these emotions as the dominating thoughts in one's mind, and *discouraging* the presence of all the destructive emotions. The mind is a creature of habit. It thrives upon the *dominating* thoughts that are fed to it. Through the faculty of willpower, one may discourage the presence of any emotion and encourage the presence of any other. Control of the mind, through the power of will, is not difficult. Control comes from persistence and habit. The secret of control lies in understanding the process of transmutation. *When any negative emotion presents itself in one's mind, it can be transmuted into a positive, or constructive emotion, by the simple procedure of changing one's thoughts.*[14]

THERE IS NO OTHER ROAD TO GENIUS THAN THROUGH VOLUNTARY SELF EFFORT! Individuals may, for a time, attain great heights of financial, business, or other achievement solely by the driving force of sex energy, but history is filled with evidence that such people may, and usually do, carry with them certain traits of character which rob them of the ability to either keep or enjoy their fortune. This is worthy of analysis, thought, and meditation, for it states a truth, the knowledge of which may be helpful to all men and women. Ignorance of this truth has cost thousands of people their privilege of HAPPINESS, even though they possessed riches.

The emotion of love brings out and develops the artistic and one's artistic and esthetic nature. It leaves its impress upon one's very soul, even after the "fire" has been subdued by time and circumstance. Memories of love never pass. They linger, guide, and influence long after the source of stimulation has faded. There is nothing new in this. Every person who has been moved by GENUINE LOVE knows that it leaves enduring traces upon the human heart. The effect of love endures because love is spiritual in nature. Individuals who cannot be stimulated to great heights of achievement by love are, sadly, hopeless—they are dead, though they may seem to live. Even the memories of love are sufficient to lift one to a higher plane of creative effort. The major force of love may spend itself and pass away like a fire which has burned itself out, but it leaves behind indelible marks as evidence that it passed that way. Its departure often prepares the human heart for a still greater love.

So go back, at times, into your yesterdays and bathe your mind in the beautiful memories of past love. It will soften the influence of present worries and annoyances. It will give you a source of escape from the unpleasant realities of life, and just maybe—who knows?—your mind will yield to you, during this temporary retreat, some idea or plan which may change the entire financial or spiritual status of your life.

If you believe yourself unfortunate because you have loved and lost, perish the thought. One who has loved truly can never lose entirely. Love is whimsical and temperamental. Its nature is ephemeral and transitory. It comes when it pleases and goes away without warning. Accept and enjoy it while it remains, but spend no time worrying about its departure. Worry will never bring it back.

Dismiss also the thought that love never comes but once. Love may come and go, times without number, but there are no two love experiences which affect one in just the same way. There may be, and there usually is, one love experience which leaves a deeper imprint on the heart than all the others, but all love experiences are beneficial except to the person who becomes resentful and cynical when love makes its departure.

There should be no disappointment over love, and there would be none if people understood the difference between the emotion of love and the emotion of sex. The major difference is that love is spiritual, while sex is biological. Love is chemistry; sex is physics. No experience that touches the human heart with a spiritual force can possibly be harmful, except through ignorance or jealousy.

Love is, without question, life's greatest experience. It brings one into communion with Infinite Intelligence. When mixed with the emotions of romance and sex, it may lead one far up the ladder of creative effort. The emotions of love, sex, and romance are sides of the eternal triangle of achievement-building genius. Nature creates geniuses through no other force.[15]

Love is an emotion with many sides, shades, and colors. The love which one feels for parents or children is quite different from that which one feels for one's sweetheart. The one is mixed with the emotion of sex, while the other is not.

The love which one feels in true friendship is not the same as that felt for one's beloved, parents, or children, but it, too, is a form of love.

Then there is the emotion of love for things inanimate, such as the love of Nature's handiwork. But the most intense and burning of all these various kinds of love is that which is experienced in the blending of the emotions of love and sex. Marriages that are not blessed with the eternal affinity of love and sex, properly balanced and proportioned, cannot be fully happy ones — and seldom endure. Love alone will not bring happiness in marriage, nor will sex alone. But when these two beautiful emotions are blended, marriage may bring about a state of mind which is closest to the spiritual that one may ever know during earthly existence. When the emotion of romance is added to those of love and sex, the obstructions between the finite human mind and Infinite Intelligence can be removed. Genius status can be attained. And *The Tenth Step to Riches* can be mastered.

*Positive and negative emotions cannot
occupy the mind at the same time.*
ONE OR THE OTHER MUST DOMINATE.

Chapter 11

THE SUBCONSCIOUS MIND
The Connecting Link
The Eleventh Step to Riches

THE SUBCONSCIOUS MIND consists of a field of conscious-ness in which every impulse of thought or sensation that reaches the objective mind through any of the five senses is classified and recorded, and from which thoughts may be recalled or withdrawn as letters may be taken from a filing cabinet.

The subconscious mind receives and files sense impressions or thoughts regardless of their nature. You may VOLUNTARILY plant in your subconscious mind any plan, thought, or purpose which you desire to translate into its physical or monetary equivalent. The subconscious acts first on the dominating desires which have been mixed with emotional feeling, such as FAITH.

Consider this in connection with the instructions given in Chapter 1 on DESIRE for taking the six actions there outlined, and also the instructions given in Chapter 6 on formulating and executing plans, and you will understand the importance of the thought conveyed in the preceding paragraph.

THE SUBCONSCIOUS MIND WORKS DAY AND NIGHT. Through a method or procedure that is not yet understood, the subconscious mind draws upon the forces of Infinite Intelligence for the power with which it voluntarily transmutes one's desires into their physical equivalent, making use always of the most practical media by which this end may be accomplished.

You cannot *entirely* control your subconscious mind, but you can voluntarily hand over to it any plan, desire, or purpose which you wish transformed into concrete form. Read again the instructions for using the subconscious mind in Chapter 3. There is plenty of evidence to support the belief that the subconscious mind is the connecting link between the finite human mind and Infinite Intelligence. It is the intermediary through which one may draw upon the forces of Infinite Intelligence at will. It alone contains the secret process by which mental impulses are modified and changed into their spiritual equivalent. It alone is the medium through which prayer may be transmitted to the source which is capable of answering prayer.

The possibilities of creative effort connected with the subconscious mind are stupendous and imponderable. They inspire one with awe. I never approach the discussion of the subconscious mind without a feeling of littleness and inferiority, which is due, perhaps, to the fact that our entire stock of knowledge on this subject is so pitifully limited. The very fact that the subconscious mind is the medium of communication between the thinking human mind and Infinite Intelligence is in itself a thought which almost paralyzes one's reason.

After you have accepted as a reality the existence of the subconscious mind and *understand* its possibilities as a medium for transmuting your DESIRES into their physical or monetary equivalent, you will comprehend the full significance of the instructions given in Chapter 1 on DESIRE. You will also understand why you have been repeatedly admonished to MAKE YOUR DESIRES CLEAR AND TO REDUCE THEM TO WRITING. You will also understand the necessity of PERSISTENCE in carrying out instructions.

The instructions involved in *The 13 Steps to Riches* are the stimuli with which you acquire the ability to reach and to influence your subconscious mind. Do not become discouraged if you cannot do this upon the first attempt. Remember that the subconscious mind may be voluntarily directed *only through habit*, using the directions given in Chapter 2 on FAITH. You have not yet had time to master faith. Be patient. Be persistent.

A good many statements in the chapters on faith and auto-suggestion will be repeated here for the benefit of YOUR sub-conscious mind. Remember, your subconscious mind functions automatically *whether you make any effort to influence it or not*. This naturally suggests to you that thoughts of fear and poverty and all negative thoughts serve as stimuli to your subconscious mind — *unless* you master these impulses and give your subconscious mind more desirable food upon which it may feed.

The subconscious mind will not remain idle! If you fail to plant DESIRES in your subconscious mind, it will feed upon the thoughts which reach it as the *result of your neglect*. It has already been explained that thought impulses, both negative and positive, reach the subconscious mind continuously from the four sources mentioned in Chapter 10.

For the present, it is sufficient if you remember that you are living *daily* in the midst of all manner of thought impulses which are reaching your subconscious mind without your knowledge or awareness. Some of these impulses are negative, some are positive. You are now engaged in trying to help shut off the flow of negative impulses and to aid in voluntarily influencing your subconscious mind through positive impulses of DESIRE.

When you achieve this, you will possess the key which unlocks the door to your subconscious mind. Moreover, you will control that door so completely that no undesirable thought will influence your subconscious mind.

Everything which human beings create BEGINS in the form of a thought impulse. No one can create anything which he or she does not first conceive in THOUGHT. Through the aid of the imagination, thought impulses may be assembled into plans. The imagination, when under control, may be used for the creation of plans or purposes that lead to success in one's chosen occupation.

All thought impulses which are intended for transmutation into their physical equivalent and which are voluntarily planted in the subconscious mind must pass through the imagination and be mixed with faith. The mixing of faith with a plan, or purpose, intended for submission to the subconscious mind may be done ONLY through the imagination.

From these statements you will readily observe that the voluntary use of the subconscious mind calls for the coordination and application of all the principles of success explained in this book.

Ella Wheeler Wilcox[1] gave evidence of her understanding of the power of the subconscious mind when she wrote:

"You never can tell what a thought will do
  In bringing you hate or love —
For thoughts are things, and their airy wings
  Are swifter than carrier doves.

They follow the law of the universe —
  Each thing creates its kind,

And they speed o'er the track to bring you back
  Whatever went out from your mind."

Mrs. Wilcox understood the truth that thoughts which go out from one's mind also embed themselves deeply in one's subconscious mind, where they serve as a magnet, pattern, or blueprint by which the subconscious mind is influenced while translating them into their physical equivalent. Thoughts are truly things, for the reason that every material thing begins in the form of "thought-energy."

The subconscious mind is more susceptible to influence by impulses of thought which are mixed with feeling or emotion than by those originating solely in the reasoning portion of the mind. In fact, there is much evidence to support the theory that ONLY emotionalized thoughts have any ACTION influence upon the subconscious mind. It is a well-known fact that emotion or feeling rules the majority of people. If it is true that the subconscious mind responds more quickly to, and is influenced more readily by, thought impulses which are energized with emotion, then it is essential to become familiar with the more important of the emotions. There are seven major positive emotions and seven major negative emotions. The negatives automatically inject themselves into the thought impulses, which ensures their passage into the subconscious mind. The positives *must be injected*, through the principle of autosuggestion, into the thought impulses which an individual wishes to pass on to his or her subconscious mind. (Instructions for accomplishing this are given in Chapter 3 on Autosuggestion.)

These emotions, or feeling impulses, may be likened to yeast in a loaf of bread because they constitute the ACTION element which transforms thought impulses from the passive to the active state. Thus may one understand why thought impulses which have been well mixed with emotion are acted upon more readily than thought impulses originating in cold reason.

You are preparing yourself to influence and control the "inner audience" of your subconscious mind in order to hand over to it the DESIRE for money, which you wish transmuted into its monetary equivalent. It is essential, therefore, that you understand the method of approach to this inner audience. You must speak its language or it will not heed your call. It understands best the language of emotion or feeling. Let me, therefore, describe here the seven major positive emotions and the seven major negative emotions, so that you may draw upon the positives and avoid the negatives when giving instructions to your subconscious mind.

The Seven Major Positive Emotions

> The emotion of DESIRE
> The emotion of FAITH
> The emotion of LOVE
> The emotion of SEX
> The emotion of ENTHUSIASM
> The emotion of ROMANCE
> The emotion of HOPE

There are other positive emotions, but these are the seven most powerful and the ones most commonly used in creative effort. Master these seven emotions (they can be mastered only by USE), and the other positive emotions will be at your command when you need them. Remember, in this connection, that you are studying a book which is intended to help you develop money-consciousness by *filling your mind with positive emotions*. One does not become money-conscious by filling one's mind with negative emotions.

The Seven Major Negative Emotions
(To be avoided)

The emotion of FEAR
The emotion of JEALOUSY
The emotion of HATRED
The emotion of REVENGE
The emotion of GREED
The emotion of SUPERSTITION
The emotion of ANGER

Positive and negative emotions cannot occupy the mind at the same time. One or the other must dominate. It is your responsibility to make sure that positive emotions constitute the dominating influence of your mind. Here the LAW OF HABIT will come to your aid. *Form the habit* of applying and using the positive emotions! Eventually, they will dominate your mind so completely that the negatives *cannot* enter it.

Only by following these instructions literally, and continuously, can you gain control over your subconscious mind. The presence of a single powerful negative thought or feeling in your conscious mind is sufficient to *destroy* all chances of constructive aid from your subconscious mind.[2]

If you are an observant person, you must have noticed that most people resort to prayer ONLY AFTER everything else has FAILED! Or else they pray by a ritual of meaningless words. And because it is a fact that most people who pray do so ONLY AFTER EVERYTHING ELSE HAS FAILED, they go to prayer with their minds filled with FEAR and DOUBT, *which are the emotions the subconscious mind acts* upon and passes on to Infinite Intelligence. Likewise, those are the emotions which Infinite Intelligence receives and ACTS UPON.

If you pray for a thing, but have fear as you pray that you may not receive it or that your prayer will not be acted upon by Infinite Intelligence, your prayer *will have been in vain.*

Prayer does sometimes result in the realization of that for which one prays. If you have ever had the experience of receiving that for which you prayed, go back in your memory and recall your actual STATE OF MIND while you were praying, and you will know for sure that the theory here described is more than a theory.

The time may come when the schools and educational institutions of the country will teach the "science of prayer." When that time comes (it will come as soon as humanity is ready for it and demands it), no one will approach the Universal Mind (Infinite Intelligence) in a state of fear, for the very good reason that there will be no such emotion as fear. Ignorance, superstition, and false teaching will have disappeared, and human beings will have attained their true status as children of Infinite Intelligence. A few have already attained this blessing.

If you believe this prophesy is farfetched, take a look at the human race in retrospect. Less than a hundred years ago, people believed that lightning was evidence of the wrath of God and feared it. Now, thanks to the power of FAITH, we have harnessed lightning and made it turn the wheels of industry. Much less than a hundred years ago, people believed the space between the planets to be nothing but a great void, a stretch of dead nothingness. Now, thanks to this same power of FAITH, we know that far from being either dead or a void, the space between the planets is very much alive, that it is filled with mysterious substances and pulsates with energy — the highest form of energy known, except perhaps for the energy of THOUGHT! Moreover, there is evidence that this living, pulsating, vibratory energy which permeates every atom of matter and fills every niche of space,[3] connects every human brain with other human brains in mysterious ways we do not yet understand.

Why should we not believe that this same energy connects every human brain with Infinite Intelligence? There are no tollgates between the finite human mind and Infinite Intelligence. The communication costs nothing except Patience, Faith, Persistence,

Understanding, and a SINCERE DESIRE to communicate. Moreover, the approach can be made only by each individual. Paid prayers are worthless. Infinite Intelligence does no business by proxy. You either go direct or you do not communicate. You may buy prayer books and repeat them until the day of your doom without avail. Thoughts which you wish to communicate to Infinite Intelligence must undergo transformation such as can be given only through your own subconscious mind. The method by which you may communicate with Infinite Intelligence is analogous to that through which the vibration of sound is communicated by radio. If you understand the working principle of radio, you know that sound cannot be communicated through the airwaves until it has been stepped up or changed into a rate of vibration which the human ear cannot detect. The radio processing and transmitting equipment takes the sound of the human voice and scrambles or modifies it by stepping up the vibration millions of times. Only in this way can the vibration of sound be communicated hundreds or thousands of miles away. After this transformation has taken place, the original vibrations of sound—now in the form of highly energized electromagnetic waves—are broadcast across the airwaves to radio receivers, which step that energy back down to its original state so that it is recognized as sound.

Similarly, the subconscious mind is the intermediary which translates one's prayers into terms which Infinite Intelligence utilizes, presents the message, and receives back the answer in the form of a definite plan or idea for procuring the object of the prayer. Understand this principle and you will know why mere words read from a prayer book—while they may provide comfort and give one cause for reflection and meditation—cannot and will never serve as an agency of active communication between the human mind and Infinite Intelligence. Before your prayer will "reach" Infinite Intelligence (a statement of this author's theory only), it is transformed in some way from its original "thought vibration" into terms of "spiritual vibration."

Faith is the only known agency which will give your thoughts a spiritual nature in this way. FAITH and FEAR make poor bedfellows. Where one is found, the other cannot exist.

Chapter 12

THE BRAIN
A Broadcasting and Receiving Station for Thought
The Twelfth Step to Riches

MORE THAN 20 years ago, I, working in conjunction with Dr. Alexander Graham Bell and Dr. Elmer R. Gates, observed that every human brain is both a "broadcasting" and a "receiving" station for the impulses of thought.

Under the right circumstances and in a fashion that may be likened to that employed by the radio broadcasting principle, every human brain is capable of "picking up" thought impulses which originate in the brains of others.

In connection with the statement in the preceding paragraph, compare and consider the description of the Creative Imagination as outlined in the discussion on Imagination in Chapter 5. The Creative Imagination is the receiving set of the brain, which processes thoughts released by the brains of others. It is the agency of communication between one's own conscious or reasoning mind and the four sources from which one may receive thought stimuli (i.e., Infinite Intelligence, one's own subconscious mind, the "highly energized" conscious mind of another person, and the subconscious storehouse of another person. See the discussion on the Sixth Sense in Chapter 10.)

Creative Imagination is the mechanism by which intuition and hunches seem to spring out of thin air, and by which two or more people, working closely together in a state of intense concentration and focus, seem to anticipate each other's next thoughts, actions, insights, and even actual words.[1]

When thus highly stimulated, or stepped up, the mind becomes more receptive to thought impulses that somehow reach it from sources outside itself. This stepping-up process is driven by powerful emotions, either positive or negative.

Thought manifests itself as electrical energy within the human brain. Only highly intensified or "energized" thought impulses are transmitted from one brain to another through this mysterious and still not understood process. Thought which has been modified or stepped up by any of the major emotions is the only type of thought which passes from one brain to another through the "broadcasting machinery" of the human brain.

The emotion of sex stands at the head of the list of human emotions as far as intensity and driving force are concerned. The brain which has been stimulated by the emotion of sex is much more highly energized than it is when that emotion is dormant or absent. (To reiterate an earlier point, "stimulated by the emotion of sex" refers to a sex drive that is vigorous and powerful, yet under control, channeled, and given adequate and appropriate expression.)

The result of sex transmutation is the increase of this energizing effect on thoughts and thought processes to such a pitch that the Creative Imagination becomes highly receptive to ideas, which it seems to literally pluck out of thin air. When the brain is operating in this highly energized state, it not only attracts thoughts and ideas released by other brains, but it also gives to its own thoughts that feeling which is essential before those thoughts will be picked up and acted upon by one's own subconscious mind.

Thus, you will see that the broadcasting principle is the factor through which you mix feeling or emotion with your thoughts and pass them on to your subconscious mind.

The subconscious mind is the sending station of the brain, through which thought impulses are broadcast. The Creative Imagination is the receiving set, through which thought impulses are picked up. Along with the important factors of the subconscious mind and the faculty of the Creative Imagination, which together constitute the sending and receiving sets of your mental broadcasting equipment, consider now the principle of autosuggestion, which is the medium by which you may put into operation your broadcasting station.

Through the instructions described in Chapter 3 on Autosuggestion, you were definitely and specifically shown the method by which DESIRE may be transmuted into its monetary equivalent.

Operation of your mental broadcasting station is a comparatively simple procedure. You have but three factors to bear in mind and apply when you wish to use your broadcasting station— the SUBCONSCIOUS MIND, CREATIVE IMAGINATION, and AUTOSUGGESTION. The stimuli through which you put these three forces into action have been described. The procedure begins with DESIRE.

The Greatest Forces Are Intangible

The world has been brought to the very borderline of an understanding of the forces that are intangible and unseen. Throughout history, people have depended too much upon their physical senses and have limited their knowledge to physical things they could see, touch, weigh, and measure.

We are now entering the most marvelous of all ages—an age which will teach us something of the intangible forces of the world about us. Perhaps we shall learn as we pass through this age that the "other self" is more powerful than the physical self we see when we look in a mirror.

Sometimes people speak lightly of the intangibles—the things they cannot perceive through any of their five senses—and when we hear such people speak, it should remind us that *all of us are controlled by forces which are unseen and intangible.*

The whole human race has not the power to cope with nor control the intangible force wrapped up in the rolling waves of the oceans. We still do not have the ability to understand the intangible force of gravity, which keeps this little earth suspended in mid-air and keeps us from falling from it, much less the power to control that force. We are entirely subservient to the intangible force that comes with a thunderstorm, and we are just as helpless in the presence of the intangible force of electricity — we do not even fully understand what electricity is, where it comes from, or what is its ultimate purpose!

Nor is this by any means the end of our ignorance in connection with things unseen and intangible. We do not understand the intangible force (and intelligence) wrapped up in the soil and resources of the earth — *the force which provides us with every morsel of food we eat, every article of clothing we wear, every dollar we carry in our pockets.*

The Dramatic Story of the Brain

Last, but not least, we — with all of our boasted culture and education — understand little or nothing of the intangible force (the greatest of all the intangibles) of *thought*. We know but little concerning the physical brain and its vast network of intricate structures through which the power of thought is translated into its material equivalent, but we are now entering an age which shall yield enlightenment on the subject. Already scientists have turned their attention to the study of this stupendous thing called a brain, and, while they are still in the kindergarten stage of their studies, they have uncovered enough knowledge to know that the "central switchboard" of the human brain, the number of lines which connect the brain cells one with another, equals the figure one, followed by 15 million zeros!

"The figure is so stupendous," said Dr. C. Judson Herrick of the University of Chicago, "that astronomical figures dealing with hundreds of millions of light years, become insignificant by comparison....It has been determined that there are from 10 billion to 14 billion nerve cells in the human cerebral cortex, and we know that these are arranged in definite patterns. These arrangements are not haphazard. They are orderly. Recently developed methods... draw off action currents from very precisely located cells...amplify them...and record potential differences to a millionth of a volt."

It is inconceivable that such a network of intricate equipment should be in existence for the sole purpose of carrying on the physical functions incidental to growth and maintenance of the physical body. Is it not likely that the same system that gives billions of brain cells the media for communication one with another, provides also the means of communication with other intangible forces?

After this book had been written, and just before the manuscript went to the publisher, there appeared in *The New York Times* an editorial showing that at least one great university and one intelligent investigator in the field of mental phenomena were carrying on organized research through which conclusions were reached that parallel many of those described in this and the following chapter. The editorial briefly analyzed the work carried on by Dr. Rhine and his associates at Duke University.

What is Telepathy?

A month ago we cited on this page some of the remarkable results achieved by Professor Rhine and his associates [at] Duke University from more than a hundred thousand tests to determine the existence of "telepathy" and "clairvoyance." These results were summarized in the first two articles in *Harper Magazine*. In the second that has now appeared, the author, E. H. Wright, attempts to summarize what has been learned, or what it seems reasonable to infer, regarding the exact nature of these "extrasensory" modes of perception.

The actual existence of telepathy and clairvoyance now seems to some scientists enormously probable as the result of Rhine's experiments. Various percipients were asked to name as many cards in a special pack as they could without looking at them and without other sensory access to them. About a score of men and women were discovered who could regularly name so many of the cards correctly that "there was not one chance in many a million...of their having done their feats by luck or accident."

But how did they do them? These powers, assuming that they exist, do not seem to be sensory. There is no known organ for them. The experiments worked just as well at distances of several hundred miles as they did in the same room. These facts also dispose, in Mr. Wright's opinion, of the attempt to explain telepathy or clairvoyance through any physical theory of radiation. All known forms of radiant energy decline inversely as the square of the distance traversed. Telepathy and clairvoyance do not. But they do vary through physical causes as our other mental powers do. Contrary to widespread opinion, they do not improve when the percipient is asleep or half-asleep, but, on the contrary, when he is most wide-awake and alert. Rhine discovered that a narcotic will invariably lower a percipient's score, while a stimulant will always send it higher. The most reliable performer apparently cannot make a good score unless he tries to do his best.

One conclusion Wright draws with some confidence is that telepathy and clairvoyance are one and the same gift. That is, the faculty that "sees" a card face down on a table seems to be exactly the same one that "reads" a thought residing only in another mind. There are several grounds for believing this. So far, for example, the two gifts have been found in every person who enjoys either of them. In every one so far the two have been of equal vigor, almost exactly. Screens, walls, distances, have no effect at all on either. Wright advances from this conclusion to express what he puts forward as no more than the mere hunch that other extra-sensory experiences, prophetic dreams, premonitions of disaster, and the like, may also prove to be part of the same faculty. The reader is not asked to accept any of these conclusions unless he finds it necessary, but the evidence that Rhine has piled up must remain impressive.

*   *   *

In view of Dr. Rhine's announcement in connection with the conditions under which the mind responds to what he terms "extrasensory modes of perception," I now feel privileged to add to his testimony by stating that my associates and I have discovered what we believe to be the ideal conditions under which the mind can be stimulated so that the Sixth Sense described in the next chapter can be made to function in a practical way.

The conditions to which I refer consist of a close working alliance between myself and two members of my staff. Through experimentation and practice, we discovered how to stimulate our minds (by applying the principle used in connection with the "Invisible Counselors" described in the next chapter) so that we can, by a process of "blending" our three minds into one, find the solution to a great variety of problems.

The procedure is simple. We sit down at a conference table, clearly state the nature of the problem we have under consideration, then begin discussing it. Each contributes whatever thoughts that may occur. The strange thing about this method of mind stimulation is that it places each participant in communication with unknown sources of knowledge definitely outside his own experience.

If you understand the principle described in Chapter 9 on the Master Mind, you of course recognize the round-table procedure here described as being a practical application of the Master Mind.[2] This method of mind stimulation, through harmonious discussion of definite subjects among three people, illustrates the simplest and most practical use of the Master Mind. *By adopting and following a similar plan, any student of this philosophy may come into possession of the famous Carnegie formula briefly described in the introduction.* If it means nothing to you at this time, mark this page and read it again after you have finished the final chapter.

*All individuals have become
what they are because of their*
DOMINATING THOUGHTS AND DESIRES.

Chapter 13

THE SIXTH SENSE
The Door to the Temple of Wisdom
The Thirteenth Step to Riches

THE THIRTEENTH STEP to Riches, the final step, is known as the SIXTH SENSE, through which Infinite Intelligence *may* and *will* communicate voluntarily, without any effort from or demands by the individual.

This principle is the apex of *The Think and Grow Rich Philosophy*. It can be assimilated, understood, and applied ONLY by first mastering the other 12 principles explained in the previous chapters.[1]

The SIXTH SENSE is that portion of the subconscious mind which has been referred to as Creative Imagination. It has also been referred to as the "receiving set" through which ideas, plans, and thoughts flash into the mind. These flashes are sometimes called hunches or inspirations.

The Sixth Sense defies description! It cannot be described to a person who has not mastered the other principles of this philosophy because such a person has no knowledge and no experience with which the Sixth Sense may be compared. Understanding of the Sixth Sense comes only by meditation through mind development *from within*. The Sixth Sense most likely is the medium of contact between the finite human mind and Infinite Intelligence, and for this reason *it is a mixture of both the mental and the spiritual*. It is believed to be the point at which the human mind contacts the Universal Mind.

After you have mastered all of the success principles explained in this book, you will be prepared to accept as truth a statement which may otherwise be incredible to you, namely:

Through the aid of the Sixth Sense, you will be warned of impending dangers in time to avoid them and notified of opportunities in time to embrace them.

With the development of the Sixth Sense, there comes to your aid, to do your bidding, a "Guardian Angel," who will open to you at all times the door to the Temple of Wisdom.

Whether or not this is a statement of truth you will never know except by following the instructions described in the pages of this book or some similar method of procedure.

I am not a believer in nor an advocate of miracles, for the reason that I have enough knowledge of Nature to understand that *Nature never deviates from her established laws*. Some of her laws are so incomprehensible that they produce what appear to be miracles. The Sixth Sense comes as near to being a miracle as anything I have ever experienced, and it appears so only because I do not understand the method by which this principle is operated.

This much I do know—there is a power, or a First Cause, or an Intelligence, which permeates every atom of matter and embraces every unit of energy perceptible to the human mind, and this Infinite Intelligence converts acorns into oak trees, causes water to flow downhill in response to the law of gravity, follows night with day, and winter with summer, each maintaining its proper place and relationship to the other. This Intelligence may, through the principles of *The Think and Grow Rich Philosophy*, be induced to aid in transmuting DESIRES into concrete, or material, form. I have this knowledge because I have experimented with it—and have EXPERIENCED IT.

Step by step through the preceding chapters, you have been led to this, the last principle. If you have mastered each of the preceding principles, you are now prepared to accept *without being skeptical* the stupendous claims made here. If you have not mastered the other principles, you must do so before you may determine definitely whether or not the claims made in this chapter are fact or fiction.

While I was passing through the age of hero worship, I found myself trying to imitate those whom I most admired. Moreover, I discovered that the element of FAITH, with which I endeavored to imitate my idols, gave me great capacity to do so quite successfully.

I have never entirely divested myself of this habit of hero worship, although I have passed the age commonly given over to such. My experience has taught me that the next best thing to being truly great is to emulate the great, by feeling and action, as nearly as possible.

Long before I had ever written a line for publication or endeavored to deliver a speech in public, I followed the habit of reshaping my own character by trying to imitate the nine individuals whose lives and life's work had been most impressive to me. These nine were Ralph Waldo Emerson, Thomas Paine, Thomas A. Edison, Charles Darwin, Abraham Lincoln, Luther Burbank, Napoleon Bonaparte, Henry Ford, and Andrew Carnegie. Every night over a long period of years, I held an imaginary Council meeting with this group whom I called my Invisible Counselors.

The procedure was this. Just before going to sleep at night, I would shut my eyes and see in my imagination this group of men seated with me around my Council Table. Here I had not only an opportunity to sit among those whom I considered to be great, but I actually dominated the group by serving as the chairman.

Before eyebrows are raised, let me assure you that I had a very DEFINITE PURPOSE in indulging my imagination through these nightly meetings. My purpose was to rebuild my own character so it would represent a composite of the characters of my imaginary counselors. Realizing as I did early in life that I had to overcome the handicap of being born into an environment of ignorance and superstition, I deliberately assigned myself the task of voluntary rebirth through the method here described.[2]

Building Character through Autosuggestion

Being an earnest student of psychology, I knew, of course, that all individuals have become what they are because of their

DOMINATING THOUGHTS AND DESIRES. I knew that every deeply seated desire has the effect of causing one to seek outward expression through which that desire may be transmuted into reality. I knew that self-suggestion is a powerful factor in building character, that it is, in fact, the sole principle through which character is built.

With this knowledge of the principles of mind operation, I was fairly well armed with the equipment needed to rebuild my character. In these imaginary Council meetings, I called on my Cabinet members for the knowledge I wished each to contribute, addressing myself to each member in audible words such as follows:

"Mr. Emerson, I desire to acquire from you the marvelous understanding of Nature which distinguished your life. I ask that you make an impression upon my subconscious mind of whatever qualities you possessed which enabled you to understand and adapt yourself to the laws of Nature. I ask that you assist me in reaching and drawing upon whatever sources of knowledge are available to this end.

"Mr. Burbank, I request that you pass on to me the knowledge which enabled you to so harmonize the laws of Nature that you caused the cactus to shed its thorns and become an edible food. Give me access to the knowledge which enabled you to make two blades of grass grow where but one grew before, and helped you to blend the coloring of the flowers with more splendor and harmony, for you alone have successfully 'gilded the lily.'

"Napoleon, I desire to acquire from you, by emulation, the marvelous ability you possessed to inspire men and to arouse them to greater and more determined spirit of action. Also to acquire the spirit of enduring FAITH, which enabled you to turn defeat into victory and to surmount staggering obstacles. Emperor of Fate, King of Chance, Man of Destiny, I salute you!

"Mr. Paine, I desire to acquire from you the freedom of thought and the courage and clarity with which to express convictions which so distinguished you!

"Mr. Darwin, I wish to acquire from you the marvelous patience and ability to study cause and effect, without bias or prejudice, so exemplified by you in the field of natural science.

"Mr. Lincoln, I desire to build into my own character the keen sense of justice, the untiring spirit of patience, the sense of humor, the human understanding, and the tolerance which were your distinguishing characteristics.

"Mr. Carnegie, I am already indebted to you for my choice of a life's work, which has brought me great happiness and peace of mind. I wish to acquire a thorough understanding of the principles of *organized effort* which you used so effectively in the building of a great industrial enterprise.

"Mr. Ford, you have been among the most helpful of the people who have supplied much of the material essential to my work. I wish to acquire your spirit of persistence, the determination, poise, and self-confidence which have enabled you to master poverty and to organize, unify, and simplify human effort, so that I may help others to follow in your footsteps.

"Mr. Edison, I have seated you nearest to me, at my right, because of the personal cooperation you have given me during my research into the causes of success and failure. I wish to acquire from you the marvelous spirit of FAITH with which you have uncovered so many of Nature's secrets, the spirit of unremitting toil with which you have so often wrested victory from defeat."

My method of addressing the members of the imaginary Cabinet would vary according to the traits of character in which I was for the moment most interested in acquiring. I studied the records of their lives with painstaking care. After some months of this nightly procedure, I was astounded by the discovery that these imaginary figures became apparently real.

Each of these nine men developed individual characteristics, which surprised me. For example, Lincoln developed the habit of always being late, then walking around in solemn parade. When he came, he walked very slowly with his hands clasped behind him, and once in a while, he would stop as he passed and rest his hand momentarily upon my shoulder. He always wore an expression of seriousness upon his face. Rarely did I see him smile. The cares of a sundered nation made him grave.

That was not true of the others. Burbank and Paine often indulged in witty repartee which seemed at times to shock the other members of the Cabinet. One night Paine suggested that I prepare a lecture on "The Age of Reason" and deliver it from the pulpit of a church which I formerly attended. Many around the table laughed heartily at the suggestion. Not Napoleon! He drew his mouth down at the corners and groaned so loudly that all turned and looked at him with amazement. To him the church was but a pawn of the state, not to be reformed, but to be used as a convenient inciter to mass activity by the people.

On one occasion Burbank was late. When he came, he was excited with enthusiasm and explained that he had been late because of an experiment he was conducting, through which he hoped to be able to grow apples on any sort of tree. Paine chided him by reminding him that it was an apple which started all the trouble between man and woman. Darwin chuckled heartily as he suggested that Paine should watch out for little serpents when he went into the forest to gather apples, as they had the habit of growing into big snakes. Emerson observed, "No serpents, no apples," and Napoleon remarked, "No apples, no state!"

Lincoln developed the habit of always being the last one to leave the table after each meeting. On one occasion, he leaned across the end of the table, his arms folded, and remained in that position for many minutes. I made no attempt to disturb him. Finally, he lifted his head slowly, got up and walked to the door, then turned around, came back, and laid his hand on my shoulder and said, "My boy, you will need much courage if you remain steadfast in carrying out your purpose in life. But remember, when difficulties overtake you, the common people have common sense. Adversity will develop it."

One evening Edison arrived ahead of all the others. He walked over and seated himself at my left, where Emerson was accustomed to sit, and said, "You are destined to witness the discovery of the secret of life. When the time comes, you will observe that life consists of great swarms of energy, or entities, each as intelligent as human beings *think* themselves to be. These units of life group together like hives of bees and remain together until they disintegrate *through lack of harmony*. These units have differences of opinion, the same as human beings, and often fight among themselves. These meetings which you are conducting will be very helpful to you. They will bring to your rescue some of the same units of life which served the members of your Cabinet during their lives. These units are eternal. THEY NEVER DIE! Your own thoughts and DESIRES serve as the magnet which attracts units of life from the great ocean of life out there. Only the friendly units are attracted -- the ones which harmonize with the nature of your DESIRES."

The other members of the Cabinet began to enter the room. Edison got up and slowly walked around to his own seat. Edison was still living when this happened. It impressed me so greatly that I went to see him and told him about the experience. He smiled broadly and said, "Your dream was more a reality than you may imagine it to have been." He added no further explanation to his statement.[3]

These meetings became so realistic that I became fearful of their consequences and discontinued them for several months. The experiences were so uncanny I was afraid if I continued them I would lose sight of the fact that the meetings were purely *experiences of my imagination*.

Some six months after I had discontinued the practice, I was awakened one night, or thought I was, when I saw Lincoln standing at my bedside. He said, "The world will soon need your services. It is about to undergo a period of chaos which will cause men and women to lose faith, and become panic-stricken. Go ahead with your work and complete your philosophy. That is your mission in life. If you neglect it for any cause whatsoever, you will be reduced to a primal state and be compelled to retrace the cycles through which you have passed during thousands of years."

The following morning, I was unable to tell whether I had dreamed this or had actually been awake, and I have never since found out which it was, but I do know that the dream, if it were a dream, was so vivid in my mind the next day that I resumed my meetings the following night.

At our next meeting the members of my Cabinet all filed into the room together and stood at their accustomed places at the Council Table, while Lincoln raised a glass and said, "Gentlemen, let us drink a toast to a friend who has returned to the fold."

After that, I began to add new members to my Cabinet, until soon it grew to more than 50, among them Christ, St. Paul, Galileo, Copernicus, Aristotle, Plato, Socrates, Homer, Voltaire, Spinoza, Kant, Schopenhauer, Newton, Confucius, Elbert Hubbard, Woodrow Wilson, and William James.

This is the first time that I have ever had the courage to mention this in writing. Heretofore, I have remained quiet on the subject because I knew from my own attitude in connection with such matters that I would be misunderstood if I described my unusual experience. I have been emboldened now to reduce my experience to the printed page because I am now less concerned about what "they say" than I was in the years that have passed. One of the blessings of maturity is that it sometimes brings one greater courage to be truthful, regardless of what those who do not understand may think or say.

Lest I be misunderstood, I wish here to state most emphatically that I still regard my Cabinet meetings as being purely imaginary, but I feel entitled to suggest that while the members of my Cabinet may be purely fictional and the meetings existent only in my own imagination, they have led me into glorious paths of adventure, rekindled an appreciation of true greatness, encouraged creative endeavor, and emboldened the expression of honest thought.

Somewhere in the cell structure of the human brain is an area which receives vibrations of thought ordinarily called hunches. So far, science has not discovered where this site of the Sixth Sense is located, but this is not important. The fact remains that human beings do receive accurate knowledge through sources other than the five physical senses. Such knowledge generally is received when the mind is under the influence of extraordinary stimulation. Any emergency which arouses the emotions and causes the heart to beat more rapidly than normal may, and often does, bring the Sixth Sense into action. Anyone who has experienced a near accident while driving knows that on such occasions the Sixth Sense often comes to one's rescue and aids, by split seconds, in avoiding the accident.

These facts are mentioned preliminary to a statement of fact which I shall now make, namely, that during my meetings with the Invisible Counselors I found my mind most receptive to ideas, thoughts, and knowledge which reach me through the Sixth Sense. I can truthfully say that I owe entirely to my Invisible Counselors full credit for such ideas, facts, or knowledge as I received through inspiration.

On scores of occasions when I have faced emergencies, some of them so grave that my life was in jeopardy, I have been miraculously guided past these difficulties through the influence of my Invisible Counselors.

My original purpose in conducting Council meetings with imaginary beings was solely that of impressing my own sub-conscious mind, through the principle of autosuggestion, with certain characteristics which I desired to acquire. In more recent years, my experimentation has taken on an entirely different trend. I now go to my imaginary counselors with every difficult problem which confronts me. The results are often astonishing, although I do not depend entirely on this form of counsel.

You, of course, have recognized that this chapter covers a subject with which a majority of people are not familiar. The Sixth Sense is a subject that will be of great interest and benefit to the person whose aim is to accumulate vast wealth or accomplish a great achievement of any kind, but it need not claim the attention of those whose desires are more modest.

Henry Ford undoubtedly understood and made practical use of the Sixth Sense. His vast business and financial operations made it necessary for him to understand and use this principle. Thomas Edison understood and used the Sixth Sense in connection with the development of inventions, especially those involving basic patents where he had no human experience and no accumulated knowledge to guide him, as was the case while he was working on the phonograph and the motion picture machine.

Nearly all great leaders, such as Napoleon, Bismark, Joan of Arc, Christ, Buddha, Confucius, and Mohammed understood and made use of the Sixth Sense almost continuously. The major portion of their greatness consisted of their knowledge of this principle.

The Sixth Sense is not something that one can take off and put on at will. Ability to use this great power comes slowly, through application of the other principles outlined in this book. Seldom does any individual come into workable knowledge of the Sixth Sense before the age of 40. More often, the knowledge is not available until one is well past 50 because the spiritual forces with which the Sixth Sense is so closely related do not mature and become usable except through years of meditation, self-examination, and serious thought.

No matter who you are or what may have been your purpose in reading this book, you can profit by it without understanding the principle described in this chapter. This is especially true if your major purpose is that of accumulation of money or other material things.

This chapter on the Sixth Sense was included because the book is designed to present a complete philosophy by which individuals may unerringly guide themselves in attaining whatever they ask of life. The starting point of all achievement is DESIRE. The finishing point is that brand of KNOWLEDGE which leads to understanding—understanding of self, understanding of others, understanding of the laws of Nature, and understanding and recognition of HAPPINESS.

This sort of understanding comes in its fullness only through familiarity with and use of the principle of the Sixth Sense, hence that principle had to be included as a part of this philosophy for the benefit of those who demand more than money.

Having read this chapter, you must have observed that while reading it you were lifted to a high level of mental stimulation. Splendid! Come back to this chapter again a month from now, read it once more, and observe that your mind will soar to a still higher level of stimulation. Repeat this experience from time to time, giving no concern as to how much or how little you learn at the time, and eventually you will find yourself in possession of a power that will enable you to throw off discouragement, master fear, overcome procrastination, and draw freely upon your imagination. Then you will have felt the touch of that unknown something which has been the moving spirit of every truly great thinker, leader, artist, musician, writer, scientist, or statesman. Then you will be in position to transmute your DESIRES into their physical or financial counterpart as easily as you may lie down and quit at the first sign of opposition.

Faith vs. Fear

Previous chapters have described how to develop FAITH through autosuggestion, desire, and the subconscious mind. The final pages of this book will present detailed instructions for the mastery of FEAR.

Here will be found a full description of the six fears which are the cause of all discouragement, timidity, procrastination, indifference, indecision, and the lack of ambition, self-reliance, initiative, self-control, and enthusiasm. Search yourself carefully as you study these six enemies, as they may exist only in your subconscious mind, where their presence will be hard to detect. Remember, too, as you analyze the "Six Ghosts of Fear" that they are nothing but ghosts because they exist only in one's mind. Remember also that ghosts — creations of uncontrolled imagination — have caused most of the damage people have done to their own minds; therefore, ghosts can be as dangerous as if they lived and walked on the earth in physical bodies.[4]

Without doubt, the most common weakness of all human beings is the habit of leaving their minds open to the negative influence of other people.

Epilogue

HOW TO OUTWIT THE 6 GHOSTS OF FEAR

Take Inventory of Yourself
As You Read This and Find Out
How Many of the Ghosts
Stand in Your Way

BEFORE YOU CAN put any portion of *The Think and Grow Rich Philosophy* into successful use, your mind must be prepared to receive it. The preparation is not difficult. It begins with study, analysis, and an understanding of three enemies which you shall have to clear out.

These are INDECISION, DOUBT, and FEAR!

The Sixth Sense will never function while these three negatives or any one of them remains in your mind. The members of this unholy trio are closely tied. Where one is found the other two are close at hand.

INDECISION is the seedling of FEAR! And remember this as you read. Indecision crystallizes DOUBT. The two blend and become FEAR! This blending process often is slow. This is one reason why these three enemies are so dangerous. They germinate and grow *without their presence being observed*.

The remainder of this chapter describes an end which must be attained before *The Think and Grow Rich Philosophy*, as a whole, can be put into practical use.[1] It also analyzes a condition which has reduced large numbers of people to poverty, and it states a truth which must be understood by all who would accumulate riches, whether measured in terms of money or a state of mind of far greater value than money.

Let us now turn the spotlight on the cause and the cure of the Six Basic Fears. Before we can master an enemy, we must know its name, its habits, and its place of abode. As you read, analyze yourself carefully and determine which, if any, of the six common fears have attached themselves to you. Do not be deceived by the habits of these subtle enemies. Sometimes they remain hidden in the subconscious mind, where they are difficult to locate and still more difficult to eradicate.

The Six Basic Fears

There are Six Basic Fears, with some combination of which every human being suffers at one time or another. Most people are fortunate if they do not suffer from the entire six. Named in the order of their most common appearance, they are:

The fear of POVERTY (at the heart of most people's worries)
The fear of CRITICISM
The fear of ILL HEALTH
The fear of LOSS OF LOVE OF SOMEONE
The fear of OLD AGE
The fear of DEATH

All other fears are of minor importance. They can be grouped under these six headings.

The prevalence of these fears, as a curse to the world, runs in cycles. For almost six years, while the Depression was on, we floundered in the cycle of FEAR OF POVERTY. During World War I we were in the cycle of FEAR OF DEATH. Just following the war, we were in the cycle of FEAR OF ILL HEALTH, as evidenced by the epidemic of disease which spread all over the world.[2]

Fears are nothing more than states of mind. As has been demonstrated repeatedly in the chapters of this book, one's state of mind is subject to control and direction.[3]

An individual can create nothing which he or she does not first *conceive* in the form of an impulse of thought. Following this statement comes another of still greater importance, namely, that THOUGHT IMPULSES BEGIN IMMEDIATELY TO TRANSLATE THEMSELVES INTO THEIR PHYSICAL EQUIVALENT, WHETHER THOSE THOUGHTS ARE VOLUNTARY OR INVOLUNTARY. Thought impulses which are picked up by mere chance from sources outside one's own mind (thoughts created in other minds) may determine one's financial, business, professional, or social destiny just as surely as do the thought impulses which one creates by intent and design.

We are here laying the foundation for the presentation of a fact of great importance to the person who does not understand why some people appear to be lucky while others of equal or greater ability, training, experience, and intellectual capacity seem destined to misfortune. This fact may be explained by the statement that *all human beings have the ability to completely control their own mind*, and with this control, obviously, all individuals can open their minds to the "tramp" thought impulses which derive from the brains of others, or else can close the doors tightly and admit only thought impulses of their own choice.

Nature has endowed human beings with absolute control over only one thing—and that is THOUGHT. This fact—coupled with the additional fact that everything that human beings create begins in the form of a *thought*, an IDEA – leads one very near to the principle by which FEAR may be mastered.

If it is true that ALL THOUGHT HAS A TENDENCY TO CLOTHE ITSELF IN ITS PHYSICAL EQUIVALENT (and this is true beyond any doubt), it is equally true that thought impulses of fear and poverty cannot be translated into terms of courage and financial gain.

The people of America began to think of poverty following the Wall Street crash of 1929. Slowly but surely, that mass thought was crystallized into its physical equivalent, which was known as a depression. This had to happen. It is in conformity with the laws of Nature.

The Fear of Poverty

There can be no compromise between POVERTY and RICHES! The roads that lead to poverty and riches travel in opposite directions. If you want riches, you must refuse to accept any circumstance that leads toward poverty. (The word "riches" is here used in its broadest sense, meaning financial, spiritual, mental and material estates). The starting point of the path that leads to riches is DESIRE. In Chapter 1, you received full instructions for the proper use of DESIRE. Now in this concluding discussion on FEAR you will receive complete instructions for preparing your mind to make practical use of DESIRE.

Here then is the place to give yourself a challenge which will definitely determine how much of this philosophy you have absorbed so far. Here is the point at which you can turn prophet and foretell accurately what the future holds in store for you. If, after reading what follows, you are willing to accept poverty, you may as well make up your mind to receive poverty. This is one decision you cannot avoid.

If you demand riches, determine what form of riches and how much will be required to satisfy you. You should now know the road that leads to riches. You have been given a road map which, if followed, will keep you on that road. If you neglect to make the start, or stop before you arrive, no one will be to blame but YOU. The responsibility is yours. No alibi will save you from accepting this responsibility. If you now fail or refuse to demand riches of life, it will be because of one thing—the only thing you can truly control—a STATE OF MIND. And a state of mind is something that one *assumes*. It cannot be purchased. It must be *created*.

Fear of poverty is a state of mind, nothing else! But it is sufficient to destroy one's chances of achievement in any undertaking, a truth which becomes painfully evident during any time of economic difficulty and uncertainty.

Fear of poverty paralyzes the faculty of reason, destroys the faculty of imagination, kills self-reliance, undermines enthusiasm, discourages initiative, leads to uncertainty of purpose, encourages procrastination, wipes out enthusiasm, and makes self-control impossible. It takes the charm from one's personality, destroys the possibility of accurate thinking, diverts concentration of effort, kills persistence, turns willpower into nothingness, destroys ambition, beclouds memory, and invites failure in every conceivable form. It kills love and assassinates the finer emotions of the heart, discourages friendship, invites disaster in a hundred forms, leads to sleeplessness, misery and unhappiness—and all this despite the obvious truth that we live in a world of overabundance of everything the heart could desire, with nothing standing between us and our desires except *lack of a definite purpose and the plans that derive from it.*

The Fear of Poverty is without doubt the most destructive of the Six Basic Fears. It has been placed at the head of the list because it is the most difficult fear to master. Considerable courage is required to state the truth about the origin of this fear, and still greater courage to accept the truth after it has been stated. The fear of poverty grew out of human beings' inherited tendency to PREY UPON OTHERS ECONOMICALLY. Nearly all animals are motivated by instinct, but their capacity to think is limited; therefore, they prey upon one another physically. Human beings, with their superior sense of intuition and the capacity to think and to reason, do not eat other human beings bodily—they get more satisfaction out of "eating" them FINANCIALLY. Human beings, by nature, are so avaricious that every conceivable law has been passed to safeguard them from each other.

Of all the ages of the world of which we know anything, the age in which we live seems to be one that is most characterized by "money-madness." People are almost considered less than the dust of the earth unless they can display a fat bank account. But if they have money—NEVER MIND HOW THEY ACQUIRED IT—they are "royalty" or "big shots." They seem above the law, they rule in politics, they dominate in business, and the whole world about them bows in respect when they pass.

Nothing brings a person so much suffering and humility as POVERTY! Only those who have experienced poverty understand the full meaning of this.

It is no wonder that people fear poverty. Through a long line of inherited experiences, people have learned, for sure, that some individuals cannot be trusted where matters of money and earthly possessions are concerned. This is a stinging, but true indictment.

The majority of marriages continue to be motivated by the wealth possessed by one or both of the contracting parties. It is no wonder, therefore, that the divorce courts stay busy. So eager are people to possess wealth that they will acquire it in whatever manner they can — through legal methods if possible, through other methods if necessary or expedient.

Self-analysis may disclose weaknesses which one does not like to acknowledge. This form of examination is essential for all who demand of life more than mediocrity and poverty. Remember, as you check yourself point by point, that you are both the court and the jury, the prosecuting attorney and the attorney for the defense, the plaintiff and the defendant — and it is YOU who are on trial. Face the facts squarely. Ask yourself definite questions and demand direct replies. When your examination is over, you will know more about yourself. If you do not feel that you can be an impartial judge in this self-examination, call upon someone who knows you well to serve as judge while you cross-examine yourself. You are after the truth. *Get it, no matter at what cost even though it may temporarily embarrass you!*

The majority of people, if asked what they fear most, would reply, "I fear nothing." The reply would be inaccurate because few people realize that they are bound, handicapped, and whipped spiritually and physically by some form of fear. So subtle and deeply seated is the emotion of fear that one may go through life burdened with it, never recognizing its presence. Only a courageous analysis will disclose the presence of this universal enemy. When you begin such an analysis, search deeply into your character. Here is a list of the symptoms for which you should look:

Symptoms of the Fear of Poverty

INDIFFERENCE. Commonly expressed through lack of ambition; willingness to tolerate poverty; acceptance of whatever compensation life may offer without protest; mental and physical laziness; lack of initiative, imagination, enthusiasm and self-control

INDECISION. The habit of permitting others to do one's thinking. Staying on the fence.

DOUBT. Generally expressed through alibis and excuses designed to cover up, explain away, or apologize for one's failures, sometimes expressed in the form of envy of those who are successful or by criticism of them.

WORRY. Usually expressed by finding fault with others, a tendency to spend beyond one's income, neglect of personal appearance, scowling and frowning; intemperance in the use of alcoholic, sometimes through the use of narcotics; nervousness, lack of poise, self-consciousness and lack of self-reliance.

OVER-CAUTION. The habit of looking for the negative side of every circumstance, thinking and talking of possible failure instead of concentrating upon the means of succeeding. Knowing all the roads to disaster, but never searching for the plans to avoid failure. Waiting for the "right time" to begin putting ideas and plans into action, until the waiting becomes a permanent habit. Remembering those who have failed, and forgetting those who have succeeded. Seeing the hole in the doughnut, but overlooking the doughnut. Pessimism, leading to indigestion, poor elimination, autointoxication, bad breath and bad disposition.

PROCRASTINATION. The habit of putting off until tomorrow that which should have been done last year. Spending enough time in creating alibis and excuses to have done the job. This symptom is closely related to over-caution, doubt, and worry. Refusal to accept responsibility when it can be avoided. Willingness to compromise rather than put up a stiff fight. Compromising with difficulties instead of harnessing and using them as steppingstones to advancement. Bargaining with life for a penny, instead of demanding prosperity, opulence, riches, contentment, and happiness. Planning what to do IF AND WHEN OVERTAKEN BY FAILURE, INSTEAD OF BURNING ALL BRIDGES AND MAKING RETREAT IMPOSSIBLE. Weakness of, and often total lack of, self-confidence, definiteness of purpose, self-control, initiative, enthusiasm, ambition, thrift, and sound reasoning ability. EXPECTING POVERTY INSTEAD OF DEMANDING RICHES. Association with those who accept poverty instead of seeking the company of those who demand and receive riches.

Money Talks!

Some will ask, "Why did you write a book about money? Why measure riches in dollars alone?" Some will believe, and rightly so, that there are other forms of riches more desirable than money. Yes, there are riches which cannot be measured in terms of dollars, but there are millions of people who will say, "Give me all the money I need, and I will find everything else I want."

The major reason I wrote this book on how to get money is the fact that the world has but lately passed through an experience that left millions of men and women paralyzed with the FEAR OF POVERTY. What this sort of fear does to one was well described by Westbrook Pegler in the *New York World-Telegram*:[4]

Money is only clam shells or metal discs or scraps of paper, and there are treasures of the heart and soul which money cannot buy, but most people, being broke, are unable to keep this in mind and sustain their spirits. When a man is down and out and on the street, unable to get any job at all, something happens to his spirit which can be observed in the droop of his shoulders, the set of his hat, his walk and his gaze. He cannot escape a feeling of inferiority among people with regular employment, even though he knows they are definitely not his equals in character, intelligence or ability.

These people — even his friends — feel, on the other hand, a sense of superiority and regard him, perhaps unconsciously, as a casualty. He may borrow for a time, but not enough to carry on in his accustomed way, and he cannot continue to borrow very long. But borrowing in itself, when a man is borrowing merely to live, is a depressing experience, and the money lacks the power of earned money to revive his spirits. Of course, none of this applies to bums or habitual ne'er-do-wells, but only to men of normal ambitions and self-respect.

Women in the same predicament must be different. We somehow do not think of women at all in considering the down-and-outers. They are...not recognizable in crowds by the same plain signs which identify busted men. Of course, I do not mean the shuffling hags of the city streets who are the opposite number of the confirmed male bums. I mean reasonably young, decent and intelligent women. There must be many of them, but their despair is not apparent....

When a man is down and out he has time on his hands for brooding. He may travel miles to see a man about a job and discover that the job is filled or that it is one of those jobs with no base pay but only a commission on the sale of some useless knickknack which nobody would buy.... Turning that down, he finds himself back on the street with nowhere to go but just anywhere. So he walks and walks. He gazes into store windows at luxuries which are not for him, and feels inferior and gives way to people who stop to look with an active interest. He wanders into the railroad station or puts himself down in the library to ease his legs and soak up a little heat, but that isn't looking for a job, so he gets going again. He may not know it, but his aimlessness would give him away even if the very lines of his figure did not. He may be well dressed in the clothes left over from the days when he had a steady job, but the clothes cannot disguise the droop....

He sees thousands of other people, bookkeepers or clerks or chemists...busy at their work and envies them from the bottom of his soul. They have their independence, their self-respect and manhood, and he simply cannot convince himself that he is a good man, too, though he argue it out and arrive at a favorable verdict hour after hour.

It is just money which makes this difference in him. With a little money he would be himself again."[5]

The Fear of Criticism

Just how humanity originally came by this fear, no one can state definitely, but one thing is certain — people have it in a highly developed form. I am inclined to attribute the basic fear of criticism to that part of inherited human nature which prompts people not only to take away the goods and wares of others, but to justify their action by CRITICISM of their victims' character. It is a well-known fact that thieves will criticize those from whom they steal and that politicians seek office not by displaying their own virtues and qualifications, but by attempting to besmirch their opponents.

The Fear of Criticism takes on many forms, the majority of which are petty and trivial.[6] The astute manufacturers of clothing have not been slow to capitalize on this basic fear, with which all humanity has been cursed. Every season the styles in many articles of wearing apparel change. Who establishes the styles? Certainly not the purchaser of clothing, but the manufacturers. Why do they change the styles so often? The answer is obvious. They change the styles so they can sell more clothes.

For the same reason the manufacturers of automobiles (with a few rare and very sensible exceptions) change styles of models every season. No one wants to drive an automobile which is not of the latest style, although the older model may actually be the better car.

We have been describing the manner in which people behave under the influence of the Fear of Criticism as applied to the small and petty things of life. Let us now examine human behavior when this fear affects people in connection with the more important events of human relationship. Take, for example, practically any person who has reached the age of mental maturity (from 35 to 40 years of age, as a general average), and if you could read the secret thoughts of his or her mind, you would find a very decided disbelief in most of the fables taught by the majority of the dogmatists and theologians a few decades back.

Not often, however, will you find an individual who has the courage to openly state his or her belief on this subject. Most people will, if pressed far enough, tell a lie rather than admit that they do not believe all of the stories associated with a religion, particularly if their religion (or sect) is one of those which are rigidly dogmatic and intolerant of questioning.

Why does the average person, even in this day of enlightenment, shy away from denying his or her belief in those aspects of religious dogma that are almost surely "fabulous," or fable-like? The answer is "the Fear of Criticism." Men and women have been burned at the stake for daring to express their disbelief in ghosts. It is no wonder we have inherited a consciousness which makes us fear criticism. The time was, and not so far in the past, when criticism carried severe punishments—and still does in many countries.

The Fear of Criticism robs people of their initiative, destroys their power of imagination, limits their individuality, takes away their self-reliance, and does them damage in a hundred other ways. Parents often do their children irreparable injury by criticizing them. The mother of one of my boyhood chums used to punish him with a switch almost daily, always completing the job with the statement, "You'll land in the penitentiary before you are 20." He was sent to a reformatory at the age of 17.

Criticism is the one form of "service" of which everyone has too much. Everyone has a stock of it which is handed out gratis, whether asked for or not. One's nearest relatives often are the worst offenders. It should be recognized as a crime (in reality, it is a crime of the worst nature) for any parent to create an inferiority complex in the mind of a child through unnecessary criticism. Employers who understand human nature get the best there is in their employees not by criticism, but by constructive suggestion. Parents may accomplish the same results with their children. Criticism will plant FEAR in the human heart, or resentment, but it will not build love or affection.

Symptoms of the Fear of Criticism

This fear is almost as universal as the Fear of Poverty, and its effects are just as fatal to personal achievement, mainly because this fear destroys initiative and discourages the use of imagination. The major symptoms of the fear are:

SELF-CONSCIOUSNESS. Generally expressed through nervousness, timidity in conversation and in meeting strangers, awkward movement of the hands and limbs, shifting of the eyes.

LACK OF POISE. Expressed through lack of voice control, nervousness in the presence of others, poor posture of body, poor memory.

WEAK PERSONALITY. Lacking in firmness of decision, personal charm, and ability to express opinions definitely. The habit of sidestepping issues instead of meeting them squarely. Agreeing with others without careful examination of their opinions.

INFERIORITY COMPLEX. The habit of expressing self-approval by word of mouth and by actions, as a means of covering up a feeling of inferiority. Using big words to impress others (often without knowing the real meaning of the words). Imitating others in dress, speech and manners. Boasting of imaginary achievements. This sometimes gives a surface appearance of a feeling of superiority.

EXTRAVAGANCE. The habit of trying to keep up with the Jones, spending beyond one's income.

LACK OF INITIATIVE. Failure to embrace opportunities for self- advancement, fear to express opinions, lack of confidence in one's own ideas, giving evasive answers to questions asked by superiors, hesitancy of manner and speech, deceit in both words and deeds.

LACK OF AMBITION. Mental and physical laziness, lack of self- assertion, slowness in reaching decisions, tendency to be easily influenced by others, the habit of criticizing others behind their backs and flattering them to their faces, the habit of accepting defeat without protest, quitting an undertaking when opposed by others, being suspicious of other people without cause, lacking tact in manner and speech, unwillingness to accept the blame for mistakes.

The Fear of Ill Health

This fear may be traced to both physical and social heredity. As to its origin, it is closely associated with the causes of the Fear of Old Age and the Fear of Death because it leads us closely to the border of terrible worlds of which we know not, but concerning which we have been taught some discomforting stories. Also, certain unethical people engaged in the business of "selling health" have had not a little to do with keeping alive the Fear of Ill Health.

In the main, we fear ill health because of the terrible pictures which have been planted in our mind of what may happen if death should overtake us. We also fear it because of the economic toll which it may claim.

A reputable physician estimated that 75 percent of all people who visit physicians for professional service suffer from hypochondria (imaginary illness). It has been shown most convincingly that the fear of disease, even where there is not the slightest cause for fear, often produces the physical symptoms of the disease feared.

Powerful and mighty is the human mind! It builds or it destroys.

Playing upon this common weakness of Fear of Ill Health, dispensers of patent medicines have reaped fortunes. This form of imposition upon credulous humanity became so prevalent some years ago that *Colliers' Weekly Magazine*[7] conducted a bitter campaign against some of the worst offenders in the patent medicine business.[8]

Through a series of experiments conducted some years ago, it was demonstrated that people can be made ill by suggestion alone. We conducted this experiment by causing three acquaintances to visit the "victims." Each visitor asked the question, "What ails you? You look terribly ill." The first questioner usually provoked a grin and a nonchalant "Oh, nothing, I'm all right," from the victim. The second questioner usually was answered with the statement, "I don't know exactly, but I do feel badly." The third questioner was usually met with the frank admission that the victim was actually feeling ill. Try this on acquaintances if you doubt that it will make them uncomfortable, but do not carry the experiment too far because some people may actually develop serious physical symptoms in response to suggestion. (There is a certain religious sect whose members take vengeance upon their enemies by the "hexing" method. They call it placing a spell on the victim, and there are reliable reports that some individuals have actually died after being hexed.)

There is overwhelming evidence that disease sometimes begins in the form of negative thought impulse. Such an impulse may be passed from one mind to another, by suggestion, or created by an individual in his or her own mind.

A man who was blessed with more wisdom than this incident might indicate, once said, "When anyone asks me how I feel, I always want to answer by knocking him down."

Physicians sometimes send patients into new climates for their health because a change of mental attitude is necessary. The seed of the Fear of Ill Health lives in every human mind. Worry, fear, discouragement, and disappointment in love and business affairs cause this seed to germinate and grow. Every form of negative thinking may cause ill health.

Disappointments in business and in love stand at the head of the list of causes of the Fear of Ill Health. A young man suffered a devastating disappointment in love which eventually resulted in his being hospitalized. For months he suffered a debilitating depression. A psychotherapist[9] was called in. The psychotherapist changed nurses, placing the patient under the care of a *very charming young woman* who began (by prearrangement with the therapist) to coddle him and shower him with affection beginning the first day of her arrival on the job. Within three weeks the patient was discharged from the hospital, still suffering, but with an entirely different malady. HE WAS IN LOVE AGAIN. The remedy was a hoax, but the patient and the nurse were later married. Both are in good health at the time of this writing.

Symptoms of the Fear of Ill Health

The symptoms of this almost universal fear are:

INAPPROPRIATE AUTOSUGGESTION. The habit of negative use of self- suggestion by looking for and expecting to find the symptoms of all kinds of disease. "Enjoying" imaginary illness and speaking of it as being real. The habit of trying all fads and "isms" recommended by others as having therapeutic value. Dwelling on the details of operations, accidents, and other forms of illness. Experimenting with diets, physical exercises, and reducing schemes without professional guidance. Over-reliance or experimentation with home remedies, patent medicine, and quack remedies.

HYPOCHONDRIA. The habit of talking about illness, concentrating the mind upon disease, and expecting its appearance until a nervous condition occurs. Nothing that comes in bottles can cure this condition. It is brought on by negative thinking and nothing but positive thought can effect a cure. Hypochondria (a medical term for imaginary disease) is said to do as much damage on occasion as the disease one fears might do. Most so-called cases of nerves come from imaginary illness.

LACK OF EXERCISE. Fear of ill health often interferes with proper physical exercise and results in one's being overweight by causing one to avoid outdoor life.

SUSCEPTIBILITY TO ILLNESS. Fear of ill health breaks down the body's natural resistance and creates a favorable condition for any form of disease one may contact.[10] The Fear of Ill Health often is related to the Fear of Poverty, especially in the case of the hypochondriac who constantly worries about the possibility of having to pay doctor's bills, hospital bills, etc. This type of person spends much time preparing for sickness, talking about death, saving money for cemetery lots, burial expenses, etc.

SELF-CODDLING. The habit of making a bid for sympathy using imaginary illness as the lure. (People often resort to this trick to avoid work.) The habit of feigning illness to cover plain laziness or to serve as an alibi for lack of ambition.

INTEMPERANCE. The habit of using alcohol or narcotics to deaden pains such as headaches, neuralgia, etc., instead of eliminating the cause. The habit of reading about illness and worrying over the possibility of being stricken by it. The habit of reading, listening to, or viewing patent medicine advertisements.

The Fear of Loss of Love

The original source of this inherent fear needs but little description. It obviously (on the male side) grew out of males' early and, apparently, inherently polygamous nature and the propensity to steal the mates of other males. It also derives (on the female side) from woman's maternal instincts and need for protection during periods of pregnancy and early child nurturing. Both men and women, therefore, have a biological and behavioral basis to fear the loss of love or "mate companionship."

Jealousy and other similar forms of neurosis thus grow out of human beings' inherited fear of the loss of security that the loss of love and companionship of another person represents. This fear is the most painful of all the Six Basic Fears. It plays more havoc with the body and mind than any of the other basic fears, and it can lead to severe mental problems.

As indicated above, the Fear of Loss of Love probably dates back to the Stone Age, when males stole females by brute force. They continue to do so in modern civilizations, but their technique has changed. Instead of force, they now use the lure of romantic persuasion, the promise of fine clothes, expensive automobiles and jewelry, access to economic power, and other bait much more effective than physical force. Males' habits are the same as they were at the dawn of civilization, but are expressed differently.

Careful analysis has shown that women generally are more susceptible to the Fear of Loss of Love than are men. This fact is easily explained. Women through the ages have learned from experience that men, considered as a group, are polygamous by nature, that they are not to be trusted in the hands of rivals.

Symptoms of the Fear of Loss of Love

The distinguishing symptoms of this fear are:

JEALOUSY. The habit of being suspicious of friends and loved ones without any reasonable evidence of sufficient grounds. (Jealousy is a form of neurosis which sometimes becomes violent without the slightest cause.) The habit of accusing wife or husband of infidelity without grounds. General suspicion of everyone, absolute faith in no one.

FAULT FINDING. The habit of finding fault with friends, relatives, business associates, and loved ones upon the slightest provocation or without any cause whatsoever.

GAMBLING. The habit of gambling, stealing, cheating, and otherwise taking risky chances to provide money for loved ones with the belief that love can be bought.

The habit of spending beyond one's means or incurring debts to provide gifts for loved ones, with the object of making a favorable showing. Insomnia, nervousness, lack of persistence, weakness of will, lack of self-control, lack of self- reliance, bad temper.

The Fear of Old Age

In the main, this fear grows out of two sources: First, the thought that old age may bring with it POVERTY. Secondly, and by far the most common source of origin, thoughts arising from false and cruel teachings of the past, which have been too well mixed with fire and brimstone and other "bogeymen" cunningly designed to enslave people through fear.

In the basic Fear of Old Age, people have two very sound reasons for their apprehension — one growing out of their distrust of others, who may seize whatever worldly goods they may possess, and the other arising from the terrible pictures of the "world beyond" which were planted in their minds through "social heredity" before they came into full possession of their powers of reason.

The possibility of ill health, which is more common as people grow older, is also a contributing cause of this common Fear of Old Age. Eroticism also enters into the cause of the Fear of Old Age, as no one cherishes the thought of diminishing sexual attraction and activity.

The most common cause of Fear of Old Age is associated with the possibility of poverty. "Poorhouse" — and everything the term conveys — is not a pretty word.[11] It throws a chill into the mind of every person who faces the possibility of having to spend his or her declining years impoverished and worried constantly about meeting both the necessities of daily life and the special needs of old age.

Another contributing cause of the Fear of Old Age is the possibility of loss of freedom and independence, as old age may bring with it the loss of both physical and economic freedom.

Symptoms of the Fear of Old Age

The commonest symptoms of this fear are:

THE TENDENCY TO SLOW DOWN and develop an inferiority complex at the age of mental maturity, around the age of 50, falsely believing oneself to be "slipping" because of age. (The truth is that one's most useful years, mentally and spiritually, are those between 50 and 60.)

THE HABIT OF SPEAKING APOLOGETICALLY of oneself as being old merely because one has reached the age of 60 or 70, instead of reversing the rule and expressing gratitude for having reached the age of wisdom and understanding.

THE HABIT OF KILLING OFF INITIATIVE, imagination, and self- reliance by falsely believing oneself too old to exercise these qualities. The habit of the man or woman of 50 or 60 dressing with the aim of trying to appear much younger and affecting mannerisms of youth, thereby inspiring ridicule by both friends and strangers.

The Fear of Death

To some this is the cruelest of all the basic fears. The reason is obvious. In the majority of cases, the terrible pangs of fear associated with the thought of death may be charged directly to religious fanaticism. So-called "heathen" are less afraid of death than are the more civilized. For thousands of years, human beings have been asking the still unanswered questions, "Whence?" and "Whither?" "Where did I come from, and where am I going?"

During the darker ages of history, the more cunning and crafty were not slow to offer the answer to these questions—FOR A PRICE. Witness, now, the major source of the origin of the FEAR OF DEATH:

"Come into my tent, embrace my faith, accept my dogmas, and I will give you a ticket that will admit you straightaway into heaven when you die," cries a leader of sectarianism. "Remain out of my tent," says the same leader, "and may the devil take you and burn you throughout eternity."

ETERNITY is a long time. FIRE is a terrible thing. The thought of eternal punishment by fire not only causes people to fear death, it often causes them to lose their reason. It can destroy interest in life and make happiness impossible.

During my research I reviewed a book entitled *A Catalogue of the Gods* in which were listed the 30,000 gods which humankind has worshipped through the ages. Think of it! Thirty-thousand of them, represented by everything from a crawfish to a man. It is little wonder that people have become frightened at the approach of death.

While the religious leader may not be able to provide safe conduct into heaven, nor by lack of such provision force the unfortunate to descend into hell, the possibility of the latter seems so terrible that the very thought of it lays hold of the imagination in such a realistic way that it paralyzes reason and sets up the Fear of Death.

In truth, NO ONE KNOWS for certain what heaven or hell is like or in what sense either exists. This very lack of positive knowledge opens the door of people's minds to the charlatans so that they may enter and control those minds with their stock of legerdemain and various brands of pious fraud and trickery.

The fear of DEATH is not as common now as it was during the age when there were no great colleges and universities. Scientists have turned the spotlight of truth upon the world, and this truth is rapidly freeing men and women from this terrible fear of DEATH. The young men and women who attend our colleges and universities are not so easily impressed by "fire" and "brimstone" any longer. Through the aid of biology, astronomy, geology, and other related sciences, the fears of the dark ages that gripped the minds of humanity and destroyed people's reason have been dispelled.

Insane asylums have been filled with people who have gone mad because of the FEAR OF DEATH.

This fear is useless. Death will come no matter what anyone may think about it. Accept it as a necessity and pass the thought out of your mind. It must be a necessity or it would not come to all. Perhaps it is not as bad as it has been pictured.

The entire world is made up of only two things, ENERGY and MATTER. In elementary physics we learn that neither matter nor energy (the only two realities known) can be created or destroyed. Both matter and energy can be transformed, but neither can be destroyed.

Life is energy, if it is anything. If neither energy nor matter can be destroyed, then life cannot truly be destroyed. Life, like other forms of energy, may be passed through various processes of transition, or change, but it cannot be destroyed. Death is a mere transition.

But if death is *not* a mere change, or transition, then nothing comes after death except a long, eternal, peaceful sleep, and sleep is nothing to be feared. Either way, you may thus wipe out forever the fear of death.

Symptoms of the Fear of Death

The general symptom of this fear is the habit of THINKING about dying instead of making the most of LIFE, a habit which is due generally to lack of purpose or lack of a suitable occupation. This fear is more prevalent among the aged, but sometimes the more youthful are victims of it.

The greatest of all remedies for the Fear of Death is a BURNING DESIRE FOR ACHIEVEMENT, backed by useful service to others. Busy people seldom have time to think about dying. They find life too thrilling to worry about death. Sometimes the Fear of Death is closely associated with the Fear of Poverty, where one's death would leave loved ones poverty-stricken. In other cases, the Fear of Death is caused by illness and the consequent breaking down of physical body resistance. The commonest causes of the Fear of Death are poor health, poverty, lack of appropriate occupation, disappointment over love, insanity, and religious fanaticism.

Old Man Worry

Worry is a state of mind based upon fear. It works slowly but persistently. It is insidious and subtle. Step by step it digs itself in until it paralyzes one's reasoning faculty and destroys self-confidence and initiative. Worry is a form of sustained fear caused by indecision, therefore, it is a state of mind which can be controlled.

An unsettled mind is helpless. Indecision makes an unsettled mind. Most individuals lack the willpower to reach decisions promptly and to stand by them after they have been made, even during normal business conditions. During periods of economic distress (such as the world has recently experienced), individuals are handicapped not solely by their inherent nature to be slow at reaching decisions, but by the influence of the *indecision of others around them* who have created a state of mass indecision.

During an international economic downturn, the whole atmosphere all over the world can be filled with "Fearenza" and "Worryitis," two mental disease germs which can spread rapidly. There is only one known antidote for these germs. It is the habit of prompt and firm DECISION. Moreover, it is an antidote which every individual must apply for himself or herself.

We do not worry over conditions once we have reached a decision to follow a *definite line of action*. I once interviewed a man who was to be electrocuted two hours later.[12] The condemned man was the calmest of some eight men who were on death row with him. His calmness prompted me to ask him how it felt to know that he was going into eternity in a short while. With a smile of confidence on his face, he said, "It feels fine. Just think, brother, my troubles will soon be over. I have had nothing but trouble all my life. It has been a hardship to get food and clothing. Soon I will not need these things. I have felt fine ever since I learned FOR CERTAIN that I must die. I made up my mind then to accept my fate in good spirit."

As he spoke he devoured a dinner of proportions sufficient for three men, eating every mouthful of the food brought to him and apparently enjoying it as much as if no disaster awaited him. DECISION gave this man resignation to his fate! Decision can also prevent one's acceptance of undesired circumstances.

Through indecision, the Six Basic Fears become translated into a state of worry and anxiety. Relieve yourself *forever* of the Fear of Death by reaching a decision to accept death as an inescapable event. Whip the Fear of Poverty by reaching a decision to get along with whatever wealth you can accumulate WITHOUT WORRY. Put your foot upon the neck of the Fear of Criticism by reaching a decision NOT TO WORRY about what other people think, do, or say. Eliminate the Fear of Old Age by reaching a decision to accept it not as a handicap, but as a great blessing which carries with it wisdom, self-control, and understanding not known to youth. Acquit yourself of the Fear of Ill Health by the decision to forget symptoms. Master the Fear of Loss of Love by reaching a decision to get along without love if that is necessary.

Kill the habit of worry in all its forms by reaching a general, blanket decision that nothing which life has to offer is worth the price of worry. With this decision will come poise, peace of mind, and calmness of thought which will bring happiness.

Those whose minds are filled with fear not only destroy their own chances of intelligent action, but they transmit these destructive vibrations to the minds of all who come into contact with them and destroy also their chances.

Even a dog or a horse knows when its master lacks courage. Moreover, a dog or a horse will pick up the vibrations of fear thrown off by its master and behave accordingly. Lower down the line of intelligence in the animal kingdom, one finds this same capacity to pick up the vibrations of fear. The vibrations of fear pass from one mind to another just as quickly and as surely as the sound of the human voice passes from the broadcasting station to the receiving set of a radio.[13]

The person who gives expression, by word of mouth, to negative or destructive thoughts is practically certain to experience the results of those words in the form of a destructive kickback. The release of destructive thought impulses alone, without the aid of words, produces also a kickback in more ways than one. First of all, and perhaps most important to be remembered, the person who releases thoughts of a destructive nature must suffer damage through the breaking down of the faculty of Creative Imagination. Secondly, the presence in the mind of any destructive emotion develops a negative personality which repels people and often converts them into antagonists. The third source of damage to the person who entertains or releases negative thoughts lies in this significant fact: Negative thought impulses are not only damaging to others, but they also EMBED THEMSELVES IN THE SUBCONSCIOUS MIND OF THE PERSON RELEASING THEM and there become a part of his or her character.

One is never through with a thought, merely by releasing it. When a thought is released, it spreads in every direction, but it also plants itself permanently in the subconscious mind of the person releasing it.

Your business in life is presumably to achieve success. To be successful, you must find peace of mind, acquire the material needs of life, and above all, attain HAPPINESS. All of these evidences of success begin in the form of thought impulses.

You may control your own mind. You have the power to feed it whatever thought impulses you choose. With this privilege goes also the responsibility of using it constructively. You are the master of your own earthly destiny just as surely as you have the power to control your own thoughts. You may influence, direct, and eventually control your own environment, making your life what you want it to be—or you may neglect to exercise the privilege which is yours to make your life to order, thus casting yourself upon the broad "Sea of Circumstance," where you will be tossed hither and yon like a chip on the waves of the ocean.

THE DEVIL'S WORKSHOP

The Seventh Basic Evil

In addition to the Six Basic Fears, there is another evil by which people suffer. It constitutes a rich soil in which the seeds of failure grow abundantly. It is so subtle that its presence often is not detected. This affliction cannot properly be classed as a fear. IT IS MORE DEEPLY SEATED AND MORE OFTEN FATAL THAN ALL OF THE SIX FEARS. For want of a better name, let us call this evil SUSCEPTIBILITY TO NEGATIVE INFLUENCES.

Individuals who accumulate great riches always protect themselves against this evil! The poverty stricken never do! Those who succeed in any calling must prepare their minds to resist the evil. If you are reading this philosophy for the purpose of accumulating riches in whatever form, you should examine yourself very carefully to determine whether you are susceptible to negative influences. If you neglect this self-analysis, you will forfeit your right to attain the object of your desires.

Make the analysis searching. After you read the questions prepared for this self-analysis, hold yourself to a strict accounting in your answers. Go at the task as carefully as you would search for any other enemy you knew to be awaiting you in ambush and deal with your own faults as you would with a more tangible enemy.

You can easily protect yourself against robbers because the law provides organized cooperation for your benefit, but the "Seventh Basic Evil" is more difficult to master because it strikes when you are not aware of its presence, when you are asleep and while you are awake. Moreover, its weapon is intangible because it consists of merely a STATE OF MIND. This evil is also dangerous because it strikes in as many different forms as there are human experiences. Sometimes it enters the mind through the well-meant words of one's own relatives. At other times it bores from within, through one's own mental attitude. Always it is as deadly as poison, even though it may not kill as quickly.

How to Protect Yourself Against Negative Influences

To protect yourself against negative influences, whether of your own making or the result of the activities and thoughts of negative people around you, recognize that you have WILLPOWER and put it into constant use until it builds a wall of immunity against negative influences in your own mind.

Recognize the fact that you and every other human being are by nature lazy, indifferent, and susceptible to all suggestions that harmonize with your weaknesses.

Recognize that you are, by nature, susceptible to all the Six Basic Fears, and set up habits for the purpose of counteracting all these fears.

Recognize that negative influences often work on you through your subconscious mind, therefore, they are difficult to detect, and keep your mind closed against all people who depress or discourage you in any way.

Clean out your medicine chest, throw away all pill bottles, and stop pandering to colds, aches, pains, and imaginary illness.

Deliberately seek the company of people who influence you to THINK AND ACT FOR YOURSELF.

Do not EXPECT troubles, as they have a tendency not to disappoint.

Without doubt, the most common weakness of all human beings is the habit of leaving their minds open to the negative influence of other people. This weakness is all the more damaging because most people do not recognize that they are cursed by it, and many who acknowledge it neglect or refuse to correct the evil until it becomes an uncontrollable part of their daily habits.

To aid those who wish to see themselves as they really are, the following list of questions has been prepared. Read the questions and state your answers aloud so that you can hear your own voice. This will make it easier for you to be truthful with yourself.

Self-Analysis Test Questions

Do you complain often of feeling bad, and if so, what is the cause?

Do you find fault with other people at the slightest provocation?

Do you frequently make mistakes in your work, and if so, why?

Are you sarcastic and offensive in your conversation?

Do you deliberately avoid the association of anyone, and if so, why?

Do you suffer frequently with indigestion? If so, what is the cause?

Does life seem futile and the future hopeless to you? If so, why?

Do you like your occupation? If not, why?

Do you often feel self-pity, and if so, why?

Are you envious of those who excel you?

To which do you devote most time, thinking of SUCCESS or of FAILURE?

Are you gaining or losing self-confidence as you grow older?

Do you learn something of value from all mistakes?

Are you permitting some relative or acquaintance to worry you? If so, why?

Are you sometimes "in the clouds" and at other times "in the depths" of despondency?

Who has the most inspiring influence upon you? What is the cause?

Do you tolerate negative or discouraging influences which you can avoid?

Are you careless of your personal appearance? If so, when and why?

Have you learned how to drown your troubles by being too busy to be annoyed by them?

Would you call yourself a "spineless weakling" if you permitted others to do your thinking for you?

Do you neglect internal bathing until autointoxication makes you ill-tempered and irritable?[14]

How many preventable disturbances annoy you, and why do you tolerate them?

Do you resort to liquor, pills, narcotics, or cigarettes to quiet your nerves? If so, why do you not try willpower instead?

Does anyone nag you, and if so, for what reason?

Do you have a DEFINITE CHIEF AIM IN LIFE, and if so, what is it and what plan have you for achieving it?

Do you suffer from any of the Six Basic Fears? If so, which ones?

Have you a method by which you can shield yourself against the negative influence of others?

Do you make deliberate use of autosuggestion to make your mind positive?

Which do you value most, your material possessions or your privilege of controlling your own thoughts?

Are you easily influenced by others, against your own judgment?

Has today added anything of value to your stock of knowledge or state of mind?

Do you face squarely the circumstances which make you unhappy, or do you sidestep the responsibility?

Do you analyze all mistakes and failures and try to profit by them, or do you take the attitude that this is not your duty?

Can you name three of your most damaging weaknesses? What are you doing to correct them?

Do you encourage other people to bring their worries to you for sympathy?

Do you choose, from your daily experiences, lessons or influences which aid in your personal advancement?

Does your presence have a negative influence on other people as a rule?

What habits of other people annoy you most?

Do you form your own opinions, or permit yourself to be influenced by other people?

Have you learned how to create a mental state of mind with which you can shield yourself against all discouraging influences?

Does your occupation inspire you with faith and hope?

Are you conscious of possessing spiritual forces of sufficient power to enable you to keep your mind free from all forms of FEAR?

Does your religion help you to keep your own mind positive?

Do you feel it your duty to share other people's worries? If so, why?

If you believe that birds of a feather flock together, what have you learned about yourself by studying the friends whom you attract?

What connection, if any, do you see between the people with whom you associate most closely and any unhappiness you may experience?

Could it be possible that some person whom you consider to be a friend is, in reality, your worst enemy because of his or her negative influence on your mind?

By what rules do you judge who is helpful and who is damaging to you?

Are your intimate associates mentally superior or inferior to you?

How much time out of every 24 hours do you devote to:
   a. your occupation
   b. sleep
   c. play and relaxation
   d. acquiring useful knowledge
   e. plain waste

Who among your acquaintances:
   a. encourages you most
   b. cautions you most
   c. discourages you most
   d. helps you most in other ways

What is your greatest worry? Why do you tolerate it?

When others offer you free, unsolicited advice, do you accept it without question or analyze their motive?

What, above all else, do you most DESIRE? Do you intend to acquire it? Are you willing to subordinate all other desires for this one? How much time daily do you devote to acquiring it?

Do you change your mind often? If so, why?

Do you usually finish everything you begin?

Are you easily impressed by other people's business or professional titles, college degrees, or wealth? Are you easily influenced by what other people think or say of you?

Do you cater to people because of their social or financial status?

Whom do you believe to be the greatest person living? In what respect is this person superior to yourself?

How much time have you devoted to studying and answering these questions? (At least one day is necessary for the thoughtful analysis and the full answering of the entire list.)

If you have answered all these questions truthfully, you know more about yourself than the majority of people. Study the questions carefully, come back to them once each week for several months, and be astounded at the amount of additional knowledge of great value to yourself you will have gained by the simple method of answering the questions truthfully. If you are not certain concerning the answers to some of the questions, seek the counsel of those who know you well, especially those who have no motive in flattering you, and see yourself through their eyes. The experience will be astonishing.

You have ABSOLUTE CONTROL over but one thing, and that is your thoughts. This is the most significant and inspiring of all known facts! It reflects the divine nature of humanity. This divine prerogative is the sole means by which you may control your own destiny. If you fail to control your own mind, you may be sure you will control nothing else.

If you must be careless with your possessions, let it be in connection with material things. *Your mind is your spiritual estate!* Protect and use it with the care to which divine royalty is entitled. You were given WILLPOWER for this purpose.

Unfortunately, there is no legal protection against those who, either by design or ignorance, poison the minds of others by negative suggestion. This form of destruction should be punishable by heavy legal penalties because it may and often does destroy one's chances of acquiring material things which are protected by law.

People with negative minds tried to convince Thomas Edison that he could not build a machine that would record and reproduce the human voice "because," they said, "no one else had ever produced such a machine." Edison did not believe them. He knew that THE MIND CAN PRODUCE ANYTHING THE MIND CAN CONCEIVE AND BELIEVE.[15] And that knowledge was what lifted the great Edison above the common herd.

People with negative minds told F. W. Woolworth he would go broke trying to run a store on five and ten cent sales. He did not believe them. He knew that he could do anything within reason if he backed his plans with FAITH. Exercising his right to keep other people's negative suggestions out of his mind, he piled up a fortune of more than a hundred million dollars.

People with negative minds told George Washington he could not hope to win against the vastly superior forces of the British, but he exercised his divine right to BELIEVE; therefore, this book was published under the protection of the Stars and Stripes, while the name of Lord Cornwallis has been all but forgotten.

Doubting Thomases scoffed when Henry Ford tried out his first crudely built automobile on the streets of Detroit. Some said the thing never would become practical. Others said no one would pay money for such a contraption. FORD SAID, "I'LL BELT THE EARTH WITH DEPENDABLE MOTOR CARS," AND HE DID! His decision to trust his own judgment piled up a fortune far greater than generations of his descendants could squander. For the benefit of those seeking vast riches, let it be remembered that practically the sole difference between Henry Ford and a majority of the more than 100,000 people who worked for him is this—FORD HAD A MIND AND CONTROLLED IT, WHILE MOST OF THE OTHERS HAD MINDS WHICH THEY DID NOT TRY TO CONTROL.

Henry Ford has been repeatedly mentioned because he is an astounding example of what individuals with a mind of their own, and a will to control it, can accomplish. His record knocks the foundation from under that time-worn alibi, "I never had a chance." Ford never had a chance either, but he CREATED AN OPPORTUNITY AND BACKED IT WITH PERSISTENCE UNTIL IT MADE HIM RICHER THAN CROESUS.[16]

Mind control is the result of self-discipline and habit. You either control your mind or it controls you. There is no halfway compromise. The most practical of all methods for controlling the mind is the habit of keeping it busy with a definite purpose, backed by a definite plan. Study the records of any individuals who achieve noteworthy success, and you will observe that they have control over their own mind, moreover, that they exercise that control and direct it toward the attainment of definite objectives. Without this control, success is not possible.

57 Famous Alibis

By Old Man IF

People who do not succeed have one distinguishing trait in common. They know *all the reasons for failure* and have what they believe to be airtight alibis to explain away their own lack of achievement.

Some of these alibis are clever, and a few are justifiable by the facts. But alibis cannot be used for money. The world wants to know only one thing—HAVE YOU ACHIEVED SUCCESS?

A character analyst compiled a list of the most commonly used alibis. As you read the list, examine yourself carefully and determine how many of these alibis, if any, are your own property. Remember, too, the philosophy presented in this book makes every one of these alibis obsolete:

IF I didn't have a wife and family . . .

IF I had enough "pull" . . .

IF I had money . . .

IF I had a good education . . .

IF I could get a job . . .
IF I had good health . . .
IF I only had time . . .
IF times were better . . .
IF other people understood me . . .
IF conditions around me were only different . . .
IF I could live my life over again . . .
IF I did not fear what "THEY" would say . . .
IF I had been given a chance . . .
IF I now had a chance . . .
IF other people didn't have it in for me . . .
IF nothing happens to stop me . . .
IF I were only younger . . .
IF I could only do what I want . . .
IF I had been born rich . . .
IF I could meet the right people . . .
IF I had the talent that some people have . . .
IF I dared assert myself . . .
IF only I had embraced past opportunities . . .
IF people didn't get on my nerves . . .
IF I didn't have to keep house and look after the children . . .
IF I could save some money . . .
IF the boss only appreciated me . . .
IF I only had somebody to help me . . .
IF my family understood me . . .
IF I lived in a big city . . .
IF I could just get started . . .
IF I were only free . . .
IF I had the personality of some people . . .
IF I were not so fat . . .
IF my talents were known . . .
IF I could just get a break . . .
IF I could only get out of debt . . .
IF I hadn't failed . . .
IF I only knew how . . .
IF everybody didn't oppose me . . .

IF I didn't have so many worries . . .

IF I could marry the right person . . .

IF people weren't so dumb . . .

IF my family were not so extravagant . . .

IF I were sure of myself . . .

IF luck were not against me . . .

IF I had not been born under the wrong star . . .

IF it were not true that "what is to be will be" . . .

IF I did not have to work so hard . . .

IF I hadn't lost my money . . .

IF I lived in a different neighborhood . . .

IF I didn't have a "past" . . .

IF I only had a business of my own . . .

IF other people would only listen to me . . .

IF—and this is the greatest of them all—I had the courage to see myself as I really am, I would *find out what is wrong with me and correct it*, then I might have a chance to profit by my mistakes and learn something from the experience of others, for I know that there is something WRONG with me or I would now be where I WOULD HAVE BEEN IF I had spent more time analyzing my weaknesses and less time building alibis to cover them.

Building alibis with which to explain away failure is a national pastime. The habit is as old as the human race and is fatal to success! Why do people cling to their pet alibis? The answer is obvious. They defend their alibis because THEY CREATE them! An alibi is the child of one's own imagination. It is human nature to defend one's own brain-child.

Building alibis is a deeply rooted habit. Habits are difficult to break, especially when they provide justification for something we do. Plato had this truth in mind when he said, "The first and best victory is to conquer self. To be conquered by self is, of all things, the most shameful and vile."

Another philosopher had the same thought in mind when he said, "It was a great surprise to me when I discovered that most of the ugliness I saw in others was but a reflection of my own nature."

"It has always been a mystery to me," said Elbert Hubbard, "why people spend so much time deliberately fooling themselves by creating alibis to cover their weaknesses. If used differently, this same time would be sufficient to cure the weakness, then no alibis would be needed."

In parting, I would remind you that "Life is a chessboard, and the player opposite you is TIME. If you hesitate before moving, or neglect to move thoughtfully and decisively, your pieces will be wiped off the board by TIME. You are playing against a partner who will not tolerate INDECISION!"

Previously you may have had a logical excuse for not having forced life to come through with whatever you asked, but that alibi is now obsolete because you are in possession of the Master Key that unlocks the door to life's bountiful riches.

The Master Key is intangible, but it is powerful! It is the privilege of creating, *in your own mind*, a BURNING DESIRE for a definite form of riches. There is no penalty for the use of the Key, but there is a price you must pay if you do not use it. The price is FAILURE. There is a reward of stupendous proportions if you put the Key to use. It is the satisfaction that comes to all *who conquer self and force life to pay whatever is asked.*

The reward is worthy of your effort. Will you make the start and be convinced?

"If we are related," said the immortal Emerson, "we shall meet." In closing, may I borrow his thought and say, "If we are related, we have, through these pages, met."

THE END

APPENDIX

APPENDIX A

A Soaring Spirit

Napoleon Hill was born on October 26, 1883, in a two-room log cabin in the mountains of Wise County in southwest Virginia, the son of James Monroe and Sara Sylvania Blair Hill. He died at age 87 on November 8, 1970, at his retirement home on Paris Mountain near Greenville, South Carolina, where he spent the last 13 years of his life. He was in relatively good health up until his sudden death and had recently undergone a successful cataract operation — the better to allow him to continue his lifelong habit of reading, research, and reflection on the principles of success. His death came the day before that of Charles DeGaulle of France, a towering world figure whom Hill would no doubt have relished interviewing about his life, philosophy, and particular path to success.

Dr. Hill was survived by his wife, Annie Lou N. Hill, a native South Carolinian; three sons, James H. Hill and Blair H. Hill of Lumberport, West Virginia, and David H. Hill of Clarksburg, West Virginia; two brothers, Vivian O. Hill of Washington and Dr. Paul Hill of Harrisburg, Virginia; and one sister, Mrs. Willie Wise of Wise, Virginia. The November 12, 1970, edition of *The Greenville (S. C.) News* published the following editorial after his death:

Napoleon Hill chose to settle down in Greenville about 18 [*sic*, should be "13"] years ago after an active life in which he came to know many of America's most famous people. He himself became famous for the books he published after moving here.

His works on the power of thought achieved best-seller status and were published after the author had attained an age at which most people were in complete retirement.

Mr. Hill acquired a vast amount of information and wisdom which he was able to reduce to easily-grasped form in the books he wrote. He had the refreshing ability to keep growing and to remain outgoing as the years rolled by.

He was one of the best exponents of the power of positive thinking, an attribute the world needs in an age when negative thought appears to be gaining popularity. Greenville and the nation lost a valuable citizen when Napoleon Hill died recently at age 87.

Napoleon and Annie Lou Hill today lie buried side by side in Frederick Memorial Gardens, located on the Cherokee Foothills Scenic Highway just off Interstate 85 and about one and a half miles from the city limits of Gaffney, South Carolina. If you ever pass that way, and if Napoleon Hill has meant something to you, a trip to Memorial Gardens will be a memorable experience.

The gravesites of Napoleon and his beloved Annie Lou—who died December 21, 1984, at the age of 90—lie in section B-1, lot 16, under the shade of a stately Florida maple. A four-foot-by-16-inch bronze marker, embellished with etched dogwood flowers, rests above their individual markers. The main marker reads simply, "Napoleon Hill – Author." The exposed roots of the old maple have gradually fingered their way over the ground's surface and, seemingly, almost down into Hill's very grave—a living metaphor for how his life's work has provided and continues to provide sustenance, inspiration, and energy to the lives of so many people all these years.

A second aspect of the landscape in Frederick Memorial Gardens provides, equally fortuitously, another metaphoric statement about what Napoleon Hill's life and work have meant to the world. Across the curving cemetery road from Hill's grave rests a monument designed by John Erwin Ramsay, an architect from Salisbury, North

Carolina. It is a Christian monument, full of symbolism about the ultimate futility of human striving—a trylon or "triangular stele" (a tall triangular shaft tapering to a point), representing the Holy Trinity; water at the base representing the "water of life"; and so on. There is also a soaring concrete arch fronting the trylon, like the parabolic trajectory of a steep Roman candle shot, frozen in time—a small-scale St. Louis Gateway Arch. It symbolizes birth and death, and mankind's need for relationship with God, but the dramatic upward "soaring" of this parabola—and the inscription relating to its skyward thrust—in some unexpected way call to mind *The Think and Grow Rich Philosophy* of Napoleon Hill and his belief in the power of individuals to shape their own destiny. In part, the inscription reads:

"From the earth, man *through his own efforts* soars upward in search of eternal life...."

APPENDIX B

Tributes to the Author*
From Great American Leaders

Here is what some American leaders in finance, education, government, and politics had to say about Napoleon Hill's research and writings on the principles of success:

Supreme Court of the United States
Washington, D. C.

Dear Mr. Hill:
...I wish to express my appreciation of the splendid work you have done in the organization of this philosophy.

It would be helpful if every politician in the country would assimilate and apply the... principles upon which your lessons are based. It contains some very fine material which every leader in every walk of life should understand.

I am happy to have had the privilege of rendering you some slight measure of help in the organization of this splendid course of "common sense" philosophy.

Sincerely yours,
[signature]
William H. Taft

(Former President and former Chief Justice of the United States)

---

* Adapted from the 1937 edition of *Think and Grow Rich!*.

"Allow me to express my appreciation of the compliment you have paid me in sending the original manuscript...I can see you have spent a great deal of time and thought in its preparation. Your philosophy is sound and you are to be congratulated for sticking to your work over so long a period of years. Your students will be amply rewarded for their labor."

-- THOMAS A. EDISON, inventor and entrepreneur

"Your work and mine are peculiarly akin. I am helping the laws of Nature to create more perfect specimens of vegetation while you are using those same laws...to build more perfect specimens of thinkers."

-- LUTHER BURBANK, father of scientific plant breeding

"Certainly I will supply you with the information you request. This I consider to be not only a duty, but it is a pleasure as well. You are laboring in behalf of the people who have neither the time nor the inclination to ferret out the causes of failure and success."

-- THEODORE ROOSEVELT, President

"If I had a young son I would insist that he read every word... by Napoleon Hill, [one of the two] most inspirational writers in the world. I know your...fundamentals of success are sound because I have been applying them in my business for more than 30 years."

-- JOHN WANAMAKER, department store founder

"Our entire business policy, in the management of our hotels, is based upon [your success fundamentals] of which I am a student."

-- E. M. STATLER, hotel magnate

"I feel greatly indebted for the privilege of reading your law of success philosophy. If I had had this fifty years ago, I suppose I could have accomplished all that I have done in less than half the time. I sincerely hope the world will discover and reward you."

-- ROBERT DOLLAR, steamship magnate

"Napoleon Hill has produced what I believe to be the first practical philosophy of achievement. Its major distinguishing feature is the simplicity in which it has been presented."

-- DAVID STARR JORDAN, president of Stanford University

"Mr. Curtis...has built one of the greatest publishing businesses in the world by applying the principles of this philosophy."

-- EDWARD BOK, editor of *Ladies Home Journal*, speaking about Cyrus H. K. Curtis, founder of Curtis Publishing Company, publisher of *Ladies Home Journal* and *The Saturday Evening Post*

"You may say for Mr. Rockefeller that he endorses Mr. Hill's... principles of success, and that he recommends them to those who are seeking the highway to achievement."

-- Secretary to JOHN D. ROCKEFELLER, founder of Standard Oil Co.

"By applying many of the...fundamentals of the law of success philosophy, we have built a great chain of successful stores. I presume it would be no exaggeration of fact if I said that the Woolworth Building might properly be called a monument to the soundness of these principles."

-- F. W. WOOLWORTH, founder of Woolworth "5-and-10-cent" department store chain

"Mastery of the law of success philosophy is the equivalent of an insurance policy against failure."

-- SAMUEL GOMPERS, American labor leader

"May I not congratulate you on your persistence. Any man who devotes that much time...must of necessity make discoveries of great value to others. I am deeply impressed by your interpretation of the 'Master Mind' principles which you have so clearly described."

-- WOODROW WILSON, President of the United States

"I know that you are doing a world of good....I would not care to set a monetary value on this training because it brings to the student qualities which cannot be measured by money alone."

-- GEORGE EASTMAN, founder of Eastman-Kodak Co.

"Whatever success I may have obtained I owe, entirely, to the application of your...fundamental principles of the law of success. I believe I have the honor of being your first student."

--WILLIAM WRIGLEY, JR., founder of the William Wrigley Jr. Company, world's largest manufacturer of chewing gum products

EVIDENCE THAT MONEY COULD NOT BUY

The foregoing is evidence and praise seldom accorded *any* course of education. Money could not buy such letters of endorsement from individuals who are, or have been, leaders of our times.

Think and Grow Rich! is a liberating, power-radiating book that will shape your destiny, enrich your future, and turn your hopes and dreams into solid success-realities.

Don't waste your own precious years blindly searching for the hidden road to the heights. Profit by the dearly bought experience of America's leaders. More than 500 great and prominent Americans were minutely analyzed — their methods, motives, strategy — to find out the secrets that put them on top.

No matter whether you are rich or poor, you have one asset as great as the richest person on earth — and that is TIME. But with each setting sun, you become one day older and have *one day less* in which to attain the success and wealth you desire. Thousands of progressive people throughout the North American continent have realized this mighty truth and have sought the help so clearly and inspiringly taught by Napoleon Hill.

You cannot afford to let day after day slip into eternity without getting possession of the principles of success. You will profit greatly from the lessons in *Think and Grow Rich!* The cost is trifling. The benefits are tremendous.

APPENDIX C

Original Publisher's Preface*

This book conveys the experience of more than 500 individuals of great wealth, who began at scratch, with nothing to give in return for riches except THOUGHTS, IDEAS and ORGANIZED PLANS.

Here you have the entire philosophy of money-making, just as it was organized from the actual achievements of the most successful individuals known to the American people during the early part of the twentieth century. It describes WHAT TO DO, also, HOW TO DO IT!

It presents complete instructions on HOW TO SELL YOUR PERSONAL SERVICES.

It provides you with a perfect system of self-analysis that will readily disclose what has been standing between you and "the big money" in the past.

It describes the famous Andrew Carnegie formula of personal achievement by which he accumulated hundreds of millions of dollars for himself and made no fewer than a score of millionaires of people to whom he taught his secret.

Perhaps you do not need all that is to be found in the book — no one of the 500 individuals from whose experiences it was written did — but you may need ONE IDEA, PLAN or SUGGESTION to

---

* Adapted from the 1937 edition of *Think and Grow Rich!*.

start you toward your goal. Somewhere in the book you will find this needed stimulus.

The book was inspired by Andrew Carnegie after he had made his millions and retired. It was written by the man to whom Carnegie disclosed the astounding secret of his riches — the same man to whom the 500 wealthy individuals revealed the source of their riches.

In this volume will be found *The 13 Steps to Riches* essential to every person who accumulates sufficient money to guarantee financial independence. It is estimated that the research — covering more than 25 years of continuous effort — which went into the preparation of this book could not be duplicated at a cost of less than $1 million.

Moreover, the knowledge contained in the book never can be duplicated, at any cost, for the reason that more than half of the 500 persons who supplied the information it brings have passed on.

Riches cannot always be measured in money!

Money and material things are essential for freedom of body and mind, but there are some who will feel that the greatest of all riches can be evaluated only in terms of lasting friendships, harmonious family relationships, sympathy and understanding between business associates, and introspective harmony which brings one peace of mind measurable only in spiritual values!

All who read, understand and apply this philosophy will be better prepared to attract and enjoy these higher estates which always have been and always will be denied to all except *those who are ready for them.*

Be prepared, therefore, when you expose yourself to the influence of this philosophy, to experience a CHANGED LIFE which may help you not only to negotiate your way through life with harmony and understanding, but also to prepare you for the accumulation of material riches in abundance.

THE PUBLISHER

APPENDIX D

This Standing Army

Is at Your Service*

It Will Bring You Fame, Fortune, Peace of Mind or Whatever You Demand of Life!

In this picture you see the most powerful army on earth.

Observe the emphasis on the word POWERFUL. This army is standing at attention, ready to do the bidding of any person who will command it. It is YOUR army if you will take charge of it.

---

* Adapted from the 1937 version of *Think and Grow Rich!*.

These soldiers are named DEFINITE CHIEF AIM...HABIT OF SAVING...SELF-CONFIDENCE...IMAGINATION...INITIATIVE... LEADERSHIP...ENTHUSIASM... SELF-CONTROL...DOING MORE THAN PAID FOR...PLEASING PERSONALITY...ACCURATE THOUGHT...CONCENTRATION...COOPERATION...FAILURE... TOLERANCE...THE GOLDEN RULE...THE MASTER MIND.

A long, searching study of the lives of 500 great American men and women — as well as actual endorsement from nationally known leaders — proves that these are the *basic principles* upon which all true and lasting success is built.

POWER comes from organized effort. You see in this picture — in these "soldiers" — the forces which enter into all organized effort. Master these sixteen forces or personal qualities *and you may have whatever you want in life.*

NAPOLEON HILL HAS WRITTEN A SUCCESS COURSE FOR YOU!

Think and Grow Rich! presents, for the first time in the history of the world, the true philosophy upon which all lasting success is built. Ideas, when translated into intelligent plans of action, are the beginning of all successful achievement. So *Think and Grow Rich!* proceeds to show you how to create practical ideas for every human need. It does so in easy-to-understand steps.

Napoleon Hill spent the better part of 25 years in perfecting this philosophy of success. During the long years he worked on it, some parts or the whole of it were reviewed and praised by many of the greatest Americans of our times.

Among them are included four Presidents of the United States, Theodore Roosevelt, Woodrow Wilson, Warren G. Harding, and

William H. Taft; Also, Thomas Edison, Luther Burbank, William J. Wrigley, Alexander Graham Bell, Judge E. H. Gary, Cyrus H. K. Curtis, Edward Bok, E. M. Statler—dozens of other glowing names in politics, finance, education, and invention.

ANDREW CARNEGIE STARTED IT

More than 25 years ago, Napoleon Hill, then a young special investigator for a nationally known business magazine, was sent to interview Andrew Carnegie. During that interview Carnegie slyly dropped a hint of a certain master power he used—a magic law of the human mind, a little known psychological principle—which was amazing in its power.

Carnegie suggested to Hill that upon that principle he could build the philosophy of all personal success—whether it be measured in terms of money, power, position, prestige, influence, or accumulation of wealth.

That part of the interview never went into Hill's magazine. But it did launch the young author upon more than 20 years of research. And today we open to YOU the discovery and methods of using the revolutionary force which Carnegie quietly hinted at.

In the trail of the lessons of success found in *Think and Grow Rich!* come accomplishments, not mere entertainment and time-killing diversion. There come larger businesses; bigger bank accounts; fatter pay envelopes; small, struggling enterprises given new life and power to grow; and low-pay employees shown how to gain advancement by leaps and bounds.

APPENDIX E

What Do You Want Most?*

*Is It Money, Fame, Power, Contentment, Personality,
Peace of Mind, Happiness?*

The Thirteen Steps to Riches described in this book offer the shortest dependable philosophy of individual achievement ever presented for the benefit of the man or woman who is searching for a definite goal in life.

Before beginning the book you will profit greatly if you recognize the fact that *the book was not written to entertain*. You cannot digest the contents properly in a week or a month.

After reading the book thoroughly, Dr. Miller Reese Hutchison, nationally known consulting engineer and long-time associate of Thomas A. Edison, said:

"This is not a novel. It is a textbook on individual achievement that came directly from the experiences of hundreds of America's most successful individuals. It should be *studied, digested, and meditated upon*. No more than one chapter should be read in a single night. Readers should underline the sentences which impress them most. Later, they should go back to these marked lines and read

---

* Adapted from the original 1937 edition of *Think and Grow Rich!*.

them again. *A real student will not merely read this book,* but will absorb its contents and make them his or her own. This book should be adopted by all high schools and no boy or girl should be permitted to graduate without having satisfactorily passed an examination on it. This philosophy will not take the place of the subjects taught in schools, but it will enable one to *organize and apply* the knowledge acquired, and convert it into useful service and adequate compensation without waste of time."

Dr. John R. Turner, dean of the College of The City of New York, after having read the book, wrote to Napoleon Hill: "The very best example of the soundness of this philosophy is your own son, Blair, whose dramatic story you have outlined in the chapter on Desire."

Dr. Turner had reference to the author's son, who, born without normal hearing capacity, not only avoided becoming a deaf mute, but actually converted his disability into a priceless asset by applying the philosophy here described. After reading Blair's story, you will realize that you are about to come into possession of a philosophy which can be transmuted into material wealth, or serve as readily to bring you peace of mind, understanding, spiritual harmony, and in some instances, as in the case of the author's son, it can help you master physical affliction.

The Most Profitable Way to Use This Book

The author discovered, through personally analyzing hundreds of successful men and women, that *all* of them followed the habit of exchanging ideas through *conferences.* When they had problems to be solved, they sat down together and talked freely until they discovered, from their joint contribution of ideas, a plan that would serve their purpose.

You who read this book will get the most out of it by putting into practice the Master Mind principle described in the book. This you can do (as others are doing so successfully) by forming a study club, consisting of any desired number of people who are friendly and harmonious. The club should have a meeting at regular periods, as often as once each week. The procedure should consist of reading one chapter of the book at each meeting, after which the contents of the chapter should be freely discussed by all members. All members should make notes, putting down *ALL IDEAS OF THEIR OWN* inspired by the discussion.   Each member should carefully read and analyze each chapter several days prior to its open reading and joint discussion in the club. The reading at the club should be done by someone who reads well and understands how to put color and feeling into the lines.

By following this plan, readers will get from its pages not only the sum total of the best knowledge organized from the experiences of hundreds of successful people, but more important by far, *they will tap new sources of knowledge in their own minds, as well as acquire knowledge of priceless value FROM EVERY OTHER PERSON PRESENT.*

If you follow this plan *persistently,* you will be almost certain to uncover and appropriate the secret formula by which Andrew Carnegie acquired his huge fortune, as referred to in the author's introduction.

APPENDIX F

Early Sources

Napoleon Hill did not write in a vacuum. The late 19th century and early twentieth century witnessed the publication of a vast variety of motivational and "success oriented" books, pamphlets, and magazines. Hill no doubt availed himself of many of them in his personal reading and research for *Think and Grow Rich!*.

The following excerpts from a small 332-page pocketbook published in 1896 by Louis Klopsch (New York) are instructive. Just as echoes of Napoleon Hill can be found in every "success" book or other "how to achieve" resource produced since the 1950s, so can glimpses be found in pre-*Think and Grow Rich!* books of rhetorical and other techniques Hill would use in his landmark work.

In the excerpt below, note the use of inspirational quotations from well-known individuals. Note the emphatic, forceful language ("Very well, *I will be a king!*"). Note the emphasis on faith as a source of empowerment, the discussion about "dogged determination," persistence in the face of tough obstacles, and "invincible will." Here Napoleon Bonaparte is quoted as saying, "'Impossible' is a word only to be found in the dictionary of fools." Hill in *Think and Grow Rich!* reports that he once took a dictionary and immediately cut out the word "impossible." Ideas and techniques such as these certainly foreshadow *Think and Grow Rich!*. Hill's genius lay in how he artfully blended and integrated such narrative and rhetorical techniques with the very practical, applicable "how to do it" principles of success that he developed during his more than 20 years of research.

The excerpt that follows is from Chapter XV, "Willpower," from *How to Succeed; or, Stepping-Stones to Fame and Fortune* by Dr. Orison Swett Marden.

CHAPTER XV
WILLPOWER.

In the moral world there is nothing impossible if we can bring a thorough will to do it. –W. HUMBOLDT.

It is firmness that makes the gods on our side. – VOLTAIRE

People do not lack strength they lack will. – VICTOR HUGO

Perpetual pushing and assurance put a difficulty out of countenance and make a seeming difficulty give way. – JEREMY COLLIER.

When a firm, decisive spirit is recognized, it is curious to see how the space clears around a man and leaves him room and freedom. – JOHN FOSTER

"Do you know," asked Balzac's father, "that in literature a man must be either a king or a beggar?" "Very well," replied his son, "*I will be a king.*" After ten years of struggle with hardship and poverty, he won success as an author.

"Why do you repair that magistrate's bench with such great care?" asked a bystander of a carpenter who was taking unusual pains. "Because I wish to make it easy against the time when I come to sit on it myself," replied the other. He did sit on that bench as a magistrate a few years later.

"*I will be marshal of France and a great general,*" exclaimed a young French officer as he paced his room with hands tightly clenched. He became a successful general and a marshal of France.

"There is so much power in faith," says [Edward] Bulwer [-Lyton],* "even when faith is applied but to things human and

---

* (1803-1873) English dramatist, novelist, and politician.

earthly, that let a man but be firmly persuaded that he is born to do some day, what at the moment seems impossible, and it is fifty to one but what he does it before he dies."

There is about as much chance of idleness and incapacity winning real success, or a high position in life, as there would be in producing a *Paradise Lost* by shaking up promiscuously the separate words of *Webster's Dictionary*, and letting them fall at random on the floor. Fortune smiles upon those who roll up their sleeves and put their shoulders to the wheel; upon men who are not afraid of dreary, dry, irksome drudgery, men of nerve and grit who do not turn aside for dirt and detail.

"Is there one who difficulties dishearten?" asked John Hunter. "He will do little. Is there one who will conquer? That kind of man never fails."

"Circumstances," says Milton, "have rarely favored famous men. They have fought their way to triumph through all sorts of opposing obstacles."…

The simple truth is that a will strong enough to keep a man continually striving for things not wholly beyond his powers will carry him in time very far toward his chosen goal.

At nineteen, Bayard Taylor walked to Philadelphia, thirty miles, to find a publisher for fifteen of his poems. He wanted to see them printed in a book; but no publisher would undertake it. He returned to his home whistling, however, showing that his courage and resolution had not abated.

In Europe he was often forced to live on twenty cents a day for weeks on account of his poverty. He returned to London with only thirty cents left. He tried to sell a poem of twelve hundred lines, which he had in his knapsack, but no publisher wanted it. Of that time he wrote: "My situation was about as hopeless as it is possible to conceive." But his will defied circumstances and he rose above them.…

We are told of a young New York inventor who about twenty years ago spent every dollar he was worth in an experiment, which, if successful, would introduce his invention to public notice and insure his fortune, and what he valued more, his usefulness. The next morning the daily papers heaped unsparing ridicule upon him. Hope for the future seemed vain. He looked around the shabby room where his wife, a delicate little woman, was preparing breakfast. He was without a penny. He seemed like a fool in his own eyes; all these years of hard work were wasted. He went into his chamber, sat down, and buried his face in his hands.

At length, with a fiery heat flashing through his body, he stood erect. "It *shall* succeed!" he said, shutting his teeth. His wife was crying over the papers when he went back. "They are very cruel," she said. "They don't understand." "I'll make them understand," he replied cheerfully. "It was a fight for six years," he said afterward. "Poverty, sickness and contempt followed me. I had nothing left but the *dogged determination* that is should succeed." It did succeed. The invention was a great and useful one. The inventor is now a prosperous and happy man.

Napoleon was a terrible example of what the power of will can accomplish. He always threw his whole force of body and mind direct upon his work. Imbecile rulers and the nations they governed went down before him in succession. He was told that the Alps stood in the way of his armies. "There shall be no Alps," he said, and the road cross the Simplon* was constructed, through a district formerly almost inaccessible. "Impossible," said he, "is a word only to be found in the dictionary of fools." He was a man who toiled terribly, sometimes employing and exhausting four secretaries at a time. He spared no one, not even himself. His influence inspired other men, and put a new life into them. "I made my generals out of mud," he said.

To think we are able is almost to be so — to determine upon attainment, is frequently attainment itself. Thus, earnest resolution has often seemed to have about it almost a savor of omnipotence.

---

* The Simplon Pass is 6,590 feet (2,009 meters) high in the Lepontine Alps in Southern Switzerland. Napoleon had his troops build the Simplon Road here between 1800 and 1806 as an entryway to Italy. The Pass has been a major trade route between southern and northern Europe since the 13th century.

The strength of Suwarrow's* character lay in his power of willing, and, like most resolute persons, he preached it up as a system....

What has chance ever done in the world? Has it built any cities? Has it invented any telephones, and telegraphs? Has it built any steamships, established any universities, any asylums, any hospitals? Was there any chance in Cæsar's crossing the Rubicon? What had chance to do with Napoleon's career, with Wellington's, or Grant's...? Every battle was won before it was begun. What had luck to do with Thermopylæ, Trafalgar, Gettysburg? Our successes we ascribe to ourselves; our failures to destiny.

A vacillating man, no matter what his abilities, is invariably pushed to the wall in the race of life by a determined will. It is he who resolves to succeed, and who at every fresh rebuff begins resolutely again, that reaches the goal. The shores of fortune are covered with the stranded wrecks of men of brilliant ability, but who have wanted courage, faith and decision, and have therefore perished in sight of more resolute but less capable adventurers, who succeeded in making port. Hundreds of men go to their graves in obscurity, who have been obscure only because they lacked the pluck to make a first effort, and who, could they only have resolved to begin, would have astonished the world by their achievements and successes. The fact is, as Sydney Smith[†] has well said, that in order to do anything in this world that is worth doing, we must not stand shivering on the bank, and thinking of the cold and the danger, but jump in and scramble through as well as we can.

Is not this a grand privilege of man, immortal man, that though he may not be able to stir a finger; that though a moth may crush

---

* The Russian Aleksandr V. Suvorov (1729-1800) was one of the greatest military commanders of all time, ranking with Alexander the Great, Hannibal, and George Patton, J. Others have labeled him a butcher who was more interested in destroying than defeating his enemies. His battle record was 63 victories, no defeats, frequently against numerically superior enemies.

[†]Smith (1771-1845) was an English clergyman, essayist, and lecturer considered by many as the wittiest man of his era. He was a founder of the *Edinburgh Review*.

him; that merely by a righteous will, he is raised above the stars; that by it he originates a good in the universe, which the universe could not annihilate; a good which can defy extinction, though all created energies of intelligence or matter were combined against it?

A man whose moral nature is ascendant is not the subject, but the superior of circumstances. His is free; nay, more, he is a king; and though this sovereignty may have been won by many desperate battles, once on the throne, and holding the sceptre with a firm grasp, he has a royalty of which neither time nor accident can strip him.

What can you do with a man who has an invincible purpose in him; who never knows when he is beaten; and who, when his legs are shot off, will fight on the stumps. Difficulties and opposition do not daunt him. He thrives upon persecution; it only stimulates him to more determined endeavor. *The world always listens to a man with a will in him.* You might as well snub the sun as such men as Bismarck and Grant.

Hope would storm the castle of despair; it gives courage when despondency would give up the battle of life. He is the best doctor who can implant *hope* and courage in the human soul. So he is the greatest man who can inspire us to the grandest achievements.

Our remedies oft in ourselves do lie
   Which we ascribe to heaven; the fated sky
Gives us free scope; and only backward pulls
   Our slow designs when we ourselves are dull.
How much I could do if I only tried.

APPENDIX G

Works by Napoleon Hill
(Chronologically)

Hill's Golden Rule magazine (1919-1920)
Napoleon Hill's Magazine (1921-1923)
The Law of Success (1928, 1979)
The Magic Ladder to Success (1930)
Inspiration Magazine (1931)
Think and Grow Rich! (1937, 1960)
Mental Dynamite (1941) — 16-volume textbook
How to Raise Your Own Salary (1953)
Science of Success (1953) — six volumes (textbooks)
PMA Science of Success (1956)
Success through a Positive Mental Attitude (1960, 1977),
    with W. Clement Stone
Your Right to Be Rich (1961, 1990) — An Interactive Study
    Guide
The Master Key to Riches (1965)
Grow Rich with Peace of Mind (1967)
Succeed And Grow Rich Through Persuasion (1970), with
    E. Harold Keown
You Can Work Your Own Miracles (1971) —
    How to Condition Yourself for Success

APPENDIX H

"It Couldn't Be Done"

One of Annie Lou Hill's (Mrs. Napoleon Hill's) favorite poems was "It Couldn't Be Done," written by Edgar Guest in 1914. With its emphasis on Positive Mental Attitude, can-do spirit, enthusiasm, perseverance, and refusal to let scoffers and doubters dissuade one from one's dreams and desire for achievement, this delightful verse captures in poetic form the essence of Napoleon Hill's *Think and Grow Rich Philosophy*.

"It Couldn't Be Done"

Somebody said that it couldn't be done,
    But he with a chuckle replied
That "maybe it couldn't," but he would be one
    Who wouldn't say so till he'd tried.
So he buckled right in with the trace of a grin
    On his face. If he worried he hid it.
He started to sing and he tackled the thing
    That couldn't be done, and he did it.

Somebody scoffed: "Oh, you'll never do that;
    At least no one has ever done it";
But he took off his coat and he took off his hat,
    And the first thing we knew he'd begun it.

With a lift of his chin and a bit of a grin,
  Without any doubting or quiddit,
He started to sing and he tackled the thing
  That couldn't be done, and he did it.

There are thousands to tell you it cannot be done,
  There are thousands to prophesy failure;
There are thousands to point out to you, one by one,
  The dangers that wait to assail you.
But just buckle it in with a bit of a grin,
  Just take off your coat and go to it;
Just start to sing as you tackle the thing
  That "cannot be done," and you'll do it.

Edgar Guest (1881-1959) was an English immigrant who arrived in Detroit in 1891. He began supporting his family as a newspaper copy boy and went on to become a career newspaperman and radio personality who wrote more than 20 volumes of poetry. At his death, he was mourned as "the poet of the people" because he wrote popular sentimental poems about everyday family life and values. He composed some 11,000 poems during his career. (The word "quiddit" in verse 2, line 6, is actually "quiddity" and means "quibbling.")

A Hill nephew came across "It Couldn't Be Done," checked in pencil, in a book titled *It Can Be Done: Poems of Motivation and Inspiration*—more than 50 years after the book had been given to Annie Lou Hill, in 1923, by her sister Mary.

APPENDIX I

The Mindpower Press

What the World Needs Is More Winners!

Thousands upon thousands of men and women, through the years and throughout the world, have credited their success in life largely, if not entirely, to the application of the practical lessons of achievement Dr. Hill teaches in *Think and Grow Rich!*. It has been an extraordinary philosophy that has been steadily spreading and slowly helping change the landscape of human potential and achievement, individual by individual, decade by decade.

Thanks to the work of Napoleon Hill, the rungs on the ladder to high success and great riches — in the fullest, most meaningful sense of those words — are within reach of anyone who can read or hear, think, and be motivated to action. And an organization called The Mindpower Press will be dedicated to helping make sure that such individuals' reach does not exceed their grasp.

The Press will be an educational organization whose mission is to perpetuate *The Think and Grow Rich Philosophy* and to develop and disseminate timely, practical information about the science of success and achievement.

The goal of The Press is to make the principles and skills involved in this philosophy, and the book from which it is derived, available to every individual and community in America and eventually throughout the world.

The Press will be composed of, and supported by, success-oriented, achievement-focused individuals. Its members and supporters will have this in common: Their lives, in one way or another, have been positively and dramatically influenced by *Think and Grow Rich!*, and they would like to repay that debt by helping spread the word to others who have the potential to *think and grow rich* in all ways that matter.

THE WINNING COMBINATION

Napoleon Hill often wrote about the power of the Master Mind Principle. In his words, "Whenever two or more minds are blended in a spirit of perfect harmony, for the pursuit of a definite purpose, there is born of that alliance a power which is greater than that of all the individual minds combined."

The Mindpower Press invites you to consider becoming a part of an ambitious, far-reaching new Master Mind Alliance. You can join thousands of individuals whose lives have been touched by *Think and Grow Rich!* and who want to help perpetuate and further develop the book's teachings and research.

Would you like to learn about future developments concerning *Think and Grow Rich!* and the philosophy of success it entails?

Would you be interested in sharing with a national audience the story of what *Think and Grow Rich!* has meant to you—how it has specifically helped you along the road to success?

Would you like to receive information about a future fully interactive website that will be devoted to developing and sharing success information and ideas?

If you would, please write to us to let us know. We will add your name to our mailing and resource lists, and we will keep you informed of new programs, publications, and services as they are developed. Our address is:

The Mindpower Press
P.O. Box 1732
Clemson, South Carolina 29633
(864) 654-4642

May great success be yours—live your dream!

ACKNOWLEDGEMENTS

This new version of *Think and Grow Rich!* was made possible with the help and support of many individuals in many places. I want to thank my partner, Del Gurley, and his wife (and my sister) Barbara Cornwell Gurley. Del, who epitomizes *The Think and Grow Rich Philosophy*, has believed in this project, supported it in numerous ways, and provided financing and encouragement that helped make it happen. I cherish the many "Master Mind Alliance" hours the Gurleys and I discussed the project, traded ideas, and dreamed the dream of making *Think and Grow Rich!* more relevant and understandable for future generations of high achievers.

Thanks are due also to Dr. Caron St. John, director of the Spiro Center for Entrepreneurial Leadership at Clemson University. Her guidance, intelligent counsel, and sage advice, especially in the "proposal stage" of our project, were valuable and are greatly appreciated.

An unusual venture such as this required the services of a good intellectual property attorney. I found one in Jim Bagarazzi of the Dority & Manning law firm, who helped us avoid the pitfalls and get through the minefields of copyright questions, contract negotiations, and trademark law. Thanks, Jim, for helping us protect the tremendous investment we have made in this project.

Tonya Flemming performed magnificently in helping type and format the manuscript, while Patsy Melsheimer did a wonderful job at the thankless task of proofreading it and keeping its editor from looking foolish.

Beth Moore of Gurley Management made sure the bills got paid on time, shared generously of her computer resources, and could always be counted on, with a wonderful smile and laugh, to bring sunshine into many gloomy days at the office. To Elaine Payne and Lynn Whitfield, founders of the Low Carb Connoisseur, thanks for being a source of "Internet inspiration" and ideas, and for helpful suggestions about publishing resources and options.

Many friends and acquaintances have supported me as I sought to complete this work. They were always interested in, and always asked about, how things were going, and they never ceased to offer encouragements along the way. Chief among these many faithful are Don and Marietta Bolt (brother- and sister-in-law *nonpareil*), David Bryan Martin (another special brother-in-law), Jim and Sally Richardson, the late Bobby Abrams and his wife, Alice Gene, John and Joyce Geer, and Sonny and Gervais Emanuel. Special thanks are due to Dr. Jerry and Sally Trapnell for so many kindnesses extended. Thanks also to Dr. Don McKale of Clemson University's History Department, Professor Bill Koon of its English Department, children's book author Betsy Byars, and Jim and Kate Palmer for their advice about publishers and the use of literary agents. Thanks also to Rives "Boo" Cheney for an early collaboration through which we were first introduced to *Think and Grow Rich!*.

I would be remiss in not expressing my gratitude to Bob Proctor, Paul Martinelli and all the LifeSuccess Consultants they have trained around the globe. Their support of this book and their work in initiating and spreading Master Mind Study Groups throughout the world is a great and momentous service to humanity. No one knows better than they that this book can change people's lives—and it can help change the world.

While this project is not associated or affiliated with the Napoleon Hill Foundation, I would also be remiss in not expressing thanks to three individuals long associated with it: its late chairman, W. Clement Stone, for not vetoing my service for three years as the first executive editor of *Think & Grow Rich Newsletter* (and for contributing a monthly column to it); Michael J. Ritt, Jr., retired executive director of the Foundation, for insights about

Napoleon Hill and his work, derived from dinner and many other conversations; and Dr. Charles Johnson, who is Hill's nephew and current chairman of the Foundation, for sharing personal anecdotes and observations about his uncle and for letting me sit at the oaken desk at which Hill wrote many of his books.

In undertaking a research project like this, one quickly comes to understand the virtues and value of good research librarians. I owe thanks to many for their dedicated efforts to assist me in tracking down some obscure fact, bit of biographical detail, or piece of arcana. Special thanks to Lois Sill and Jan Comfort of the Robert Muldrow Cooper Library at Clemson University; to Pamela Gibson of The Eaton Florida History Room, Manatee County (Florida) Central Library; Sharon Sumpter, assistant archivist, Archive Department, and Hector Escobar of the Theodore M. Hesburgh Library, University of Notre Dame; Rose Donoway and Debby Bennett of the Caroline County (Maryland) Public Library; Leslie Litoff of the Wilmette (Illinois) Public Library; and Rick Stringer of the Schreyer Business Library, Penn State University. These individuals went out of their way to assist me with general research on Napoleon Hill and *Think and Grow Rich!* and specialized research on the likes of Edwin C. Barnes, Stuart Austin Wier, Dan Halpin, and the elusive Mr. R. U. Darby — not to mention numerous other individuals and matters too numerous to relate.

Also appreciated are the kind assistance of Lois Carroll, Aimee Duncan, and manager Felicia Hardy of the Rourk Branch of the Brunswick County Library in Shallotte, North Carolina, where I spent many fruitful hours engaged in early marketing tasks for the book; the genealogical research conducted so graciously by Ronda Darbie (unrelated to R. U., as it turned out); and a brief biographical sketch, included in the endnotes, which was written for me by Dan D. Halpin about his father, who had a fascinating connection to the Hill family and was an exemplar of *Think and Grow Rich!* success. Thanks, too, to Joseph IsaacValenzuela, Ann Martin, and Ursula Segalla for pointing out citation and other errors that have now been corrected and which get us closer to the always elusive goal of a perfect manuscript.

(An aside: Neither I, nor any of my research librarian friends, were able to find any biographical information about the enigmatic R. U. Darby, who is featured so prominently in two of Napoleon Hill's key anecdotes. I hope some reader of this book knows who Darby was and what he did later in life, and will get in touch with me so that I can include that information in a subsequent edition of this book.)

I feel a deep sense of gratitude to my late parents, John and Vivian Cornwell, who had an enormous influence on my life, outlook, and personality. They nourished my curiosity, engendered in me a love of reading, and always believed in me. I also owe a great debt to the late David Martin and his wife, Thelma, for sharing their love and values and for allowing me to wed their daughter almost four decades ago.

Finally, I would like to thank three persons whose love and support mean everything to me and who were my inspiration for undertaking my work on this book—my Betty, my beautiful wife, for her unbelievable patience throughout the long "ordeal" of getting the book finished; my firstborn, Johannah, who is well on her way to becoming the kind of success story that Napoleon Hill would have loved to write about; and my daughter and namesake, Anne-Ross. "Little Dipper," you believed in this book more than any of us, and your positive attitude and encouragement truly gave me a reason to get this job done.

Ross Cornwell
July 2007

ENDNOTES

Author's Preface
PAGE
1   **The secret was brought**   Hill, at age 25, was a freelance journalist trying to earn money to go to law school at Georgetown University when his famous interview with the industrialist took place. Carnegie (1835-1919) was in the middle of his philanthropic years, busy giving away $350 million of his vast fortune for charitable purposes (more than $6.5 billion in today's dollars). It was the fall of 1908, and Hill had visited Carnegie for an interview for *Bob Taylor's Magazine*. The rapport that developed between the old industrialist and the young journalist resulted not merely in a three-hour interview, but a three-day, three-night marathon discussion (with time out for sleep and meals) in which Carnegie enthusiastically spelled out in detail the principles he had followed and the practical steps he had taken in amassing one of America's and the world's greatest fortunes.

The old Scotsman was a fascinating figure. He had immigrated to the United States from Scotland at age 13, settling with his family in Allegheny, Pennsylvania. Poor and with little formal education, he went to work first in a cotton factory, then (like Thomas Edison) in a telegraph office, and then for the Pennsylvania Railroad. By 1859 he had become head of the railroad's western division, at the age of 24.

It is clear from his rapid advancement that Carnegie had keen powers of observation, great personal initiative, and an almost instinctive grasp of the principles of success. He used all those traits, plus an enormous capacity for hard work, to create a thriving steel-making business after leaving the railroad in 1865. By 1899 he had consolidated various holdings into the Carnegie Steel Company. In 1901 he sold the company to a group headed by financier-industrialist J. P. Morgan for some $400 million ($7.4 billion in today's dollars).

Carnegie devoted the remainder of his life to philanthropic causes. He established some 2,500 public libraries, founded the Carnegie Institute of Technology (later Carnegie-Mellon University), and in 1911 established his major philanthropy, the Carnegie Foundation, to promote "the advancement and diffusion of knowledge." One of his most significant, if less well-publicized and recognized achievements was, of course, starting the young Napoleon Hill off on the journey that led to Hill's interviews with some of the world's greatest achievers—and to the systematic development of the principles of success and *The Think and Grow Rich Philosophy*, which Carnegie wished to make available to all individuals, no matter what their background or personal circumstances.

2   **Arthur Nash**   Arthur Nash (1870-1927) was originally a minister (Disciples of Christ) who left the pulpit for a career in the garment industry. After only seven years in the business, he had founded the Arthur Nash Company, a wholesale tailoring concern in Cincinnati. The "Nash Plan," in which workers co-owned the business, was one of his management innovations. Nash is the author of *The Golden Rule of Business*, a popular business book in the early 1920s.

3   **The secret was passed**   Stuart Austin Wier (1894-1959) was an attorney, engineer, inventor, lecturer, and a prolific writer. According to Hill's official biographer, Michael J. Ritt, Jr. (*A Lifetime of Riches* written with Kirk Landers, 1995), Hill first met Wier in an oil field in Texas, and Wier became a lifelong confidant and Hill's closest friend. Wier was a native of Avoyelles Parish, Louisiana, and was educated at Louisiana State Normal College, Rice Institute, the University of Chicago, Southern Methodist University, Cornell University, and George Washington University. He served in the U. S. Army Engineer Corps in World War I and from 1917 to 1920 was a construction engineer in Dallas, Wichita Falls (Texas), and Chicago. After the war he was a public lecturer under the auspices of the Chicago Welfare League and Chicago newspapers. Wier and Hill were both well known on the lecture circuit. In 1925, after receiving his law degree, Wier became a patent attorney who himself eventually held 40 U. S. and foreign patents. He was an author of wide-ranging interests,

publishing books on law, Shakespeare, one titled *How to Remember*, and two that were no doubt of great interest to Hill — *The Art and Science of Selling* and *The Science and Art of Influence*.

4   **While serving as** Jesse Grant Chapline (1870-1937) was an educator and writer on sales and business topics. He founded LaSalle Extension University in 1908. The school eventually offered correspondence courses on the professional level in such subjects as accounting, law, business, and other fields. LaSalle Extension University advertisements were a staple of American home life in the 1950s and 1960s. LaSalle was purchased by Crowell-Collier Publishing Company in 1961. Originally based in Chicago on Dearborn Street, the school later moved to Wilmette, a suburb 15 miles north of the city.

5   **This secret was used** According to at least one account, Hill and Wilson first met when Wilson was serving as president of Princeton University and Hill came to interview him bearing one of Andrew Carnegie's letters of introduction. According to Hill's biographer, when America entered World War I, Hill wrote to President Wilson to offer his services and was assigned to Wilson's staff as a volunteer public information/public relations aide. It is not completely clear what Hill was referring to here concerning the troop training and war funds effort. However, Wilson was obviously impressed by Hill's work. Years later, he would write to Hill: "May I congratulate you on your persistence. Any man who devotes that much time [to the study of success]...must of necessity make discoveries of great value to others. I am deeply impressed by your interpretation of the 'Master Mind' principles which you have so clearly described."

6   **In the early days** Since it was first published in 1937, *Think and Grow Rich!* has had a profound, if seldom publicized effect on many business and public leaders throughout the world. Manuel L. Quezon (1878-1944) is one of the first examples on the international scene. He was elected president of the Philippine Commonwealth in 1935, the year the Commonwealth was established to prepare that country for political and economic independence from the United States. In 1909 he was appointed Resident Commissioner of the Philippines, entitled to speak, but not vote, in the U. S. House of Representatives. During the Japanese occupation in World War II, he headed the Philippine government in exile in the United States, and it was during his stay in America that he was exposed

to *Think and Grow Rich!*. He died of tuberculosis in 1944, two years before his dream of full independence for the Philippines was realized.

7   **While I was performing** The doors Carnegie opened for Napoleon Hill would lead the latter to more than two decades of study and face-to-face discussions with an almost unbelievable array of business, professional, and public leaders and philanthropists, including four Presidents of the United States. All of them are fascinating individuals in their own right, but some may be somewhat obscure to readers today. Therefore, in this and in other endnotes that follow, additional biographical details are provided about many of these individuals, either to underscore the magnitude and uniqueness of their achievements, to shed further light (if only indirectly) on a success principle or point, or to "breathe some life" into these historic figures who have long since passed from the scene. Providing these details will also, perhaps, help recapture some of that sense of excitement and enthusiasm that Napoleon Hill clearly experienced in probing these unique achievers' lives and minds.

7   **WILLIAM WRIGLEY, JR.** William J. Wrigley, Jr. (1861-1932), at age 13, was a traveling salesman for his father's soap company. In 1891 he peddled soap with baking powder as a sales premium. In 1892, as a sideline, he began selling baking powder with *chewing gum* as a premium. The response was so good he dropped the soap and baking powder to focus exclusively on selling gum, eventually making "Wrigley's" a familiar name on every American street corner. He pioneered in the use of sales incentives, offering dealers such things as clocks, coffee grinders, and fishing tackle. In 1893 he introduced Wrigley's Spearmint Gum. By 1908 the company's sales had hit $1 million per year.

7   **JOHN WANAMAKER** John Wanamaker's (1838-1922) was a new kind of store. In 1875 he bought a freight depot from the Pennsylvania Railroad to house his new sales operation, which featured a variety of specialty shops under one roof. To market this "department" store idea, he became one of the first retailers to employ an advertising agency. In addition to his business interests, he also served as Postmaster General of the United States under President Benjamin Harrison.

7   **GEORGE S. PARKER** At the age of 16, George S. Parker (1867-1953), encouraged by his elder brother Charles, established his own game publishing company. George was an avid game player who had invented

and sold almost 500 sets of a game called Banking. By 1888, Charles joined the company and, thus, Parker Brothers was created. (Their elder brother, Edward, joined the company in 1898.) George wrote the rules for all the games they produced (29 by the late 1880s) and was responsible for placing ads about the games in magazines and newspapers, a practice unheard of at the time. In addition to board games, Parker Brothers produced card games such as Flinch and Rook, and in 1935, two years before Napoleon Hill published *Think and Grow Rich!*, the company introduced one of the most popular games of all time — Monopoly. In all, George Parker invented more than 100 games.

7   **E. M. STATLER** E. M. Statler's (1863-1928) hotels were the first to have running water and private baths in each room. By the mid-1920s, the Statler properties were the largest in America owned by a single individual. The slogan of his company has become a byword in American business: "The customer is always right."

7   **HENRY L. DOHERTY** Henry Doherty (1870-1939) in 1910 organized and became president of Cities Services Company, a holding company for more than 100 public utilities and petroleum businesses with total assets exceeding $1 billion ($17 billion in today's dollars). He was a leader in the oil conservation movement and he held numerous patents for combustion procedures and equipment related to the manufactured gas industry.

7   **CYRUS H. K. CURTIS** Cyrus H. K. Curtis (1850-1933) founded the magazine *Tribune and Farmer* in Philadephia in 1876 with his wife, Louise Knapp Curtis, in charge of the women's column. The latter was so popular that Curtis expanded it into *Ladies' Home Journal* in 1883. He established the Curtis Publishing Company in 1890 and seven years later bought *The Saturday Evening Post* for the sum of $1,000. With his marketing savvy, both magazines went on to become two of the biggest success stories in periodical history, with *Ladies' Home Journal* hitting one million in circulation by 1893 and *The Saturday Evening Post* doing so in 1909.

7   **GEORGE EASTMAN** George Eastman (1854-1932), whose hand-held Kodak camera and $1 Brownie Camera for kids opened photography up to the masses, in 1924 gave away half his fortune, about $75 million (more than $790 million today), for such institutions as the University of Rochester and Massachusetts Institute of Technology. He was the first large-scale manufacturer to use profit sharing as an employee benefit.

7   **JOHN W. DAVIS**   John W. Davis (1873-1955), like Napoleon Hill a Virginian, served as Solicitor General of the United States, Ambassador to Great Britain, and as an advisor to Woodrow Wilson at the Paris Peace Conference. He was soundly beaten by Coolidge in a run for the Presidency. In 1952 he won a landmark Supreme Court case when he convinced the Court that President Harry Truman had exceeded his constitutional powers in seizing the steel mills.

7   **WILBUR WRIGHT**   Wilbur Wright (1867-1912) got the idea for the design of his and brother Orville's famous aircraft after watching buzzards flying. As he watched the graceful arcs the birds made during flight, he suddenly realized that to fly successfully, an airplane must be capable of moving on three axes—banking, moving up and down, and steering right and left.

7   **WILLIAM JENNINGS BRYAN**   William Jennings Bryan (1860-1925) was a silver-tongued orator with tremendous charisma, though not quite enough to win the White House in three attempts. He served as prosecuting attorney in the famous evolution-centered Scopes Monkey Trial, squared off against the legendary defense attorney Clarence Darrow.

7   **DR. DAVID STARR JORDAN**   David Starr Jordan (1851-1931) was the world's foremost scientific authority on fish. He named more than 2,500 species of the finny creatures. In his later career (after his tenure as Stanford's president), he served as chief director of the World Peace Foundation.

7   **DANIEL WILLARD**   In addition to his railroad responsibilities, Daniel Willard (1861-1942) served as a member of the Board of Visitors of the U. S. Naval Academy and as chairman of the War Industries Board in 1917.

7   **KING GILLETTE**   On one of his trips as a traveling hardware salesman, King Camp Gillette (1855-1932) was advised by some wag to invent "something that would be used and thrown away." Such an idea—a thin double-edged steel razor blade secured in a T-handle—flashed into his mind while he was honing a permanent straight edge razor. In 1903 he sold 51 razors and 168 blades. By the end of 1904, his American Safety Razor Company (later the Gillette Company) had sold 90,000 razors and 12.4 million blades.

7   **JOHN D. ROCKEFELLER**   John D. Rockefeller's (1839-1937) Standard Oil Company dominated the oil industry and was America's first great

business trust. His near monopoly in oil led directly to the passage of the Sherman Antitrust Act of 1890. By 1910 Rockefeller's fortune was equal to almost 2.5 percent of the entire U. S. economy—about $250 billion in today's dollars. In 1911 the courts broke up Standard Oil into several huge companies—Standard Oil of New Jersey (Esso, then EXXON), Standard Oil of New York (Socony, then Mobil), Standard Oil of California (Chevron), Standard Oil of Indiana (Amoco, then part of BP), and Standard Oil of Ohio. His donations made possible the founding of the University of Chicago, Rockefeller University, and the Rockefeller Foundation. He gave away $500 million to philanthropic causes during his lifetime, and his total charitable gifts, together with those of his son John D. Jr., amounted to $2.5 billion by 1955 (approximately $17 billion in today's dollars).

7 **FRANK A. VANDERLIP** Frank A. Vanderlip (1864-1937) was a financial reporter and later financial editor of the *Chicago Tribune* prior to becoming a banker. He also served as chairman of the War Savings Committee, which coordinated the sale of war savings certificates for World War I, and he was a trustee of the Carnegie Foundation.

7 **F. W. WOOLWORTH** Franklin W. Woolworth (1852-1919) opened his first five-and-ten-cent variety store in 1879 in Lancaster, Pennsylvania. By the end of 1904, he was operating 120 stores in 21 states, and by the time of his death the company had more than a thousand stores. He pioneered in volume buying and artful counter display merchandising. The Woolworth empire eventually expanded to Britain and Ireland and several other countries, but by the late 1990s the chain had lost a long battle against the big discounters, and in 1997 the Woolworth Corporation announced it was closing its last 400 F. W. Woolworth stores with 9,000 employees, ending a venerable business that had simply become unprofitable.

7 **COL. ROBERT A. DOLLAR** Col. Robert A. Dollar (1844-1932) was born in Falkirk, Scotland, in1844. He immigrated with his family to the United States in 1856. By age 13 he was working in a Canadian lumber camp. He made his way to San Francisco and went on to develop extensive foreign trading and lumber businesses, becoming in the process one of the largest operators of ocean vessels in the world. Before his death in 1932, he had received keys to the cities of Falkirk, Boston, New York, and Shanghai.

7   **EDWARD A. FILENE** Edward A. Filene (1860-1937), along with brother Lincoln (1865-1957), made Filene's department store in Boston world-famous. Known for its high quality fashion merchandise, it is best known for its Automatic Bargain Basement, which opened in 1909. The Basement featured distressed merchandise at bargain prices which were automatically reduced 25% after 12 selling days, then 25% more after 18 days, 25% more after 24 days, and, after 30 days, the clothing was donated to charity. Filene's pioneered the charge-plate system, cycle billing, and branch store operations. The firm joined with F. & R. Lazarus and Company and Abraham and Strauss in 1929 to form Federated Department Stores, Inc. Edward Filene was also the co-inventor of the "Filene-Finlay Simultaneous Translator," used at the war crimes trials at Nuremburg and later at sessions of the United Nations. Because of his 30-year crusade to establish credit unions in the United States, Filene is known today as the "Father of the U. S. Credit Union Movement."

7   **ARTHUR BRISBANE** In his day, Arthur Brisbane (1864-1936) was the highest paid newspaper editor in the United States and one of the world's most widely read editorialists, as managing editor of William Randolph Hearst's *The New York Evening Journal*. He was known as the master of sensationalism, and he wrote the syndicated "Today" editorial column, which was written from 1917 until the day he died in 1936. While he was famous for blaring headlines and stories about atrocities, he also campaigned for better schools, labor law, and prison reform, and against the death penalty, crime, and Prohibition.

7   **LUTHER BURBANK** During a horticultural career that lasted 55 years, Luther Burbank (1849-1926) developed more than 800 varieties and strains of plants. These included more than 200 varieties of fruits (including the Freestone peach), numerous vegetables, grains, nuts, and a host of ornamentals. He was known worldwide as one of the world's most innovative and prolific plant-breeding scientists. In 1871 he developed the Burbank potato, which was used in Ireland in the battle against the ravages of the blight epidemic. He was a friend of both Thomas Edison and Henry Ford. His legacy inspired the City of Santa Rosa's annual Rose Parade, which celebrates his memory.

7   **EDWARD W. BOK** Edward W. Bok (1863-1930) edited *Ladies Home Journal* for three decades. He won the editorship after successfully

developing and syndicating, through his Bok Syndicate Press, a regular full page of women's interest material for use by newspapers. He was a strong crusader for suffrage for women, wildlife conservation, clean cities, and elimination of highway billboards. His greatest crusade was against the excesses of the patent medicine industry, which led to passage of the Pure Food and Drug Act in 1906. *Ladies Homes Journal* was the first American magazine to mention venereal disease, which is one indication of the strength of his convictions about keeping the public informed about issues that might affect their families. Bok, the son of poor immigrants from the Netherlands, won the 1921 Pulitzer Prize for his autobiography, *The Americanization of Edward Bok.*

7   **FRANK A. MUNSEY** Frank Munsey (1854-1925) was a master of media consolidation and mergers. In addition to his newspaper-publishing career, he published America's first inexpensive (10 cents per copy) general circulation, illustrated magazine, *Munsey's Magazine.* At his death in 1925, he left most of his $40 million (more than $412 million in today's dollars) to the Metropolitan Museum of Art in New York City.

7   **JULIUS ROSENWALD** Julius Rosenwald (1862-1932), a clothing merchant in New York and then Chicago, bought a one-quarter interest in Sears, Roebuck and Company, becoming its president in 1910 and chairman in 1925. Under his leadership, Sears began the innovative custom of manufacturing its own products for sale. He also came up with Sears' soon-to-be-famous "satisfaction guaranteed or your money back" policy. He turned out to be a "challenging" philanthropist. He objected to the notion of "perpetual endowments" such as those Andrew Carnegie established, advocating instead the concept of "matched giving." One of his bequests led to the establishment of 5,000 schools in 15 Southern states for the education of blacks. He also established the Museum of Science and Industry in Chicago and donated heavily to the young University of Chicago.

7   **CLARENCE DARROW** After nine years as a small-town lawyer in Ohio, Clarence S. Darrow (1857-1938) relocated to Chicago in search of more challenging work as a defense attorney. His liberal views led him to take some of the most famous cases of the early 20th century, including the Leopold-Loeb Case, where he saved the two men from the death penalty; the Sweet Case, where he successfully defended a black family in Detroit

who had been charged for violence against a mob that tried to force them out of a white area; and the Scopes "Monkey Trial" involving Tennessee teacher John T. Scopes, who was charged with teaching evolution, instead of creationism. His main opponent was William Jennings Bryan, former three-time presidential candidate. Despite the widespread view that Darrow had won the contest, Scopes was found guilty.

7   **JENNINGS RANDOLPH** Jennings Randolph (1902-1998) was graduated from Salem College in 1924. As a young man, he, like Napoleon Hill, worked for a time as a journalist. He served seven terms as a U. S. Congressman from West Virginia (1933 to 1947) and four full terms as United States Senator (1958 to 1985). Fondly remembered as "the last of the New Deal Democrats," he gained renown as chairman of the Senate's Public Works Committee, and he was the legislative father of the National Air and Space Museum in Washington, D. C. After his death, his Senate colleague, Robert C. Byrd, recalled Randolph's love of flight:

> "On November 6, 1948, with a professional pilot at the controls, Jennings...flew from Morgantown, West Virginia, to Washington National Airport in a propeller plane fueled with gasoline made from coal. Now, that was just like Jennings Randolph—out there pioneering, not only in flight, but also in the use of fuel in that plane that had a West Virginia source—coal. Certainly, that project was an act of faith, for which many remember Senator Randolph."

Randolph authored the 26th Amendment to the Constitution that gave 18-year-olds the right to vote. He was considered the father of the Appalachian Regional Commission, and one of his last major acts was to sponsor legislation preserving it. He served for many years as a member of the Board of Directors of the Napoleon Hill Foundation, established in 1962 by Hill and his wife, Annie Lou. Randolph died of pneumonia at a retirement nursing home in St. Louis on May 8, 1998, at the age of 96, and was buried in Seventh-Day Baptist Cemetery in Salem, West Virginia, the town of his birth. He had the distinction of being the last surviving person (non-Hill family member) mentioned by name in the original edition (1937) of *Think and Grow Rich!*.

8   **As far as schooling** Steam locomotives replenished their boilers by stopping along the railway periodically to "take on water" from storage tanks.

Introduction
MINDPOWER: The Man Who "Thought" His Way

1   **Edwin C. Barnes discovered**   Interestingly, Hill's original working title for *Think and Grow Rich!* was *The Thirteen Steps to Riches*. According to one story, perhaps apocryphal, Hill's publisher, Andrew Pelton, wanted the book to be titled *Use Your Noodle to Win More Boodle*. While the origin of the final title may never be completely clear, it seems logical that, in the end, it may have been suggested by this second sentence in the introduction.

2   **How much actual cash**   If Hill was referring to 1937 dollars, the amount of "actual cash" Barnes' original DESIRE might have been worth to him was anywhere from $25 million to $37.5 million in today's dollars (Consumer Price Index inflation rate).

3   **But the amount, whatever**   The notion of "transmutation" — literally, the process by which some object is changed into another nature, form, or condition — is crucial to an understanding of Napoleon Hill's philosophy of success. Hill uses the term to describe the process by which intangible thought is translated, or translates itself, into physical activity that results in a physical change in the world. He also uses it to describe the process of converting one kind of mental state into another. The best way to understand precisely what Hill means by "transmutation" is to read the book through in its entirety, letting the particular "spin" he puts on the term sink into your mind.

4   **He had no money**   Edwin C. Barnes was born in Jefferson City, Wisconsin, in 1876 and died at the age of 78 in Bradentown (now Bradenton), Florida, in 1954. His relationship with the Edison organization made him independently wealthy, and at one time he had offices in New York, Indiana, Milwaukee, and other cities in addition to his "Edison Voice Writer" main office in Chicago. He moved to Bradenton from Chicago during the building boom of the 1920s and became the primary developer of the luxurious Palma Sola Park subdivision. An article in the August 21, 1924, edition of the *Manatee River Journal-Herald* gives a hint of the close relationship that existed between Barnes and Edison until the latter's death in 1931:

Edwin C. Barnes of Bradentown and Chicago "broke into" the front page of the New York *Times* in company with Thomas Edison the other day. The immaculate Edwin demonstrated that he could kick a hat held shoulder high, and Mr. Edison, who is Mr. Barnes' senior by about thirty-five years, demonstrated that he could do the same thing....Mr. Barnes, who is the principal owner of the Palma Sola Park Company of this city...has for years been connected with the Edison organization and he and the "wizard" are close friends. They have another interest in common — their love for Florida....Mr. Edison owns a home at Fort Myers, to which he repairs each winter, and Mr. Barnes owns one of the finest homes in Bradentown.

Barnes was also a long-time and close friend of Napoleon Hill. Hill dedicated his book *Law of Success* to three persons — Andrew Carnegie, Henry Ford, and Edwin C. Barnes. About the latter, he wrote in the dedication "...a business associate of Thomas A. Edison, whose close personal relationship over a period of more than fifteen years served to help the author 'carry on' in the face of a great variety of adversities and much temporary defeat met with in organizing the...[*Law of Success*]."

5   **An uncle of** R. U. Darby is the only person identified by name in *Think and Grow Rich!* about whom the editor could find no independent biographical information.

6   **One day President** William Rainey Harper (1856-1906) was the first president of the University of Chicago, leaving a post as professor of semitic languages at Yale University to assume the Chicago presidency. He was an innovator who initiated extension courses, studies in new disciplines such as psychology and sociology, and was also instrumental in the establishment of junior colleges.

7   **The Ford DETERMINATION** Henry Ford (1863-1947), the son of Irish immigrants, was a school dropout. At age 15 he was a machinist's apprentice in Detroit and later worked as chief engineer of the Edison Company in Detroit until 1899, when he and others founded the Detroit Auto Company. In 1903 he struck out on his own, founding the Ford Motor Company. He introduced the Model T in 1908, assembly line production in 1913, the Model A in 1927, and the V-8 engine in 1932. He ran for a U. S. Senate seat and lost and at one time considered a Presidential bid.

8   **Many years ago, I** Napoleon Hill had an abiding interest in higher
education, and post-secondary education in general, throughout his adult
life, and he was associated with a variety of teaching institutions. His
constant theme was that education should not simply focus on "imparting
knowledge," but on teaching students how to organize knowledge and
apply it to accomplish specific objectives.

After he was graduated from high school, he completed business
school in Tazewell, Virginia, and studied law at Georgetown University
Law School In Washington, D. C., but dropped out the first year because
of financial reasons. In 1913 he began working in the advertising and
sales department of LaSalle Extension University in Chicago, where he
discovered a talent for motivating students and teaching them how to
sell. In 1916 he established the George Washington Institute to teach a
correspondence course in salesmanship. In 1923 he made arrangements to
purchase and operate the Metropolitan Business College in Cleveland (it
was during this period that he was invited to deliver the commencement
address at Salem College).

Hill in 1931 established the International Publishing Corporation of
America and the related International Success University to distribute
"success" resources, including a new publication he launched, *Success
Magazine*. In 1941 he became a resident lecturer in psychology at
Presbyterian College in Clinton, South Carolina, delivering talks to
undergraduates on "The Philosophy of American Achievement." He
received an honorary doctorate from Pacific International University in the
late 1940s and was appointed head of that university's new Department
of Industrial Philosophy.

In 1962 Hill and his wife, Annie Lou, established the Napoleon Hill
Foundation, a charitable organization heavily steeped in educational
mission. The Foundation—along with the associated Napoleon Hill
World Learning Center—is today headquartered at Purdue University
Calumet in Hammond, Indiana. Through the years the Foundation has
been associated with several institutions of higher learning, including
Johnson Wales College (formerly in Rhode Island), Salem International
University in West Virginia, the University of the Pacific, University of
Texas, and University of Northern Iowa. A college professor, Judith
Williamson (who also heads the Hill World Learning Center), currently

sits on the Board of Directors of the Napoleon Hill Foundation, and a college president, Dr. Bill L. Atchley, and a future college president, Dr. Horace Fleming (University of Southern Mississippi), have also served on the board.

Here is a "footnote to a footnote," which in a tenuous "Six Degrees of Separation" way leads from higher education, to the Napoleon Hill Foundation, to one of the top names in the broadcasting industry. Bill Lee Atchley was born in 1932 in Cape Girardeau, Missouri, five years before the publication of *Think and Grow Rich!*. He was the son of Cecil Atchley, a cement plant laborer, and his wife, a laundry worker. Employing many of the success principles of *The Think and Grow Rich Philosophy* from an early age, Atchley ("Billy" in his youth) went on to overcome the meager circumstances of his birth and play professional baseball in the New York Giants organization, get a doctorate in engineering, and then become president of Clemson University in South Carolina (during which time he served on the Hill Foundation). He also later was named president of the University of the Pacific in Stockton, California, and then Southeast Missouri State University. As it turns out, Atchley's widow, Pat (he died in 2000), is the former Pat Limbaugh, also of Cape Girardeau. Her cousin from Cape Girardeau is none other than Rush Limbaugh III, who has presided over what many consider to be the most successful, and profitable, program in the history of radio broadcasting. Limbaugh, credited with virtually reinventing the national radio talk show beginning in 1988, is one of the best examples of how using a "Definite Chief Aim" to guide one's decisions and actions can lead to extraordinary success in life. He has certainly proved Hill's prediction that "There is plenty of room in radio for those who can produce or recognize IDEAS." (See endnote 6 on pages 343 - 345.)

9   **JENNINGS RANDOLPH** Randolph later would write this endorsement of Napoleon Hill's work: "I knew Napoleon Hill in 1922 when I was a student in Salem College in the town of my birth. Mr. Hill came to our campus as the commencement speaker in that year. As I listened to him, I heard something other than just the words he spoke, I felt the substance — the wisdom — and the spirit of a man and his philosophy. Mr. Hill said, 'The most powerful instrument we have in our hand is the power of our mind.' Napoleon Hill compiled this philosophy of American achievement for the benefit of all people. I strongly commend this philosophy to you for achievement and service in your chosen field."

Chapter 1
DESIRE: The Starting Point of All Achievement

1   **The morning after** Fed by wooden buildings and sidewalks and coming
     on the heels of a long dry spell, the Chicago Fire raged from October 8-
     10, 1871, destroying four square miles, including the business district.
     Two hundred and fifty lost their lives, 90,000 were left homeless, and
     property damage was estimated at $200 million. As he wrote about the
     Chicago Fire, Hill must surely have had in the back of his mind another
     catastrophe, a personal catastrophe, also involving a fire in the Windy
     City. In 1923, after losing control of *Napoleon Hill's Magazine*, which he
     had founded, he returned to Chicago to get his belongings that had been
     stored there, only to find the building they were in had been destroyed
     by fire. The loss was devastating. Gone were autographed photographs,
     many of his most important letters, including some from Presidents of the
     United States, and, worst of all, questionnaires that had been filled out by
     hundreds of the most eminent and successful individuals in America who
     had agreed to participate in Hill's research. Ever the positive thinker, Hill
     carried on, determined to complete his project, and 14 years later *Think
     and Grow Rich* was published.

2   **When the going was hard** As a young man, Marshal Field (1835-1906)
     had left the family farm in Conway, Massachusetts, to become a dry goods
     clerk. Moving to Chicago in 1856, he became first a junior partner, then a
     senior partner in the firm known as Field, Palmer & Leiter. When Palmer
     and Leiter retired, he became head of Marshal Field and Co., a thriving
     wholesale and retail dry goods business. He devoted much of his later life
     to philanthropy, particularly in support of the University of Chicago.

3   **It may be helpful**   More than $1 billion in today's dollars. Actually, Hill
     speaks conservatively here, for Carnegie in his waning years gave away
     more than three and a half times that amount (again, in today's dollars) to
     charitable causes.

4   **Practical dreamers** In the original version of *Think and Grow Rich!*, the
     Edison example is followed by this one: "Whelan dreamed of a chain
     of cigar stores, transformed his dream into action, and now the United
     Cigar Stores occupy the best corners in America." Unlike Napoleon Hill's
     philosophy and the success principles he developed, corner cigar stores

have generally not withstood the test of time. George Whelan was a U. S. financier who in 1912, after the American Tobacco Trust was broken up, put his United Cigar Stores under a holding company—Tobacco Products Corporation—and began acquiring small tobacco companies. In 1919 he bought the U.S. business of London's Philip Morris Company (begun in 1847) and formed a new American corporation, Philip Morris & Company, Inc. Whelan's wheeling and dealing led to financial collapse in 1929, but the new company survived under new management. It would go on, under its flagship product, Marlboro cigarettes, to diversify and become by the 21st century the world's largest producer and marketer of packaged consumer goods, with subsidiaries such as Kraft Foods and Miller Brewing Company.

5   **Marconi dreamed** Guglielmo Marconi (1874-1937) invented the first apparatus used for wireless telegraphy and was awarded the 1909 Nobel Prize in physics for his efforts. His work freed long distance communications from the restraints of wires and other physical transmission media and laid the foundation for the broadcasting industry.

Napoleon Hill, in discussing Marconi's work here and in explaining certain other concepts later, uses the term "ether," rather than "electromagnetic spectrum," in both the original and several subsequent edition of *Think and Grow Rich!*. In so doing, he was simply reflecting the popular scientific concepts and, thus, the scientific vocabulary of the day. In the latter 19th and early 20th century, many scientists believed that an invisible substance, which they called "ether," permeated the universe, including "empty" space. Through this medium, light and other radiation were thought to travel like vibrations in a bowl of jelly. The Michelson-Morley experiments and Albert Einstein's work, which resulted in the Special Theory of Relativity, forced the scientific community to abandon the concept of ether.

Over the years, the universe with its incredible array of electromagnetic, nuclear, and gravitational forces and phenomena has turned out to be even more mysterious than Hill or any turn-of-the-century scientist suspected. Hill's effort to describe, in clear and understandable terms, energy phenomena—everything from broadcast waves to brain waves—gives the terminology in the original version of *Think and Grow Rich!* a more metaphysical and metaphorical "flavor" than it likely would have were he writing today. The few changes in terminology that have been made in this revised edition of *Think and Grow Rich!* – as, for example, the use of "electromagnetic spectrum" instead of "ether" – are made simply to remove stylistic "impediments" to understanding for today's reader. The sum and substance of Hill's ideas remain unchanged.

6   **The oak sleeps** The quotation is from the inspirational best-selling classic *As a Man Thinketh* by James Allen, a British-born American essayist (1864-1912). Napoleon Hill was undoubtedly familiar with the body of Allen's work, which included such other popular titles as *Eight Pillars of Prosperity*, *From Poverty to Power*, and *As a Man Does: Morning and Evening Thoughts*. Allen taught that the key to personal power lies within the mind. The opening sentence of his classic is "As a man thinketh in his heart so is he" – in other words, we are what we think, and our character is the sum of all our thoughts. Hill uses variations of that tenet repeatedly in *Think and Grow Rich!*.

7   **At one time, such** The "dreamer" President was Franklin D. Roosevelt. The Tennessee Valley Authority, or TVA, is a federal agency that was established in 1933 under the Roosevelt Administration to control floods, improve navigation, raise living standards on nearby farms, and generate electric power on the Tennessee River and along its tributaries. The project was visionary in concept, gigantic in undertaking. The Tennessee River drainage basin covers parts of seven Southern states. TVA included nine major dams, 51 dams in all, interconnecting navigation locks, port facilities stretching along the route of the river, 12 coal-fired generating plants, and, later on, two nuclear plants. Combined generating capacity was more than 30 million kilowatts. TVA was a prototypical natural resource planning and management agency. Early in the New Deal, Hill – as he had with Woodrow Wilson – served as an unpaid public relations adviser to Roosevelt, according to Hill's official biographer. He developed plans to shape public opinion, offered ideas for Roosevelt's fireside chats, and there is some suggestion that he may have been responsible for the president's famous phrase from his inauguration speech, "the only thing we have to fear is fear itself." Senator Jennings Randolph was responsible for Roosevelt's asking Hill to visit the White House.

8   **O. Henry discovered** O. Henry was the pen name of William Sydney Porter (1862-1910), master of irony and the surprise ending and romanticizer

of the commonplace. He had embezzled money from the bank where he worked, but received a light prison sentence and served only three years and three months in an Ohio penitentiary, with time off for good behavior. (Interestingly, work with the incarcerated is one of the primary goals of the Napoleon Hill Foundation, which sponsors courses in prisons to teach inmates the principles for success in life. Studies have shown that recidivism is significantly reduced among prisoners who complete the studies.)

9   **Strange and varied are** "Infinite Intelligence" is the term Hill uses to describe "God," or "Divine Power," or the "Supreme Being" at work in the universe and whose influence is felt everywhere within it. His conception of God, or Infinite Intelligence, is richly textured and multi-faceted. God, to Hill, is more than a divinely spiritual, personal, moral force. God is a source of intelligence, direct communication, and exchange of information — between the Supreme Intelligence itself and the individual, and even between individuals. It is clear that Hill writes primarily from a Judeo-Christian perspective, but his view of Infinite Intelligence is nonsectarian and widely encompassing. As you read the book, notice how Hill sees Infinite Intelligence at work in the lives of Jesus, Gandhi, and Mohammed, as well as in all individuals whose mental states are "attuned" to the power of Infinite Intelligence. Hill is never "preachy" about Infinite Intelligence and how one should respond to it, but to fully understand and utilize *The Think and Grow Rich Philosophy*, it is necessary to understand the part that Infinite Intelligence — God — plays in it.

10 **Edison, the world's** "Tramp" here means "itinerant," "roving," or "traveling."

11 **That tragedy produced** Two days after Dickens' twelfth birthday, his father was jailed in a London debtor's prison. His mother sent Dickens (1812-1870) to work in a blacking factory, which manufactured black shoe polish. For four to six months, Dickens labored 12-hour days in a dirty, rat-ridden warehouse, earning only six to seven shillings per week. It was the same sort of wretched experience which many of the successful people that Hill studied had undergone early in their lives. Dickens never forgot it and drew upon it many times in his novels, but he never revealed the story to anyone but his wife, and the story did not come out until after his death. The "tragedy" Dickens suffered involved a failed love relationship

with one Maria Beadwell, daughter of an English banker. In 1830, when Dickens was 18 and working as a low-paid shorthand reporter in the law courts, he fell madly, hopelessly in love with Maria, who was 19. Her parents considered Dickens unworthy as a suitor and eventually packed Maria off to finishing school in Paris. Dickens loved her for a period of four years, but his passion was unrequited, and Maria treated him with what amounted to heartless indifference. Critics and biographers have speculated that the intense passion and inspiration he felt, followed by such bitter suffering and disappointment, both sharpened his artistic sensibilities and rendered him thereafter immensely sympathetic to the luckless and the downtrodden. Maria Beadwell, it is believed, was the inspiration for the character of Dora in *David Copperfield*.

12 **Once you have** Hill originally added the following: "Let Emerson state the thought in these words, 'Every proverb, every book, every byword that belongs to thee for aid and comfort shall surely come home through open or winding passages. Every friend whom not thy fantastic will, but the great and tender soul in thee craveth, shall lock thee in his embrace.'"

13 **I sold him the idea** The original manuscript continued: "For example, the teachers in school would observe that he had no ears, and, because of this, they would show him special attention and treat him with extraordinary kindness. They always did. His mother saw to that, by visiting the teachers and arranging with them to give the child the extra attention necessary. I sold him the idea, too, that when be became old enough to sell newspapers, (his older brother had already become a newspaper merchant), he would have a big advantage over his brother, for the reason that people would pay him extra money for his wares, because they could see that he was a bright, industrious boy, despite the fact he had no ears."

14 **He did not go** Hill originally wrote, "He [Blair] did not go to a school for the deaf." Perceptions and attitudes about persons with hearing and other disabilities are today, of course, vastly different from what they were in the era in which Hill wrote. Hill's whole approach to his son's disability may have been far different had he faced them today, although that is by no means certain, given Hill's always positive approach and attitude about overcoming obstacles and meeting challenges. Despite Blair Hill's disability and apparent lack of facility in signing, he went on to become a highly successful individual.

15 **For the first time in his life** The first electric hearing aid, the Acousticon, had been patented in 1901. It was an unwieldy apparatus with a telephone-type receiver held to the ear and a large housing for batteries about the size of a large portable radio or a big lunch box. The first hearing aid designed to be worn on the person was the Amplivox, introduced in London in 1935, which weighed two-and-a-half pounds. It is uncertain whether either of these is one of those mentioned by Hill.

16 **As this chapter was** Ernestine Schumann-Heink (1861-1936) was the most famous contralto of her generation, noted for her big, robust voice. Born in Lieben, Germany, she was selected at age 15 to sing the contralto part in Beethoven's *Ninth Symphony* in Graz. Following a successful career in Europe, she made her U. S. debut in 1899 at the Metropolitan Opera as Ortrud in Wagner's *Lohengrun*. She headlined there until 1932. She died in Hollywood in 1936 during the time Hill was writing *Think and Grow Rich!.*

Chapter 2
FAITH: Visualization and the Attainment of Desire

1 **When FAITH is blended** "Vibration of thought" is how Hill chose to describe the complex, little understood process by which electrochemical impulses in the brain create and convey "thoughts" and "emotions." "Vibration" must be understood in a descriptive and metaphoric, as well as "physical" sense here and elsewhere in Hill's writings. In any event, what is significant is not the imperfection of the words Hill uses in the effort to describe the process — all language is imperfect — but the *insight* he offers into how thoughts, bolstered by the power of faith, can affect the subconscious mind and create within it new capabilities and powers of communication. It would be a mistake to attempt to understand such terms as "vibration of thought" in a strictly literal sense. The key is to read and re-read such statements, in context, "moving with the flow" of Hill's ideas. Doing so will soon produce within you the full sense of what Hill means to convey.

2 **Understand this truth** Dr. Norman Vincent Peale (1898-1993) and others would go on to popularize this "power of positive thinking," as did Hill

and his later collaborator, friend, and patron, W. Clement Stone, in their book *Success through a Positive Mental Attitude* (1960). Whenever you listen to a motivational CD or tape, or hear a speaker extolling the virtues of positive thinking and a positive mental attitude, you are listening to an echo from Napoleon Hill.

3   **All down the ages** Neither here nor anywhere else in his book does Hill engage in "religion bashing." To the contrary, he has strong beliefs about God, or Infinite Intelligence, but he has little regard for dogmatics and sectarians, those who are convinced that they and they alone understand divine intentions and purposes and religious "truth." To Hill, nothing — no dogma, creed, or teaching — should stand in the way of, or is necessary to, direct communication between the individual and Infinite Intelligence. It is not religion that bothers Hill. It is *religionists*.

4   **Fourth. I have clearly** Examples abound of people's applying Hill's ideas and principles to attain great success in life. A fascinating instance of someone who followed Hill's advice by writing down, in the clearest terms, his definite chief aim in life was found a few years ago on a wall in the Planet Hollywood Restaurant located just off Highway 17 Bypass in Myrtle Beach, South Carolina. (Planet Hollywood restaurants were known for their collections of movie and celebrity memorabilia.) On the wall was a handwritten note with the title in red — "My Definite Chief Aim." Also written in red, at the bottom, was the word "secret," with the bulk of the note, in blue ink, saying this:

My Definite Chief Aim

I, Bruce Lee, will be the first highest paid Oriental super star in the United States. In return I will give the most exciting performances and render the best of quality in the capacity of an actor. Starting 1970 I will achieve world fame and from then onward till the end of 1980 I will have in my possession $10,000,000. I will live the way I please and achieve inner harmony and happiness.

Bruce Lee
Jan. 1969
(secret)

Lee, of course, went on to achieve his goals, becoming the most famous — and richest — martial arts movie star in the world during his time. His success on the screen spawned a worldwide industry of self-instructional CD, DVD, audio and video tapes. Unfortunately, he died in 1973 at the age of 33 from an adverse brain reaction to a medication—the same year his most famous film, "Enter the Dragon," was released. *Time* magazine wrote of him: "With nothing but his hands, feet and a lot of attitude, he turned the little guy into a tough guy." He clearly attributed a great deal of credit for his success to his belief in *The Think and Grow Rich Philosophy*.

5   **Observe the words** Some sources attribute this poem to W.D. Wintle. Others give the author as "Anonymous."

6   **Let us consider** Mohandas K. Gandhi ("Mahatma" is a Hindu title of respect meaning "great-souled") was born in 1869 and assassinated by an Indian extremist in 1948. Considered the "Father of His Country," he led the Indian nationalist movement for independence from British rule. His philosophy of nonviolent civil disobedience has been widely influential, especially on the civil rights movement in the United States. Albert Einstein said this about him: "The moral influence which Gandhi has exercised upon thinking people may be far more durable than would appear likely in our present age, with its exaggeration of brute force. We are fortunate and grateful that fate has bestowed upon us so luminous a contemporary, a beacon to generations to come." To Hill, Gandhi was the modern epitome of the power of an idea—and the human mind—to change the world.

7   **Moreover—and** Throughout this discussion, Hill uncannily foreshadows modern participatory management, labor-management teams, productivity programs and profit sharing—just about the whole scope of modern management theory and practice.

8   **If you have any doubt** Napoleon Hill obviously was not superstitious, having no qualms about the number 13. It is certainly possible that he chose it intentionally as an attention-grabber, although, more likely, it was simply the number of the most basic "success" principles he arrived at after distilling his years of research and analysis down to the most elemental level. One can almost hear him emphatically saying, "Well, if 13 is how many principles there are, then 13 they shall be!" While Hill at times exhibits mystical qualities, he is first and foremost a rationalist. He states emphatically in Chapter 13: " I am not a believer in nor an advocate

of 'miracles,' for the reason that I have enough knowledge of Nature to understand that *Nature never deviates from her established laws.* Some of her laws are so incomprehensible that they produce what appear to be 'miracles.'"

9   **Even John Pierpoint Morgan**   Investment banker J. P. Morgan (1837-1913) is the most powerful figure in the history of American finance. He reshaped the landscape of American industry and manufacturing, reorganizing the railroad industry and serving as the driving force behind the creation of the General Electric and International Harvester corporations, and, as will be seen, the world's first billion-dollar corporation, U. S. Steel.

10   **And still later**   The federal government sued in an attempt to break up U. S. Steel, but the U. S. Supreme Court ruled in 1920 that the corporation was not a monopoly that had restrained trade in violation of anti-trust laws. U. S. Steel in 2001 celebrated the centennial of its founding and was at that time the largest integrated steel producer in the United States, with its headquarters in Pittsburg, Pennsylvania.

11   **"If you had asked**   Morgan also reportedly told Carnegie when the deal was struck: "Mr. Carnegie, I want to congratulate you on being the richest man in the world."

12   **AFTER IT HAD BEEN**   Approximately $11 billion in today's dollars (Consumer Price Index inflation adjustment).

Chapter 3
AUTOSUGGESTION: The Medium for Influencing the Subconscious Mind

1   **If you repeat a million**   Coue/ (1857-1926) was a French pharmacist and psychologist who developed a system of psychotherapy known as "Couéism" that stressed the use of autosuggestion to effect positive changes in the subject's health and general well-being. The system was characterized by the repetition of the Coue/ formula, another familiar version of which is "Every day, and in every way, I am becoming better and better." The power of autosuggestion, bolstered by strong desire and faith, has enormous implications for human mental and physical health. Television commentator-producer Bill Moyers explored the amazing

mind-body connection and its role in healing in a popular book and PBS TV series, *Healing and the Mind* (1993).

2   **When visualizing** Hill understood the tremendous power of visualization long before it became a staple of modern sports and motivational courses. Jack Nicklaus, who is generally regarded as the greatest golfer in the history of the sport, has often said he never strikes a golf ball until he has an ideal picture, in his mind's eye, of the ball struck perfectly by his club, flying through the air, and landing precisely where he intends it to land. The visualization technique seems to have worked. Nicklaus has won more major championships, 18, than anyone else in the history of golf.

3   **Third. Place a written** The value of writing down and repeatedly referring to "action instructions" was brought home to the editor several years ago. A small group of us were having dinner at the Commerce Club in Greenville, South Carolina. The group included an entrepreneur by the name of Leighton Cubbage, who has made a huge fortune in the telecommunications industry; Bill Lee, a national business consultant who was a principal architect of the success of Builder Marts of America, the largest non-cooperative buying group for lumber and building materials in the United States; myself (at that time editor-in-chief of *Think & Grow Rich Newsletter*); Boo Cheney, president of Imagine, Inc., a publishing firm; and Mike Ritt, who at that time was executive director of the Napoleon Hill Foundation and later became Napoleon Hill's official biographer. Throughout dinner, Mike was peppered with questions about Napoleon Hill, and at one point I was startled to see Leighton Cubbage reach into his coat pocket and pull out small cards containing quotations from *Think and Grow Rich!*. He said he never left home without them and, in large part, had based his life and founded his businesses upon the ideas and techniques he had learned from studying *Think and Grow Rich!*. Bill Lee said much the same.

Chapter 4
SPECIALIZED KNOWLEDGE: Personal Experiences or Observations

1   **"Colleges and universities** Work-study programs, declaring a major, course advisors, and career counseling are, of course, now staples of American campus life.

2 **One advantage, in** Hill would be delighted, perhaps amazed at today's self-instructional CD, DVD, MP3, podcast, audio and video tape industries, whose products enable career people to acquire knowledge and develop new skills both at home and "on the go."

3 **The SELF-DISCIPLINE** The original version of the book has the following at this point:

> Correspondence schools are highly organized business institutions. Their tuition fees are so low that they are forced to insist upon prompt payments. Being asked to pay, whether the student makes good grades or poor, has the effect of causing one to follow through with the course when he would otherwise drop it. The correspondence schools have not stressed this point sufficiently, for the truth is that their collection departments constitute the very finest sort of training on DECISION, PROMPTNESS, ACTION and the HABIT OF FINISHING THAT WHICH ONE BEGINS.

4 **The aggregate annual** Hill originally had in mind providing this service to the many thousands of people who were unemployed during the Depression, but his comments are equally valid for people today who find themselves without jobs during periods of corporate downsizing and other economic dislocations. Today's thriving small-shop graphic arts and desktop publishing firms, which crank out business cards, flyers, logos and letterheads for self-employed people throughout the country, attest to the lasting validity of Hill's idea.

5 **Dan Halpin is** Daniel D. Halpin was born June 14, 1906, and grew up in New Haven, Connecticut. He was apparently the first student from New Haven to attend Notre Dame, and on the way out on the train, he stayed up all night in hopes of seeing Indians (he didn't).

Once on campus, he found several jobs to help defray the cost of his tuition and living expenses. His parents were in no position to pay his college costs, but an uncle, who owned Dunster Books in Cambridge, Massachusetts, gave him a number of leather-bound books on the classics, and he was thus known to have one of the finest personal libraries on the campus.

Halpin was fascinated by accounts about the famous Knute Rockne and the Notre Dame football team, which led to his choice of Notre Dame for his college education. He worked his way up the athletic manager system until he was named senior manager at the end of the 1930 school year. He was Rockne's last manager, and he also served as Rockne's secretary and what would today be considered a business manager. He became close to the Rockne family and assisted them frequently in their liaison with the university.

Halpin's leadership applied to more than sports. After a year or two, he realized the campus needed a laundry service, so he started one. He also created the logo for the business, and every piece of their equipment had stenciled on it: "La UND ry." The business was so profitable that the University eventually took it over and has run it ever since.

After the tragic Rockne plane crash in March 1931, Halpin was deputized by the president of the university to fly out to Kansas and escort Rockne's remains back to Notre Dame. Upon his graduation in June 1931, he was hired by MGM to serve as the "Rockne expert" for the film "Knute Rockne of Notre Dame."

With that behind him, he returned to the East coast with his new bride, Margaret Hyland Halpin, and rented an apartment at 425 Riverside Drive in Manhattan at the height of the Depression. His first job was selling hearing aids on 42nd street in New York City. As Napoleon Hill relates in *Think and Grow Rich!*, Halpin was so skilled a salesman that he out-sold the major brand "Dictograph," which advertised heavily on the radio. Dictograph hired him away and made him a sales manager, then, vice president. His first child was born in 1932, and the family was financially well off at that time.

Halpin's son, Dan Halpin, Jr., says, "As to Napoleon Hill, he [the elder Halpin] mentioned him frequently, and as I recall it, Dad was the best man at Mr. Hill's son's [Blair Hill's] wedding. If memory serves me, young Mr. Hill was born without ears, and my Dad was instrumental in providing him with a hearing aid, which allowed for some ability to hear. [See the account on page 39.] Subsequent to that they became friends and remained so, as far as I know. I do remember that he always spoke highly of Napoleon Hill and was quite proud of his inclusion in *Think and Grow Rich!*. Dad mentioned that he thought *Think and Grow Rich!* was one of the first of a long line of great motivational books for the businessman."

The Halpins stayed in Manhattan until 1940. His next move was to southern New Jersey and the town of Haddonfield. He was hired as vice president and general manager of sales at the Radio Corporation of America in Camden, N. J. His new role was to market and merchandise a new entertainment system called television. He spent the next 12 years with RCA. In 1952, the family moved to Montclair, N. J., where he became vice president and general manager of DuMont Television. He ended his career as an account executive with Young & Rubicam Advertising, specializing in the General Electric television account.

While his career had many firsts, he was duly proud of being the first sales executive to convince a major hotel chain to put a television in each of its rooms, in the early 1950s. He was the creative genius who convinced owners of television sets that life would be better if they owned two televisions—the second being known as a "mother-in-law" TV. As a result, RCA sold millions of sets. He was also known in the industry as the primary force behind the sales strategy for the introduction and merchandising of color television. He was truly a pioneer in the early days of the television industry.

Halpin died in his sleep, at age 63, on August 21, 1970, about six weeks before Napoleon Hill passed away in Greenville, South Carolina, which he made his retirement home.

6   **Halpin told me that**   Knute Rockne was one of America's most innovative and charismatic football coaches and possessed all the characteristics that Napoleon Hill found necessary for achieving real success in life. Rockne was born March 4, 1888, in Voss, Norway, and died March 31, 1931, in Bazaar, Kansas, when the airplane he was flying on from Kansas City to Los Angeles crashed into the farmlands. He was 43 years old. He was head coach of the Fighting Irish of Notre Dame from 1918 to 1931, during which time Notre Dame won 105 games and six national championships. In 13 years he lost only 12 games and had five ties. His winning percentage of .881 still ranks as the best ever at Notre Dame and ranks at the top of the list for both college and professional football. Rockne is best known for his "Four Horseman" backfield of 1924 and his inspirational "Win One for the Gipper" speech in 1928. In 1999 he was named #10 on ESPN SportsCentury's list of the ten greatest coaches of all time, in all sports.

7   **That is why so**   Hill originally added at this point:

    With the changed conditions ushered in by the world economic collapse, came also the need for newer and better ways of marketing PERSONAL SERVICES. It is hard to determine why someone had not previously discovered this stupendous need, in view of the fact that more money changes hands in return for personal services than for any other purpose. The sum paid out monthly, to people who work for wages and salaries, is so huge that it runs into hundreds of millions, and the annual distribution amounts to billions.

8   **Woolworth's Five**   Were he writing now, Hill might have chosen as examples such latter-day entrepreneurs as Sam Walton of Wal-Mart, Ray Kroc of McDonald's, Steven Jobs of Apple Computers, or Bill Gates of Microsoft. Also, at this point in the original manuscript Hill included a further lengthy discussion about the woman who prepared the personal services marketing plan for her son. He wrote:

    Those seeing OPPORTUNITY lurking in this suggestion will find valuable aid in the chapter on Organized Planning. Incidentally, an efficient merchandiser of personal services would find a growing demand for his services wherever there are men and women who seek better markets for their services. By applying the Master Mind Principle, a few people with suitable talent, could form an alliance, and have a paying business very quickly. One would need to be a fair writer, with a flair for advertising and selling, one handy at typing and hand lettering, and one should be a first class business getter who would let the world know about the service. If one person possessed all these abilities, he might carry on the business alone, until it outgrew him.

    The woman who prepared the "Personal Service Sales Plan" for her son now receives requests from all parts of the country for her cooperation in preparing similar plans for others who desire to market their personal services for more money. She has a staff of expert typists, artists, and writers who have the ability to dramatize the case history so effectively that one's personal services can be marketed for much more money than the prevailing wages for similar services. She is so confident of her ability that she accepts, as the major portion of her fee, a percentage of the *increased* pay she helps her clients to earn.

It must not be supposed that her plan merely consists of clever salesmanship by which she helps men and women to demand and receive more money for the same services they formerly sold for less pay. She looks after the interests of the purchaser as well as the seller of personal services, and so prepares her plans that the employer receives full value for the additional money he pays. The method by which she accomplishes this astonishing result is a professional secret which she discloses to no one excepting her own clients.

If you have the IMAGINATION, and seek a more profitable outlet for your personal services, this suggestion may be the stimulus for which you have been searching. The IDEA is capable of yielding an income far greater than that of the "average" doctor, lawyer, or engineer whose education required several years in college. The idea is saleable to those seeking new positions, in practically all positions calling for managerial or executive ability, and those desiring re-arrangement of incomes in their present positions.

Chapter 5
IMAGINATION: The Workshop of the Mind

1   **It is the faculty** In an interview in *Parade Magazine*, singer-songwriter Lionel Ritchie provided an excellent description of how Creative Imagination works. Asked, "Where do your melodies come from?," he replied: "I wish I knew...It's like radio stations playing in my head. I'm in the shower singing along to this great song, and then I stop one moment and go, 'Hey, it's not on the radio.' What's frightening about it is I'm not singing a song, I'm singing *along* with the song that's playing in my head." Asked if it were true that he considers God to be his co-writer, Ritchie said, "Absolutely. I believe that in life, if you're lucky enough, the universe gives you something that nobody else can do but you."

2   **It was the product** At this point in the original version of *Think and Grow Rich!*, Hill launches into what is virtually a commercial advertisement for

the famous soft drink, complete with praises for its "mind stimulation" attributes. (The soda's caffeine had a stimulative effect that cola consumers of the time felt but likely did not fully understand. Until 1892 the drink contained cocaine.) Here's what Hill wrote: "Now that you know the content of the Enchanted Kettle is a world famous drink, it is fitting that the author confess that the home city of the drink [Atlanta] supplied him with a wife, also that the drink itself provides him with stimulation of thought without intoxication, and thereby it serves to give the refreshment of mind which an author must have to do his best work."

3   **Whoever you are** Asa Candler (1851-1929) was one of the most imaginative salesmen and marketing geniuses the world has ever seen. In 1891 he quit his Atlanta, Georgia, drugstore, took a poorly selling stimulant and headache remedy he bought the right to, and went on to make it known worldwide—as "The Real Thing." He worked 14-hour days, slept only five hours at night, and was an indefatigable spokesman and pitchman for his product. He was fond of saying, "A sale of Coca-Cola lost today is not a sale that may be made tomorrow," and if one of his customers wanted only a single gallon of Coca-Cola syrup, he would prepare it himself just to make the sale. He passed out free Cokes on elevators. He gave businesses free "Push" and "Pull" signs with the Coke logo printed on them to go on their doors. His advertising budget was bigger than his sales for several years, and by 1909 Coca-Cola had become America's best-advertised consumer product., with Coke ads on 2.5 million square feet of walls of buildings in the nation.

Candler was a prototypical "Think and Grow Rich" entrepreneur. He "set and wrote goals for everything. He set sales goals by the month—both sequentially and year by year. He never started a business meeting without first writing down how he wanted the meeting to be resolved. A devout Methodist, Candler also wrote down his spiritual goals—such as his prayer topics and Bible readings.... When Candler made a plan, he stuck by it. 'He didn't think he could fail. He refused to accept it,'[Elizabeth Candler, his great-great-granddaughter] Graham said.... He lacked formal training, but he was always searching for ways to expand his mind. As a teen-ager, landing a job as a pharmacy clerk, he read medical books and studied Latin and Greek at night. All told, it was Candler's determination—not his training or intelligence—that built his business and made him a success...." (Michael Tarsala, "Coca-Cola's Asa Candler," *Investor's Business Daily*, February 1, 1999, p. A-8.) Candler, like so many successful entrepreneurs who amass great fortunes, spent the last 10 years of his life as a philanthropist donating to hospitals, orphanages, and educational institutions. He gave $8 million—more than $80 million in today's dollars—to Emory University in Atlanta.

4   **My name is** Armour (1832-1901) was a meat packer who developed the Chicago Stockyards. He pioneered in shipping hogs to Chicago for slaughter, then canning and exporting the meat. His son, J. Ogden Armour (1863-1927), later made Armour and Company the world's largest and most successful meatpacking firm. The Armour Institute of Technology, which P. D. Armour would go on to fund with almost $2 million, opened in December 1892, with Frank W. Gunsaulus as its first president. Mrs. P. D. Armour and her son, J. Ogden, would later give another $1 million to the school. The Armour Institute later merged with the Lewis Institute and became the Illinois Institute of Technology. Gunsaulus died in 1921 at age 65.

5   **This book describes** This entire anecdote demonstrates several of Hill's most significant points and principles—the power and "reach" of the subconscious mind to get the job done, the blending of a burning desire and strong faith to create a "prayer-like" state of mind, the ability of the subconscious mind, "vibrating" or operating at peak intensity, to leap out and connect with the mind of another human being in a spirit of harmony. Dr. Gunsaulus's story is the embodiment of Napoleon Hill's ideas.

6   **when they saw them** In the original version of the book, Hill at this point presents a discourse on the future of radio, suggesting to his readers that this would be a fruitful field to consider entering. His predictions about marketing-based advertising and how the demands of the new medium would affect the advertising industry turned out to be highly accurate. However, what he refers to as radio's "crooners and light chatter artists" are still very much with us today, and serious public programming never has succeeded in moving light entertainment off center stage. Here is what Hill had to say:

   The next flock of millionaires will grow out of the radio business, which is new and not overburdened with men of keen imagination. The money will be made by those who discover or create new and more meritorious radio programs and have the imagination to recognize merit, and to give the radio listeners a chance to profit by it.

The sponsor! That unfortunate victim who now pays the cost of all radio "entertainment" soon will become idea conscious, and demand something for his money. The man who beats the sponsor to the draw, and supplies programs that render useful service, is the man who will become rich in this new industry.

Crooners and light chatter artists who now pollute the air with wisecracks and silly giggles will go the way of all light timbers, and their places will be taken by real artists who interpret carefully planned programs which have been designed to service the minds of men, as well as provide entertainment.

Here is a wide-open field of opportunity screaming its protest at the way it is being butchered, because of lack of imagination, and begging for rescue at any price. Above all, the thing that radio needs is new IDEAS!

If this new field of opportunity intrigues you, perhaps you might profit by the suggestion that the successful radio programs of the future will give more attention to creating "buyer" audiences and less attention to "listener" audiences. Stated more plainly, the builder of radio programs who succeeds in the future, must find practical ways to convert "listeners" into "buyers." Moreover, the successful producer of radio programs in the future must key his features so that he can definitely show its effect upon the audience.

Sponsors are becoming a bit weary of buying glib selling talks, based upon statements grabbed out of thin air. They want, and in the future will demand, indisputable proof that the "Whoosit" program not only gives millions of people the silliest giggle ever, but that the silly giggler can sell merchandise!

Another thing that might as well be understood by those who contemplate entering this new field of opportunity [is that] radio advertising is going to be handled by an entirely new group of advertising experts, separate and distinct from the old time newspaper and magazine advertising agency men. The old timers in the advertising game cannot read the modern radio scripts because they have been schooled to SEE ideas. The new radio technique demands men who can interpret ideas from a written manuscript in terms of SOUND! It cost the author a year of hard labor, and many thousands of dollars to learn this.

Radio, right now, is about where the moving pictures were when Mary Pickford and her curls first appeared on the screen. There is plenty of room in radio for those who can produce or recognize IDEAS.

If the foregoing comment on the opportunities of radio has not started your idea factory to work, you had better forget it. Your opportunity is in some other field. If the comment intrigued you in the slightest degree, then go further into it, and you may find the one IDEA you need to round out your career.

Never let it discourage you if you have no experience in radio. Andrew Carnegie knew very little about making steel—I have Carnegie's own word for this—but he made practical use of two of the principles described in this book, and made the steel business yield him a fortune.

Chapter 6
ORGANIZED PLANNING: The Crystallization of Desire into Action

1   **Napoleon, Kaiser Wilhelm** After his crushing defeat at Waterloo, Napoleon ended up in lonely exile on the island of St. Helena in the South Atlantic, where he died in 1821. Kaiser Wilhelm abdicated his throne in 1918 after Germany was defeated in World War I and went into exile in Holland, where he lived quietly until his death in 1942. In early 1917, Nicholas II, last czar of Russia, was forced to abdicate his throne. He was subsequently executed along with his family. Spain's Alfonso XIII was deposed in 1931 following a decade of political upheaval. He died in exile 10 years later.

2   **That means, of course,** Hill was decades ahead of his time. He touted the value of the art of delegating long before it became a management buzzword.

3   **SELFISHNESS. Leaders who** It is tempting to believe that *Think and Grow Rich!* may have had some influence, direct or indirect, on Coach

Paul "Bear" Bryant (1913-1983), who led the University of Alabama to six national football titles and ended his career with 323 wins, only 85 losses, and 17 ties. One of his most characteristic sayings—"When we win, the team did it; when we lose, it was my fault"—is a virtual paraphrase of No. 6 here and No. 10 of the 11 Major Factors of Leadership listed earlier. Bryant was 24 years old when *Think and Grow Rich!* was first published.

4   **They must cease** Newspapers today are certainly less "organs of propaganda" for advertisers than they used to be, but the scandal-mongering and lewd-picture papers are still thriving. "Eventually" could mean a very long time.

5   **APPLICATION THROUGH**   Almost half a century "ahead of the pack," Hill was recommending that people master the art of networking.

6   **In the future,**   Some people will occasionally suggest that *Think and Grow Rich!* is too materialistic, with its emphasis on wealth-building skills, and too self-centered, with its emphasis on self-reliance, personal achievement, and getting ahead in the world.   Such people fail to understand how "spiritual" and altruistic Hill's philosophy of success is at heart.   The Golden Rule holds immense significance for Hill.   In 1921 he began publishing, in Chicago, *Napoleon Hill's Magazine*, subtitled "A National Monthly Magazine of Business Philosophy" and selling for a quarter a copy. Here is its editorial policy.   Note the positive, nondiscriminatory, inclusive, "inspirational" nature of his remarks ("men and women together...regardless of race or creed.... rendering service which helps to ameliorate the hardships of humanity")—all the more remarkable since he was writing decades before the civil rights or women's movements would begin.

This Magazine is the outgrowth of an idea that found a lodging in its editor's mind more than twenty years ago; namely, the belief that the GOLDEN RULE ought to become the guiding star in all human relationships, and especially in business, industry and commerce.

The sole object in publishing this magazine is to bring men and women together in a spirit of closer co-operation, regardless of race or creed, and cause them to realize the award which awaits all who place principle above the dollar and humanity above the individual; to inspire those who have not yet "arrived" and help them to realize that the rainbow's end can be found only by the pathway which leads through the field of useful service; to teach men and women the uselessness and folly of hatred and envy and intolerance; to bring men to realize that success lies not so much in owning property, as in rendering service which helps to ameliorate the hardships of humanity and deposits something to the credit of posterity; to find the secret doorway to its readers' hearts and plant wholesome thoughts where destructive ones existed before.

This is not intended as a magazine of literary supremacy. Its business is to get the message over...and its editor is willing to sacrifice literary art for the sake of reaching men's hearts by a more forceful and direct route. In the editor's personal writings the pronoun 'I' is used freely because he writes mostly of that which he has felt and experienced in his walk through the 'Valley of the Shadow,' during these past twenty years, which is an explanation more than it is an apology.

This magazine is in no way connected with any other magazine using the 'Golden Rule' name, a distinction that should be clearly borne in mind.

At the bottom of the page upon which this policy appears is this statement: "No Wealth or Position Can Permanently Endure Unless Founded Upon Truth and Justice." In another place, an "EDITORS' CREED" states: "Your editors pledge themselves, without reservation, to the task of helping people see the necessity of placing principle above the dollar and humanity above the selfish individual whose only object in life is to get without giving." It is against a backdrop of such sentiments that Hill was busy conducting his research for *Think and Grow Rich!*, which he would publish 16 years later. As a side note, it is interesting that Stuart Austin Wier is listed as "Associate Editor" of *Napoleon Hill's Magazine*. For more information on Wier, see page 314. (The last sentence above beginning "This magazine is in no way connected..." refers to *Hill's Golden Rule* magazine, which he launched in 1919, but lost control of in October 1920, when the publisher took full control in a heated dispute.)

7   **— THE PUBLIC THEY SERVED.** Hill originally added:

> The depression served as a mighty protest from an injured public, whose rights had been trampled upon in every direction by those who were clamoring for individual advantages and profits. When the debris of the depression shall have been cleared away, and business shall have been once again restored to balance, both employers and employees will recognize that they are NO LONGER PRIVILEGED TO DRIVE BARGAINS AT THE EXPENSE OF THOSE WHOM THEY SERVE.

8   **This should be kept** Excellence in customer service would recapture the spotlight, beginning in the 1980s. In his original manuscript, Hill used railroads and streetcars as an example of the negative effects of poor service:

> Nearly every railroad in America is in financial difficulty. Who does not remember the day when if a citizen inquired at the ticket office [about] the time of departure of a train, he was abruptly referred to the bulletin board instead of being politely given the information?
>
> The street car companies have experienced a "change of times" also. There was a time not so very long ago when street car conductors took pride in giving argument to passengers. Many of the street car tracks have been removed and passengers ride on a bus, whose driver is "the last word in politeness." All over the country, street car tracks are rusting from abandonment or have been taken up. Wherever street cars are still in operation, passengers may now ride without argument, and one may even hail the car in the middle of the block, and the motorman will OBLIGINGLY pick him up.
>
> HOW TIMES HAVE CHANGED! That is just the point I am trying to emphasize. TIMES HAVE CHANGED! Moreover, the change is reflected not merely in railroad offices and on streetcars, but in other walks of life as well. The "public-be-damned" policy is now passe/. It has been supplanted by the "we-are-obligingly-at-your-service, sir" policy.

9   **-your service, sir" policy.** The original manuscript at this point included the following:

The bankers have learned a thing or two during this rapid change which has taken place during the past few years. Impoliteness on the part of a bank official, or bank employee today is as rare as it was conspicuous a dozen years ago. In the years past, some bankers (not all of them, of course), carried an atmosphere of austerity which gave every would-be borrower a chill when he even thought of approaching his banker for a loan.

The thousands of bank failures during the depression had the effect of removing the mahogany doors behind which bankers formerly barricaded themselves. They now sit at desks in the open, where they may be seen and approached at will by any depositor, or by anyone who wishes to see them, and the whole atmosphere of the bank is one of courtesy and understanding.

It used to be customary for customers to have to stand and wait at the corner grocery until the clerks were through passing the time of day with friends, and the proprietor had finished making up his bank deposit, before being waited upon. Chain stores, managed by COURTEOUS MEN who do everything in the way of service, short of shining the customer's shoes, have PUSHED THE OLD-TIME MERCHANTS INTO THE BACKGROUND. TIME MARCHES ON!

10 **privilege of serving.** Hill had originally written here:

We can all remember the time when the gas-meter reader pounded on the door hard enough to break the panels. When the door was opened, he pushed his way in, uninvited, with a scowl on his face which plainly said, "what-the-hell-did-you-keep-me-waiting-for?" All that has undergone a change. The meter-man now conducts himself as a gentleman who is "delighted-to-be-at-your-service-sir." Before the gas companies learned that their scowling meter-men were accumulating liabilities never to be cleared away, the polite salesmen of oil burners came along and did a land office business.

11 **and city taxes!** The original manuscript included this curious statement about taxes and politicians:

(Here is a fact the politicians did not mention when they were crying out to the voters to throw their opponents out of office because the people were being taxed to death).

12 **we in America enjoy** It is unclear why Hill felt compelled here to add a parenthetical remark (italics his):

(And this is neither political nor economic propaganda).

13 **In Germany** Hill originally added, "In Germany, Russia, Italy, and most of the other European and Oriental countries, the people cannot travel with so much freedom and at so little cost," which is not quite the case today.

14 **For decades, it** Andrew Carnegie once said: "It will be a great mistake for the community to shoot the millionaires, for they are the bees that make the most honey, and contribute most to the hive even after they have gorged themselves full."

15 **ARE GETTING IT.** Hill originally added this wry comment: "Their idea of their rights of freedom was demonstrated in New York City, where violent complaint was registered with the Postmaster by a group of 'relief beneficiaries' because the Postmen awakened them at 7:30 a.m. to deliver Government relief checks. They DEMANDED that the time of delivery be set up to 10:00 o'clock."

16 **Always there are** Hill cited three examples—Germany and Italy, which at that time were ruled by fascist dictators, and Russia, which was under the Communist "dictatorship of the proletariat."

17 **If it is riches** This and following figures are from 2001 data, *Statistical Abstract of the Untied States.* Hill's original comments are interesting for comparison:

If it is riches you are seeking, do not overlook the possibilities of a country whose citizens are so rich that women, alone, spend over two hundred million dollars annually for lip-sticks, rouge and cosmetics. Think twice, you who are seeking riches, before trying to destroy the Capitalistic System of a country whose citizens spend over fifty million dollars a year for GREETING CARDS, with which to express their appreciation of their FREEDOM.

If it is money you are seeking, consider carefully a country that spends hundreds of millions of dollars annually for cigarettes, the bulk of the income from which goes to only four major companies engaged in supplying this national builder of "nonchalance" and "quiet nerves."

By all means give plenty of consideration to a country whose people spend annually more than fifteen million dollars for the privilege of seeing moving pictures, and toss in a few additional millions for liquor, narcotics, and other less potent soft drinks and giggle-waters.

Do not be in too big a hurry to get away from a country whose people willingly, even eagerly, hand over millions of dollars annually for football, baseball, and prize fights.

And, by all means, STICK by a country whose inhabitants give up more than a million dollars a year for chewing gum, and another million for safety razor blades.

18 **We have never**   The reference is to the crushing of individual freedoms under Hitler, Mussolini, and Stalin.

19 **There is no way**   It would be fascinating to hear Napoleon Hill's comments about the national debt situation facing the United States today.

20 **It is the point**   The reference is to mortgage foreclosures, on both residential and commercial properties, resulting from bankruptcy proceedings. The Depression was devastating, to families and businesses. For example, from 1929 to 1932, average per capita income (net) on family farms in America plunged from $2,297 to $74 — an incredible drop of almost 97 percent.

Chapter 7
DECISION: The Mastery of Procrastination

1   *This is important.* Napoleon Hill enjoyed getting in the occasional "dig" at crooks and crooked politicians as shown by the parenthetical remark he tossed in at this point in the original book: "(Racketeers and dishonest politicians have prostituted the honor for which such men as Adams died)."

Chapter 8
PERSISTENCE: The Sustained Effort Necessary to Induce Faith

1   **WITH PERSISTENCE** An "attitude is everything" conviction character-
izes just about every page Napoleon Hill wrote throughout his long career.
Marilyn vos Savant, who has one of the highest IQs in the world, agrees.
She writes in "Ask Marilyn" (her widely read column),"While I feel
completely confident that normal intellectual capacity is far greater than
is necessary for nearly all jobs, I also feel completely confident that nearly
all of us reach our limits of motivation, hard work and perseverance far
before we reach our limits of intelligence. In other words, our attitudes
hold us back more than our aptitudes."

2   **The secret of how** Fannie Hurst (1889-1968) was a novelist, dramatist,
and screenwriter. By her mid-20s, she had become an established author,
writing for and about working women. Several of her works were made
into motion pictures, including *Back Street* and *Imitation of Life*, the latter
twice, in 1933 and 1959.

3   **Kate Smith would** Kate Smith (1909-1986) was known as "The First Lady
of Radio." "The Kate Smith Show" ran on CBS Radio from 1931 to 1947,
and she hosted television's "The Kate Smith Hour" from 1950 to 1954. Her
career began with singing parts in assorted vaudeville shows. At age 8 she
was entertaining troops in Washington, D. C., during World War I. She
had two "signature" songs: "When the Moon Comes Over the Mountain,"
which was her theme song, and "God Bless America," the Irving Berlin
hit which she first recorded in 1938 and which he wrote exclusively for
her. Although she had no formal vocal training, her full, robust soprano
voice became one of the most recognized in the entertainment industry,
and she recorded more than 3,000 songs during her long career.

4   **During the Depression** W. C. Fields (born William Claude Dukenfield in
1880) ran away from home at age 11 and within three years had become
well-known as a vaudeville juggler. From 1915 to 1921 he performed
as a comic juggler in the Ziegfield Follies. He made the transition to
the stage in 1923 in *Poppy* and by 1931 had moved to Hollywood and
was writing, directing, and starring in his own films. One of America's
greatest comedians and masters of timing and the delayed response, he
is remembered for such films as *The Bank Dick* (1940), *My Little Chickadee*
(1940), and *Never Give a Sucker an Even Break* (1941). He died in 1946.

5   **Marie Dressler found** Marie Dressler (1869-1934) was one of Hollywood's most popular screen personalities in the early 1930s. She specialized in playing strong, self-sufficient, humorous old women. Her film debut was in the 1914 *Tillie's Punctured Romance,* a Mack Sennett film in which Charlie Chaplin and Mabel Norman also appeared. Dressler won an Academy Award as best actress for her work in the 1931 film *Min and Bill,* which co-starred Wallace Beery.

6   **Eddie Cantor lost** Saucer-eyed Eddie Cantor (born Edward Israel Iskowitz in 1892) did it all, starring in vaudeville, burlesque, on the legitimate stage, radio, and television. Orphaned at age two on the Lower East Side of New York City, he was raised by his grandmother. As a lad, he clowned and sang for coins on street corners. He was a black-face song and dance performer in vaudeville, later toured with several theater companies, appeared in Broadway reviews, was a hit with *The Chase and Sanborn Hour* on radio beginning in 1931 and running through 1949, and he hosted the half-hour *The Eddie Cantor Variety Theater* on television, a show that was syndicated in 1955. He died in 1964.

7   **The only "break"** "You know, it's a funny thing. The harder I work, the luckier I seem to get." This quote attributed to golfer Arnold Palmer (and in variations to many other professional athletes and other personalities) sums up what Hill means when he talks about "self-made" breaks that result from persistence that is derived from a clear, well-defined and strong sense of purpose.

8   **I have no way** The affair between the twice-divorced Wallace Warfield Simpson and Edward, Duke of Windsor, who gave up his throne to marry her, remains *the* love story of the 20th century. Edward (1894-1972) held the title of Prince of Wales in 1931, when he first met Mrs. Simpson (1896-1986), born a British subject but by then a U. S. citizen. Over time, he fell hopelessly in love. When she divorced her second husband — wealthy shipping magnate Ernest Simpson — in October 1936, Edward had been King of England for a scant nine months. His announced intention to marry Wallace Simpson offended both British traditionalists and the Church of England hierarchy and provoked a governmental crisis. On December 10, 1936, Edward abdicated the throne in a radio broadcast to the nation, with, in part, these words: "I have found it impossible to carry the heavy burden of responsibility and to discharge my duties as King as

I would wish to do without the help and support of the woman I love." The new king, George VI, created the title of Duke of Windsor for his older brother, and on June 3, 1937, Edward and Wallace were married in France. In a slight to Wallace that Edward never forgave, King George refused to grant her the title of Duchess of Windsor. From 1937 to 1939 and after 1945 when World War II ended, the Duke and "Duchess" resided mainly in France, lived a café-society existence, and became the subject of countless magazine articles and books through the years. Her memoirs, *The Heart Has Its Reasons*, were published in 1959. After the Duke's death in 1972, Wallace kept on her dressing room table a gold-framed message from the Duke. It read:

> My Friend, with thee to live alone
> Methinks were better than to own
> A crown, a scepter, and a throne.

9   **And what of King**   The Duke of Windsor-Wallace Simpson affair was an international scandal of the most notorious sort, setting tongues wagging on six continents. Today it seems almost innocent and pristine compared to the shenanigans conducted by the younger members of the British Royal Family in the early 1990s.

10   **crying out for expression.**   The original manuscript included the following lofty paragraph:

> And when he met a kindred spirit, crying out for this same Holy privilege of expression, he recognized it, and without fear or apology, opened his heart and bade it enter. All the scandal-mongers in the world cannot destroy the beauty of this international drama, through which two people found love, and had the courage to face open criticism, renounce ALL ELSE to give it *holy* expression.

11   **price was too great.**   Hill originally inserted here this aside:

> Surely not He who said, "He among you who is without sin, let him cast the first stone."

12   **the price demanded.**   Hill waxed eloquent at this point:

> If Europe had been blessed with more rulers with the human heart and the traits of honesty of ex-king Edward, for the past century, that unfortunate hemisphere now seething with greed, hate, lust, political connivance, and threats of war, would have a

DIFFERENT AND BETTER STORY TO TELL. A story in which Love and not Hate would rule.

In the words of Stuart Austin Wier we raise our cup and drink this toast to ex-king Edward and Wallis Simpson: "Blessed is the man who has come to know that our muted thoughts are our sweetest thoughts.

"Blessed is the man who, from the blackest depths, can see the luminous figure of LOVE, and seeing, sing; and singing, say: 'Sweeter far than utter lays are the thoughts I have of you.'"

In these words would we pay tribute to the two people who, more than all others of modern times, have been the victims of criticism and the recipients of abuse, because they found Life's greatest treasure, and claimed it.

13   **we demand of life.** The original version of *Think and Grow Rich!* contains the following curious footnote, which comes at the end of the story about the Duke of Windsor and his bride: "*Mrs. Simpson read and approved this analysis.*" Presumably, Hill had submitted this portion of his manuscript for her comments and suggestions.

Chapter 9
POWER OF THE MASTER MIND: The Driving Force

1   **The "Master Mind" may** W. Clement Stone, who worked closely with Napoleon Hill for a decade, had this to say about the principle: "During our ten-year association, I learned the missing number to my combination for worldwide successful achievement—the Master Mind Principle, two or more persons working together in complete harmony toward a mutual goal or goals....Napoleon Hill's philosophy teaches you what you were never taught, specifically, how to recognize, relate, assimilate, and apply principles whereby you can achieve any goal whatsoever that doesn't violate Universal Law—the Law of God and the rights of your fellow man" ("Editorial Reviews," Amazon.com website, November 12, 2003). Stone, who died in 2002 at age 100, founded Combined Insurance Co. The company merged in 1982 with Ryan Insurance, which was re-named Aon Corp. in 1987. Stone, one of the wealthiest individuals in America, was

also the president and driving force behind the Napoleon Hill Foundation for a number of years.

2   **It absorbs energy**   In the original version of the book, Hill uses the now obsolete term (and concept) of "ether," instead of "Unifying Force." Physicists and mathematicians today, almost half a century after Einstein's death, still labor to develop the "unified theory" Einstein was seeking which would explain what "ties together" the universe — from the gravitational force that structures the galaxies and space itself down to the tiniest forces found in the smallest corners of the subatomic world. Hill, of course, had little understanding of these matters, but he was confident that *something*, some mysterious force by which all things are connected, is at work in the universe. Because he was dealing with concepts that would have been, and still are, extremely difficult to comprehend and explain, he was forced to resort to analogies such as the one presented here.

3   **Go a step further**   Harvey S. Firestone (1868-1938) founded Firestone Tire and Rubber Company in 1900 with an investment of $10,000, which made him half owner of the business. The company originally sold rubber tires for carriages. In 1904 they began making tires for an emerging new form of transportation, the automobile. Firestone developed several techniques for the manufacture of pneumatic tires, which were used on Ford Motor Company's Model T. John Burroughs (1837-1921) was a nationally prominent naturalist. After a successful early career as a treasury clerk and national bank examiner, he devoted the remainder of his years to writing and fruit growing. The author of such books as *Signs and Seasons, Camping and Tramping with Roosevelt,* and *The Breath of Life,* Burroughs was a Thoreau-like figure who went on celebrated camping trips with the likes of Theodore Roosevelt and fellow naturalist John Muir. Luther Burbank was the father of modern scientific plant breeding.

4   **If you find**   Research has consistently shown that maintaining a positive attitude — about yourself and about life — can affect more than your financial condition. It can help you live longer. In a study of 1,500 boys conducted in California beginning in 1921, researchers found that "pessimists" in the group were 25 percent more likely to die before age 65 than positive thinkers. Researchers at the University of Wisconsin's Brain Imaging and Behavior Laboratory found that positive-thinking, optimistic subjects had

higher levels of "killer-cells" and had less of a decline in immune system response when faced with stressful situations. "Self-esteem has to do with self-valuing, self-respect, a kind of confidence and a willingness to speak one's truth," says Emmett E. Miller, author of *Deep Healing: The Essence of Mind/Body Medicine,* in a *USA Weekend* article. "That's a tonic to the immune system, to all the organs of the body."

Chapter 10
THE MYSTERY OF SEX TRANSMUTATION

1   **When "harnessed"** Hill's analysis leans toward the metaphysical, yet has an eminently practical aspect. "Harnessed" and "redirected" refer not only to subconscious, subliminal forces that can be mastered. They also caution the reader: "Keep sex in proper proportion in your life. Enjoy it, give it expression. But use it, control it, don't let it control you."

2   **Destroy the sex glands** Anyone who has ever had a pet neutered or spayed understands the effect described. While Hill generalizes the effect to include human beings who may have had similar surgical procedures, he was writing, of course, long before the advent of hormone replacement therapy, which can counteract the effects.

3   **When asked why** These kinds of meditative moments, drawing upon the Creative Imagination to contact "a source of superior intelligence"(or Infinite Intelligence), are given an excellent, more complete explanation in an editorial that appeared in the August 5, 1994, *Christian Science Monitor* (page 17), which uses language evocative of Napoleon Hill:

> Whether you are solitary or just alone in your thought, you make the most of thinking time when you let God direct your thinking. We can turn to God for direction, inspiration, ideas. Because God is divine Mind, which gives us our intelligence, it comes from God by reflection. We can "hear" Mind's ideas, feel God's presence, and be assured of His guidance....
>
> Prayerful thinking time is not only practical for solving problems and for gaining serenity; it is essential for doing creative work. Inspiration comes with beautiful precision when we know it comes from Mind, God, and listen for His direction.

Ideas, whether they come slowly or in deluges, need to be wisely considered. They need to be nurtured by a feeling of closeness to God. Then we perceive which ideas are right for our present use.

Thinking time can be valuable, especially if it is spent listening to God.

4   **In his laboratory** A similar process is described by broadcast journalist David Brinkley in his book *Washington Goes to War* (Alfred A. Knopf, 1988). Brinkley recounts the story of how one Beardsley Ruml, treasurer of R. H. Macy & Company, came up with the idea of income tax withholding—"pay-as-you-go" taxation—which was a radical innovation in the year 1940: "Ruml's habit, when he perceived a problem, was to lock himself in a room away from distractions—no newspapers, magazines, radio or people—recline for a few hours in a deeply upholstered chair, and allow his mind to float freely in what he called 'a state of dispersed attention.' It was during such a session that the idea of tax 'withholding' was born." Ruml may or may not have read *Think and Grow Rich!* and its account of Dr. Elmer Gates, but he availed himself of the same technique it advocates.

5   **ELBERT HUBBARD** Napoleon Hill was intimately acquainted with the work of Elbert Green Hubbard (1856-1915), who published the popular "Little Journey" booklets, which presented biographical essays on famous and successful people—similar, though nothing like as extensive, as the work Hill himself had undertaken. In 1899, Hubbard published the sensationally popular essay "A Message to Garcia" in his avant-garde magazine *The Philistine*. This may have had a profound effect on Hill, stressing as it did so powerfully the importance of perseverance in the face of adversity. The essay drew upon an incident from the Spanish American War. Hubbard died in 1915 when the liner *Lusitania* on which he was traveling was sunk by a German U-boat off the Irish coast.

6   **ELBERT H. GARY** Elbert H. Gary (1846-1927), an attorney and the first mayor of Wheaton, Illinois, gained lasting fame by helping to organize U. S. Steel Corp. He eventually became the first chairman and chief executive officer of the company.

7   **JOHN H. PATTERSON** John H. Patterson (1844-1922) was an innovative entrepreneur who popularized the "modern" cash register, the kind that "rang a bell" and popped open the cash drawer when a sale was

entered. He entered the cash register business indirectly. Convinced that clerks in his retail store had their fingers in the till, he purchased some of the newfangled registers. Realizing their potential, he bought out the individual whose firm manufactured them, renamed the enterprise the National Cash Register Company (later NCR), and proceeded to take the retail business by storm. Patterson is credited with introducing the idea of exclusive territories for his salespeople, opening the world's first sales training school, and pioneering the use of direct mail ads and big commissions for sales representatives. He promoted employee welfare programs and better working conditions in an era when to do so was considered all but unethical by the greater business community.

8   **ENRICO CARUSO** Caruso (1873-1921) was the most famous operatic tenor in the world in the early 1900s. Born in Naples, Italy, the eighteenth of 20 children, Caruso had no formal vocal training until he was 18. He made his American debut on November 23, 1903, in *Rigoletto* at the opening night of New York's Metropolitan Opera. He would open each season there for the next 17 years. Caruso was the first major musician or singer to record his work on gramophone recordings.

9   **into the "genius mode."** Hill's original manuscript at this point contains these intriguing lines:

> One of America's most able business leaders frankly admitted that his attractive secretary was responsible for most of the plans he created. He admitted that her presence lifted him to heights of creative imagination, such as he could experience under no other stimulus.

> One of the most successful men in America owes most of his success to the influence of a very charming young woman, who has served as his source of inspiration for more than twelve years. Everyone knows the man to whom this reference is made, but not everyone knows the REAL SOURCE of his achievements.

It is uncertain to whom Hill was referring in these paragraphs. The sentiments expressed may seem ingenuous to today's reader, but they convey vividly Hill's contention that sex drive has an enormous influence upon human behavior and motivation in the business world, a point which more dispassionate behavioral research has borne out.

10   **James Whitcomb Riley** Nicknamed "The Hoosier Poet," Riley (1849-1916) was famous for his poems and lecture circuit anecdotes about life in small town, rural America and particularly his home state of Indiana. A born mimic, he regaled audiences with rustic stories and imitations of Hoosier accents. Despite severe attacks of stage fright, which he never conquered, he went on to become one of the country's most popular lecturers. He also created the Little Orphan Annie character in *The Orphant Annie Book* [sic] (1908), and he published books of poetry such as *The Old Swimmin' Hole* and *'Leven More Poems*, the latter of which sold a half-million copies. Before beginning his career as an author, he worked as an itinerant sign painter, actor, Bible salesman, musician, and newspaper reporter. That he wrote under some sort of special "influence," Riley himself agreed: "My work did itself. I'm only the 'willer' [willow] bark through which the whistle comes."

11   **But let it be** Narcotics and alcohol seem to play a catalytic role in the lives of many creative people. They also often spell their doom. Actress Judy Garland, rock legend Jim Morrison of The Doors, poet Dylan Thomas, novelist Ernest Hemingway, playwright Tennessee Williams, rock guitarist Jimi Hendrix, author Truman Capote, "Beat Generation" chronicler Jack Kerouac, comedian John Belushi, actor River Phoenix—the list goes on and on of outstanding artists whose addictions ultimately cost them their lives.

12   **James J. Hill** James J. Hill (1838-1916) was a financier and railroad magnate. He was president and subsequently chairman of Great Northern Railway. He later assumed control of the First and Second National banks of St. Paul, Minnesota. Hill wrote a popular book, *Highways of Progress*, which was published in 1910.

13   **It is a well-known fact** Common table salt is the most common example. Sodium and chlorine by themselves are highly toxic substances, whereas sodium chloride is sprinkled on food every day in kitchens and at tables around the world.

14   ***When any negative emotion*** This statement, in a nutshell, represents the genesis of the positive mental attitude—or PMA—philosophy, which Napoleon Hill and later his patron, W. Clement Stone, would devote their lives to spreading.

15 **Love is, without** The power of love is much more than a romantic cliché, according to Emmett E. Miller, author of *Deep Healing: The Essence of Mind/Body Medicine*. "The evidence is piling up in many ways: Having a relationship protects against disease. When you're happy and joyful and feeling love, and feel loved and happy to be alive, you and your life are valued, that message gets transmitted right down to the immune cells." ("How we feel changes how we...feel," Patty Rhule, *USA Weekend*, September 24-26, 1999.)

Chapter 11
THE SUBCONSCIOUS MIND: The Connecting Link

1 **Ella Wheeler Wilcox** Ella Wheeler Wilcox was born in 1850 into an impoverished Wisconsin farm family. She seemed destined for a literary career from childhood, completing her first "novel" at the age of 10. After high school she studied at the University of Wisconsin, but left to return home, the source of her literary inspiration and aspirations. By age 18 her professional writings were earning enough money to double the family's income. Her 1883 *Poems of Passion* was originally rejected as immoral by publishers, but a Chicago house eventually accepted it, and it became a bestseller. Her works are filled with imagery of sexual passion, often symbolized in the figure of a tiger. She became a leader in what was known as "The Erotic School" and once remarked that "heart, not art" is what makes good poetry. She was also an essayist and editorialist, with pieces appearing in such publications as the *New York Journal* and *Cosmopolitan*. Napoleon Hill was no doubt attracted to Wilcox's work, given his strong belief in the power of romantic love and the important role the sex drive plays in human achievement. She died in 1919.

2 **Only by following** Herbert Benson of Harvard University's Mind/Body Medical Institute suggests the following technique to overcome the *physical* effects of negative emotions (from "How we feel changes how we...feel," by Patty Rhule, *USA Weekend*, September 24-26, 1999):

    1. Choose a word, sound, prayer or phrase that fits your belief system; for instance, "peace" or "the Lord is my shepherd."

    2. Sit comfortably, close your eyes, relax muscles.

3. Breathe slowly. On each out breath, refocus your word. Do 10 to 20 minutes once or twice a day; before breakfast or before dinner is best.

4. When finished, sit a moment and think pleasant thoughts.

3.   **Moreover, there is evidence**   In these sorts of discussions, which occur at a couple of key points in *Think and Grow Rich!*, Hill relies upon the now-outdated and discarded scientific concept of "the ether" as an invisible medium through which electromagnetic energy is transmitted throughout the universe. However, it is interesting to note that, philosophically and fundamentally, Hill's description of the characteristics of "space" and "energy" comes very close to that of the latest scientific theory — so-called "string theory," which suggests that space, energy, and matter are manifestations of unbelievably tiny, one-dimensional, vibrating "strings" — calculated to be a millionth of a billionth of a billionth of a billionth of a centimeter (10^{-33} centimeter). When Hill writes of "this living, pulsating, 'vibratory' energy which permeates every atom of matter and fills every niche of space," he could well be describing the kind of ultimate reality that string theory envisions. Instead of being a quiet void or vacuum, a tiny region of space at the ultramicroscopic level is a roiling, churning, violently fluctuating "place" whose environment is so frenzied that it is described as "quantum foam," according to string theory.   Physicist-mathematician Brian Greene's excellent book, *The Elegant Universe* (1999), gives the best explanation of string theory to date and is something Napoleon Hill would surely have read had it been available in his time.

Chapter 12
THE BRAIN: A Broadcasting and Receiving Station for Thought

1   **Creative Imagination is**   The phenomenon is perhaps aptly illustrated in the example of a championship professional basketball team, whose members seem to be able to anticipate each other's every move, response, and intention — no matter how fast the pace or complicated the circumstances — during stretches of top-flight play. The same is true with

members of an outstanding jazz ensemble when they improvise at their most creative level, or with members of a scientific team during "eureka moments" of mutual discovery and simultaneous insight.

2   **If you understand** This technique would today be described as "brainstorming," although Hill's concept of brainstorming—among the members of a Master Mind Group—assumes a significantly higher level of mental process and results than merely "kicking ideas around."

Chapter 13
THE SIXTH SENSE: The Door to the Temple of Wisdom

1   **This principle is**   In addition to *The 13 Steps to Riches*, Hill would later develop, along with W. Clement Stone, *The 17 Success Principles*, which were taught in classes and a popular correspondence course called *PMA Science of Success*. *The 17 Success Principles* are (they have been variously stated, and ordered, in different works):

1. A Positive Mental Attitude
2. Definiteness of Purpose
3. Going the Extra Mile
4. Accurate Thinking
5. Self-Discipline
6. The Master Mind Principal
7. Applied Faith
8. A Pleasing Personality
9. Personal Initiative
10. Enthusiasm
11. Controlled Attention (or Concentration)
12. Teamwork
13. Learning from Adversity and Defeat
14. Creative Vision (Imagination)
15. Budgeting Time and Money
16. Maintaining Sound Physical and Mental Health
17. The Law of Cosmic Habit Force (the use of universal law)

Hill and Stone's book, *Success through a Positive Mental Attitude* (written in 1960 and revised in 1977) provides a good explanation of *The 17 Success*

Principles, as does *Your Right to Be Rich,* an interactive study guide first published in 1961.

2 **Realizing as I did** Hill was born October 26, 1883, in a two-room log cabin in the mountains of Wise County, Virginia. It was a region marked by illiteracy, grinding poverty, and superstition. Its people led a hardscrabble existence, struggling to eke out a living by farming on difficult soils and challenging terrain. Most people born here lived their entire lives without ever leaving the mountains. Hill was one of the few who escaped and go on to travel the nation and live in some of its great cities.

3 **He smiled broadly** This is a mystical moment in the story of *Think and Grow Rich!*. As usual when he delves into metaphysical matters, Hill grasps for appropriate words to describe that which, in the end, cannot be described. It is interesting to note that Thomas Edison once answered a question about his religious beliefs during an interview by discussing "life forces" in terms remarkably similar to those Hill uses here. The published interview was quite controversial, and it is unclear how literally Edison meant his remarks to be taken. Presumably, Hill had either read the interview or else heard Edison describe the same ideas during one of his own interviews with the inventor. (For a further discussion of the incident, see Robert Conot, *A Streak of Luck,* Seaviews Books, New York, 1979, page 427, or Wyn Wachhorst, *Thomas Alva Edison: An American Myth,* MIT Press, Cambridge, Mass., 1981, pages 137-138.)

4 **in physical bodies.** In the original version of the book, this chapter ends with the following paragraph:

> The Ghost of the Fear of Poverty, which seized the minds of millions of people in 1929, was so real that it caused the worst business depression this country has ever known. Moreover, this particular ghost still frightens some of us out of our wits.

Epilogue
HOW TO OUTWIT THE SIX GHOSTS OF FEAR

1 **The remainder of** Napoleon Hill devoted his life to disseminating *The Think and Grow Rich Philosophy* and teaching people how to put it to practical use. W. Clement Stone, Hill's collaborator and patron, played a

key role in that purpose. "From 1952 to 1962 I employed Napoleon Hill and acted as his general manager," said Stone. "We were dedicated to spreading Hill's philosophy. He had previously authored *Law of Success, Think and Grow Rich*, and many other works. A few of the numerous achievements of our Master Mind Alliance were co-founding *Success Unlimited* magazine, co-authoring *Success through a Positive Mental Attitude*, developing the 'PMA Science of Achievement Course,' and, most importantly, laying the foundation that guaranteed the achievement of Hill's Definite Major Purpose in Life. Hill's Definite Major Purpose was to spread the philosophy of achievement…worldwide and to future generations. Together we influenced untold millions of persons on every continent" (source: Motivational Speakers Hall of Fame website at joshhinds.com/motspeakers.htm.)

2   **Just following the war,** The international epidemic referred to was the deadly Spanish influenza that struck in the autumn of 1918. By the time the epidemic had run its course in July 1919, more than 20 million people had been infected and more than 500,000 were dead. The flu and its virulent companion, pneumonia, killed half as many U. S. troops at home as died in combat in World War I. During the height of the epidemic, schools and churches were closed, and many people ventured outside only when wearing cotton masks. An elderly gentleman, reminiscing about "The Flu" epidemic at Clemson University in South Carolina, recalled the campus Trustee House being used as a temporary infirmary. "They were just bringing the bodies in like firewood," he exclaimed.

3   *Fears are nothing more* At this point in the original manuscript, Hill related the following anecdotal material:

> Physicians, as everyone knows, are less subject to attack by disease than ordinary laymen, for the reason that physicians DO NOT FEAR DISEASE. Physicians, without fear or hesitation, have been known to physically contact hundreds of people daily who were suffering from such contagious diseases as smallpox without becoming infected. Their immunity against the disease consisted, largely, if not solely, in their absolute lack of FEAR.

> While traditional medical research may suggest other explanations, it is notable that researchers and physicians have come more and more to emphasize the influence of positive attitudes on health, healing, and

general well-being. The specific example Hill uses here may not hold up. The general principle does.

4   **What this sort** Pegler was a caustic newspaper columnist whose invective and tirades against public programs were carried in more than 170 newspapers. He won a Pulitzer Prize in 1941 for his crusading pieces on labor union corruption, but his later writing focused less and less on exposing misdeed and more and more on expressing scorn—for New Deal administrators, labor leaders, and the Franklin D. Roosevelt family especially. Charles Fisher in *The Columnists* (Howell, Soskin Publishers, 1944) wrote this about Pegler: "Having read the newspapers in bed, he breakfasts and retires early to his study, whence emerges bad language, the sound of copy paper being yanked from the typewriter and ripped to bits, and considerable quantities of cigarette smoke. He spends perhaps six hours a day on a piece and has been known to hunt forty-five minutes for a word." Pegler died June 24, 1969, at the age of 74. (The *New York World-Telegram* was created in 1931 by the merger of the *World* and the *Evening Telegram*. The Scripps-Howard newspaper chain, owners of United Press International, bought the *Sun* in 1950 and merged it to form the *New York World-Telegram-Sun*. The paper ceased publication in 1966.)

5   **be himself again.**" At this point in the text, Hill originally included the following indignant remarks about the way some employers treated down-on-their-luck people during the Depression:

> Some employers take the most shocking advantage of people who are down and out. The agencies hang out little colored cards offering miserable wages to busted men—$2 a week, $15 a week. An $18 a week job is a plum, and anyone with $25 a week to offer does not hang the job in front of an agency on a colored card. I have a want ad clipped from a local paper demanding a clerk, a good, clean penman, to take telephone orders for a sandwich shop from 11 A.M. to 2 P.M. for $8 a month—not $8 a week but $8 a month. The ad says also, "State religion." Can you imagine the brutal effrontery of anyone who demands a good, clean penman for 11 cents an hour inquiring into the victim's religion? But that is what busted people are offered.

6   **The Fear of Criticism** At this point in the original manuscript, Hill offered this analysis:

> Bald-headed men, for example, are bald for no other reason than their fear of criticism. Heads become bald because of the tight fitting bands of hats which cut off the circulation from the roots of the hair. Men wear hats, not because they actually need them, but mainly because "everyone is doing it." The individual falls into line and does likewise, lest some other individual CRITICIZE him. Women seldom have bald heads, or even thin hair, because they wear hats which fit their heads loosely, the only purpose of the hats being adornment.
>
> But it must not be supposed that women are free from the fear of criticism. If any woman claims to be superior to man with reference to this fear, ask her to walk down the street wearing a hat of the vintage of 1890.

Hill was not infallible — if for no other reason than the fact that medical scientists in his day understood little about the relationship between genetics and male pattern baldness.

7   **Playing upon this** *Collier's* (which ceased publication in 1957) enjoyed a long history and was once America's leading general interest magazine. It was founded in April 1888 by Peter Fenelon Collier as *Once a Week* and sold along with his biweekly *Collier's Library,* which printed short novels and popular stories at "bargain rates" — 7 cents for 16 pages. The first edition featured pieces by Ella Wheeler Wilcox, James Whitcomb Riley, and H. Rider Haggard, the author of *King Solomon's Mines, She,* and other adventure stories. Winston Churchill, Agatha Christie, Pearl Buck, and Neville Shute are just a few of the many authors whose works would grace the magazine's pages over the years. *Collier's* gradually evolved into a weekly newsmagazine. Its crusade against injurious patent medicines — for example, a remedy called "liquozone" that was advertised to cure everything from cancer to dandruff — was a major impetus behind passage of the U. S. Food and Drug Act. Poor management and consistent red ink resulted in the magazine's sale to the Cowles publishing organization, which buried the publication and rolled its subscribers over into *Look* magazine in 1957.

8   **This form of** Hill believed firmly in "mind over matter" when it came to health issues, and medical research has since demonstrated conclusively that state of mind does play an important role in good health. However, whether he actually believed the following anecdote which he uses in the original *Think and Grow Rich!* — or was simply using it to make a crucial point — is unclear:

> During the "flu" epidemic which broke out during the world war, the mayor of New York City took drastic steps to check the damage which people were doing themselves through their inherent fear of ill health. He called in the newspaper men and said to them, "Gentlemen, I feel it necessary to ask you not to publish any *scare headlines* concerning the 'flu' epidemic. Unless you cooperate with me, we will have a situation which we cannot control." The newspapers quit publishing stories about the "flu," and within one month the epidemic had been successfully checked.

9   **A psychotherapist** Hill used the term "specialist in suggestive therapeutics."

10   **SUSCEPTIBILITY TO ILLNESS** Immune system research has since demonstrated conclusively the negative effects of stress on the body's immune system.

11   **The most common cause** "Poorhouse" is a concept alien to more recent generations in the United States. Prior to the advent of federal and state welfare programs, impoverished citizens who had no money or property often ended up living in county poorhouses, where their labor helped them "work off" their room and board. Except for imprisonment or confinement in an insane asylum, the pauper's life in the poorhouse was about as low as a person could fall in American society.

12   **I once interviewed** Hill worked for several years as a journalist. It was in that capacity that he interviewed Andrew Carnegie and was set on course to researching and writing *Think and Grow Rich!*.

13   **The vibrations of fear** Hill believed absolutely in the reality of extrasensory perception: "Mental telepathy is a reality. Thoughts pass from one mind to another, voluntarily, whether or not this fact is recognized by either the person releasing the thoughts or the persons who pick up those thoughts."

14 **Do you neglect** Autointoxication is a term popular in Hill's day to describe "poisoning" by toxic substances formed in the body itself, as, for example, during the digestive process. Proper "internal bathing" is accomplished by adequate daily intake of water and fiber and may also refer to enemas or colonic treatments.

15 **He knew that he** Hill would later refine this idea into what is perhaps his most famous statement—the bedrock concept of *The Think and Grow Rich Philosophy*: "Whatever the mind can conceive and believe, it can achieve." (An earlier incarnation had it "Whatever the mind of man can conceive and believe, it can achieve." Perhaps Hill's earliest expression of the idea is found in the third sentence of Chapter 5: "It has been said that anything can be created which a human being can imagine.") His collaborations with W. Clement Stone sometimes added the phrase "...with PMA" (Positive Mental Attitude) after "achieve," as in their book *Success through a Positive Mental Attitude*. In many of their later writings, Hill and Stone also added another qualifying phrase: "...so long as it does not violate the laws of God or the rights of others." Whatever its variation, the CONCEIVE-BELIEVE-ACHIEVE formula has become one of the most notable and widely used motivational "affirmations" in history. It even shows up in popular music. R Kelly's hit song "I Believe I Can Fly" in the late 1990s is filled with *Think and Grow Rich!* aphorisms:

> *If I can see it, then I can do it. / If I just believe it,*
> *there's nothing to it...*
> *If I can see it, then I can be it. / If I just believe it,*
> *there's nothing to it.*
> *I believe I can fly.*
> Song by R Kelly, from the movie *Space Jam*
> Copyright © 1996 WEA/Atlantic

16 **RICHER THAN CROESUS.** Croesus, who died in 546 B.C., was the last king of Lydia, famous for his tremendous wealth. He conquered the Greeks of Ionia, but later fell to the Persians. Croseus was the central figure in a tale by Herodotus, who had the king meet the renowned Athenian lawgiver Solon. The latter chastised Croseus, emphasizing that it is good fortune, not riches in themselves, that is the basis for true happiness.

INDEX

About the Author

Oliver Napoleon Hill was born October 26, 1883, in a two-room log cabin in the mountains of Wise County, Virginia, a region marked by illiteracy and grinding poverty. The gift of a typewriter from his stepmother at age 12 led to a career as a writer, first as a "mountain reporter" for local small-town newspapers, then as a reporter for *Bob Taylor's Magazine*, interviewing and writing "success profiles" of famous individuals. It was in 1908 on such an assignment that Hill met industrialist Andrew Carnegie, one of the richest men in the world. That meeting—and almost 30 years of subsequent research by Hill that was suggested and informally sponsored by Carnegie—led to the publication in 1937 of *Think and Grow Rich!*, one of the best-selling books of all time. Hill was the founder of the modern genre of personal success literature. *The Think and Grow Rich Philosophy* and the success formulas he developed through his research and in his book have helped countless people throughout the world to achieve outstanding success in every aspect of life. Hill became an informal advisor to two U. S. Presidents, Woodrow Wilson and Franklin D. Roosevelt. He would go on to author more than 30 books and textbooks, including *Success through a Positive Mental Attitude,* written with W. Clement Stone, who began a decade-long collaboration with Hill when the latter was age 69. Hill was a fixture on the motivational lecture circuit and a prolific creator of textbooks, study guides, and other success materials. He founded three magazines—*Hill's Golden Rule* in 1919, *Napoleon Hill's Magazine* in 1921, and *Inspiration Magazine* in 1931. He and Stone together founded *Success Unlimited* magazine in 1954. Dr. Hill died on November 8, 1970, at his retirement home on Paris Mountain near Greenville, South Carolina, where he spent the last 13 years of his life.

About the Editor

Ross Cornwell is a native South Carolinian. He was educated at Davidson College, Davidson, North Carolina, and Stanford University, Palo Alto, California. He is a graduate of the Goethe-Institut, Ebersberg, Germany. He has enjoyed two careers — one in public service, working in higher education, and the other in the private sector as a freelance writer/editor and consultant. His background includes stints as a journalist and columnist, and work in public relations, scriptwriting, speechwriting, newsletter publishing, corporate communications, and film criticism, both print and broadcast. He served as Executive Assistant to the President at Clemson University and later was managing editor of four national circulation newsletters, including *Think & Grow Rich Newsletter*. Projects and programs he headed won the CASE Grand Award, presented by the Ford Motor Company Fund for the nation's most outstanding "special public relations project" in higher education, and the *Newsweek* National First Place Award, presented to the university news and information program judged best in the United States. He is the author of the chapter on speechwriting for the second edition of the *Handbook for Institutional Advancement*. A video he wrote — "With the Mind of a Child" — won a 2001 Bronze WorldMedal at The New York Festivals and a 2002 Silver Screen Award at the 35th Annual U. S. International Film and Video Festival in Los Angeles. He is president and CEO of The Mindpower Institute and of Cornwell Associates, which provides corporate communications services. He has edited or written 10 books and written 35 videos. Ross Cornwell lives in Clemson, South Carolina, with his wife, Betty, a schoolteacher. They have two grown daughters, Johannah and Anne-Ross.

About the Type

This book was set in Book Antiqua™, a proportionally spaced, old style roman typeface inspired by two sources—pen-drawn letters of the Italian Renaissance and the modern typeface known as Palatino, created by the famous 20th-century type designer Hermann Zapf. It was chosen for this book because of its outstanding legibility and strong presence. It reflects a combination of keen artistic sensibility and technical understanding, and its design characteristics also make it an excellent presentation font for web pages. Book Antiqua™ is a trademark of The Monotype Corporation that may be registered in certain jurisdictions.

More Praise for *Think and Grow Rich!*

"There's one very good reason why you should get this book and read it closely: IT WORKS! My father put this book in my hands while I was a young boy and said, 'This is the one book you need to study to get rich!' Now I AM a multi-millionaire and this is the book that started me off!"

> -- Dr. Jeffrey Lant, internationally known marketer and author, co-founder of Worldprofit, Inc.

"As a professional speaker, I found many years ago that those people who studied personal development books were reading too many books and not internalizing any of them. Thus, I wondered what would happen if people read just one or two books over and over again and internalized the information. That's exactly what I recommend as a professional speaker to audiences worldwide and the results have been amazing. In order to teach the incredible concepts in *Think and Grow Rich!*, I read the book once a month, every month, for five years — 60 times in all! It is the most powerful book in the world when it comes to setting goals and achieving them. The simplicity of the concepts in the book is the reason it is so valuable. According to Hill, it all begins with a clear desire and a concrete game plan. It's no wonder this book has produced more millionaires than any other book."

> -- Boaz Rauchwerger, speaker, trainer, consultant and author of *How To Become a Debt-Free Money Magnet*

"*Think and Grow Rich!*...uses these millionaires to identify the key qualities for self-made success, and the habits that guarantee mediocrity. Most of the conclusions are obvious, but Hill expresses them with such force that reading this book is bound to inspire you to take a more positive approach to life."

> -- *The Mail on Sunday* (London, England)

"*Think and Grow Rich!* has had a tremendous impact on the thousands of people we have given it to over the years in our training seminars. It gives any reader the opportunity to copy the genius of others instead of having to create mediocrity on their own."

> -- Steven J. Anderson, President, Planned Marketing Associates, Inc.

"*Think and Grow Rich!* may be the most practical guide to a positive life ever written. Both the presentation and substance of this book make it a gem. Napoleon Hill's life's work was a gift to 20th century humanity and all generations not yet born — and this book is the fruit of his efforts."

> -- Louis J. Iacona, founder and CEO of VIT Associates software engineering company

"*Think and Grow Rich!* will change your outlook on life. It suggests that the thoughts you have today will ultimately shape the direction life will take tomorrow. Whenever life throws me a serious curveball, I pick up this book, and each time I do, I find something new to meditate about....This book works!"

> -- Susan Miller, astrologer, author of *The Year Ahead 2004*

"I went from poverty to earning over $1 million in a single year while still in my twenties. How did I do that? I followed the advice in Mr. Hill's book, *Think and Grow Rich!*. It's that simple."

> -- Gerry Robert, author of *The Millionaire Mindset*

"*Think and Grow Rich!* is THE success and millionaire-making blueprint you absolutely must devour. It deserves careful study and reading not just once or twice but over and over again. I highly recommend it to anyone looking for more out of their life."

> -- Yanik Silver, Internet entrepreneur and author of *Instant Internet Profits*

"Every day new books are published on how to grow rich. Some are not worth the cover price. For inspiration, read the classics such as *Think and Grow Rich!* by Napoleon Hill....It's the first step to devising a winning strategy."

> -- *The Sunday Times* (London, England)

"The 'how-to' messages in *Think and Grow Rich!* by Napoleon Hill… are as timeless today as they were when he wrote about them in 1937. They can be applied to managing a business, as well as a career. What makes Hill's book timeless is its 'giants of his time' sources including: Armour, Bell, Carnegie, Edison, Ford, Gillette, John D. Rockefeller, Theodore Roosevelt and Woolworth."

-- Dayton Daily News

"*Think and Grow Rich!* changed my life forever. I was working my way through college in 1959 as a second-shift machinist making ninety cents an hour. Somebody gave me a copy of the book and within a few months I got into sales, doubled and tripled my income and sharpened my wit. Since then I have fallen on hard times again and again as projects/opportunities come and go. But every time, I have taken a deep breath, re-read the Mastermind concept, and grown with each fall, which makes me one of the most successful people on earth — absolutely no fear of failure, which makes it possible to push the limits and fly out of the box."

-- Wayne Lundberg, consultant, Small Business
Development Centers, California Community Colleges

"When I meet with young people coming into public accounting, I'm stunned that they are unaware of many of the classics of success philosophy and motivation. One that should be in everyone's success library is *Think And Grow Rich!*….The source for most of today's motivational speakers remains *Think And Grow Rich!*. So why not go back to the source yourself? Be sure to include *Think And Grow Rich!* on your reading list."

-- Michael C. Gray, founder of Michael Gray, CPA

"Several months ago I came across an audiobook biography of Napoleon Hill, and it was an eye-opening adventure into the life of a man whose days were not the 'smooth sailing' I had always assumed they were. Napoleon struggled against a myriad of obstacles throughout his life — many of which were brought on by some of the earlier choices he had made. I can't count the number of times he became broke and penniless following a highly successful venture gone sour. His personal life was as spotted as his financial life, and a recounting of that could easily consume a full book.

"I would have thought that my discovery of his many flaws would cause me to lose respect for him, and thus doubt the veracity of his teachings that have influenced me for more than twenty years. But it is quite the opposite. Having listened to the struggles of this very human man has given me a whole new perspective of respect, even awe, of the incredible resilience and persistence that he displayed repeatedly against sometimes massive odds.

"I now understand that he didn't write about some 'theory' of how to think and grow rich. He wrote from experience—his numerous experiences and the experiences of America's most successful. While the casual observer would believe that this book is only about making money, those of us who have studied it for years know otherwise. It's about a better way to live a 'rich' life. And for that I am grateful that Napoleon gave so much of himself in order that he might leave us with this incredible work."

-- Vic Johnson, founder of AsAManThinketh.net

"*Think and Grow Rich!* sits atop our late founder's [Jose Silva] library. It is timeless wisdom for success."

-- Hilda Silva Rubio, Chairman/CEO, The Silva Method

"I first read *Think And Grow Rich!* over 30 years ago. While I was slow to put the lessons taught therein into practice (I worked for a large bureaucracy), when I did, the results were phenomenal, and the best part is that those lessons still work today as I share them with our team constantly. It is a timeless book."

-- Joe Turner, founder and Chairman of the FSMC chain of Wendy's restaurants, former Executive Director of IPTAY, the nation's most successful college athletic fundraising organization